ID0894630

Wearing the C

Leadership Secrets from
Hockey's Greatest Captains

Ross Bernstein

TRIUMPH
B O O K S

This book is available in quantity at special discounts for your group or organization. For further information, contact:

Triumph Books LLC
814 North Franklin Street
Chicago, IL 60610
(312) 337-0747
www.triumphbooks.com

Printed in the United States of America

ISBN: 978-1-60078-757-7

Interior design by Amy Carter
Editorial production by Prologue Publishing Services, LLC
All photos courtesy of AP Images, unless otherwise indicated

For Sara and Campbell…

Contents

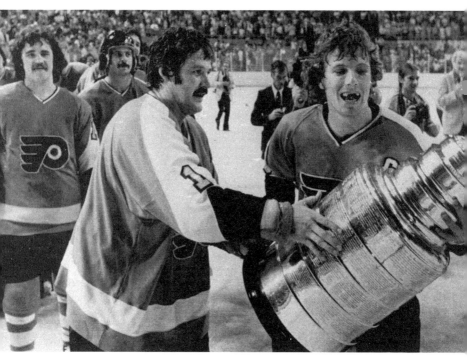

Bobby Clarke holds the Stanley Cup, with Flyers teammate Bernie Parent (left) after Philadelphia beat the Buffalo Sabres 2–0 for its second straight Finals victory in 1975.

Foreword
by Bobby Clarke

Being the captain is a responsibility to the organization and to your teammates that's carried out on a daily basis. You're a player and you have to do your job out on the ice, yet at the same time you also have to be a team leader by doing things the right way, every day. That means you practice hard every day. You have to try your hardest in every game. And you have to constantly lead by example on and off the ice. It's about doing things the right way, even when no one is looking. That's what being a captain is all about in my eyes.

I never saw myself as some great leader or anything like that. I just did what I felt was right for the team. Beyond that, I just worked really hard every day. I couldn't ask other people to work hard if I wasn't working hard myself. And I couldn't ask other people to be good if I wasn't good myself. It wasn't very complicated, but that was my philosophy. The bottom line for me was I did whatever I could to help my team win—that was it. And, truth be told, if we hadn't won the two Stanley Cups, I probably would have been just another captain.

When you're the captain, the team comes before everybody, no matter what. It's about getting everybody to buy into what's right for the team. Everybody's a little bit selfish. You don't become a good athlete without being a little bit selfish, whether it's scoring a certain number of points or wanting to make an all-star team or what have you. We all have personal goals, but if you can convince everyone to be unselfish and put the team goals ahead of individual goals, that's when amazing things can happen.

Whenever there was an issue that came up, I only had to ask myself one question: what was best for the team? If you answer that question properly, then everything usually just took care of itself. The team's job is to win hockey games. Period. Winning the Stanley Cup, that's why we play this game. So to have been fortunate enough to win not one but two of them, it's almost beyond words what it means to me. And to be the captain of those teams is very special.

Despite winning some personal awards those two seasons [1974 and 1975], I never felt above the team in any way. It was always about the team for me, and I was willing to do whatever it took to help my teammates win. I always felt that I was just part of that group, nothing special, just one piece of the puzzle. I did my job and I expected everybody else to do their jobs, as well. Luckily we did, and that was why we were able to win back-to-back championships, I think.

I tried to lead by example, whether that was trying my hardest in practice or whatever. Everybody had the same mentality. There were other players, beyond our core group of guys, who came in and out during that time. Those who embraced our work ethic and tough style of play were rewarded, and those who wouldn't or couldn't had to be pushed out. Honestly, those two championship teams were very special, and I don't think they really even needed much leadership. It was just an amazing group of selfless guys all working toward the same goal. It was such an honor to be a member of those teams, without a doubt.

As for my style of leadership, I was more quiet and reserved. I could get emotional when I needed to be, but for the most part I just did my job. As for players-only meetings, I never bothered with stuff like that because I didn't think those types of meetings had any meaning at all. There were times, however, when I would have words with a player who wasn't playing up to the expectations of what the team needed, sure. If a guy wasn't carrying his end of the load and it was hurting the team, I would talk to him about it and try to get it resolved. I wasn't ever demanding in that way, I was more laid back in asking them if they could raise their game up to the level that we needed it to be.

What was unique about those teams was how we were able to change the game by using fear and intimidation as a tactic. The "Broad Street Bullies" was what they called us, and it was our identity. It meant that we were tough, both mentally as well as physically. We were a young franchise when I got there, and they had gotten pushed around for years. That all changed when our attitude changed, though, and in the process we changed how the game of hockey was played.

Fighting was a big part of the game in those days. As the captain, I wouldn't ask a guy to go out and fight if I wasn't willing to go out and do it myself, though. So I did it. You needed a catalyst to start it and get it going, that way you can get those guys off the bench and into the game—where they can do what they do best. I remember one time when we had lost a few games and were in kind of a slump. I knew that we needed a good wake-up call, so I decided to stir things up a bit. I said to Davey [Schultz, one of the toughest hombres in hockey], "I'll get some shit going tonight, Shultzey. Just let me get it started and then you guys can go in and do what you have to do in order for us to get this thing turned around." So I started a fight early in the game, and that sort of set the tone. Some more fights followed, and sure enough we won the game. We got the momentum back on our side and carried it into the postseason. We had some tough, unselfish guys on our team, and I knew that was how they would respond. They were willing to do whatever it took to help the team win, no matter what.

We had a great coach, too, in Fred Shero, who totally supported us. As the captain, I had a great relationship with him.

I totally believed in Freddy, he was such a bright man. Just a brilliant hockey coach. He did some odd stuff and had some unorthodox ways of motivating us, but there was always a reason for whatever he did. There was a method to his madness, to be sure. I respected Freddy because he treated me like an equal. He was a smart enough coach to know that if he wanted something done, all he had to do was get me to do it. Because he knew that if I did it, then everybody would do it. Freddy understood that and used it to his advantage. Hey, more power to him. It was a win-win for all of us.

The big takeaway from my experience of being captain is in my ability now to make tough decisions. If there are decisions that have to be made and you're in charge, then you have to make them. You're not going to please everybody, that's for sure, but that's what being a leader is all about: making the decision that you feel is right and then standing behind it, one way or the other, regardless of the consequences or the outcome. You can't hem and haw and back away from them or pass the buck, either—that's not leadership. People respect that, too, when you stand behind what you say and are accountable for it. It's no different in hockey than it is if you are a manager at the office or if you are raising kids. Sometimes it's not easy making tough decisions, but they have to be made. So the better informed and prepared you can be, in whatever you are doing in life, the better the decision is going to be.

Overall, I took great pride in having worn the C. I also got to wear it as the captain of Team Canada, which was an extraordinary honor. I was the captain on a team full of captains, so it was quite humbling. Those were the best players Canada had, some of the best in the world. I learned a lot about leadership being on those teams. I learned how to become a better listener and communicator, too, which is so important when you are trying to lead a group of people and get them to accomplish a common goal.

Foreword
by Scott Stevens

Wearing the C was very, very special, truly an honor. I was asked to wear the C for New Jersey and St. Louis, and it was a sincere privilege to do so. It's also a big responsibility, though, because you're the guy everyone looks up to. So that means you've got to do things right. All I've ever wanted to do in life, since I was about four years old, was play hockey. That was my goal from a very early age, and I've always been willing to do whatever it takes to help my team win.

My parents taught me from a very early age about the value of hard work and sacrifice. There's just no substitute for hard work. They worked long hours and sacrificed a great deal in their own lives so that my brothers and I were able to play hockey. Just watching them and being around them taught me so much about the value of having a solid work ethic. I guess it was engrained in me, and that's why I worked so hard each and every day I was fortunate enough to play this great game. Growing up as a Toronto Maple Leafs fan, Darryl Sittler was a guy I really looked up to. He was a great leader, and I wanted to emulate his style.

My definition of leadership is leading by example. Period. I tried to set the tone in practice and in games, and as the captain you hope that your teammates simply follow your lead. If everybody sees you doing all the little things, making sacrifices,

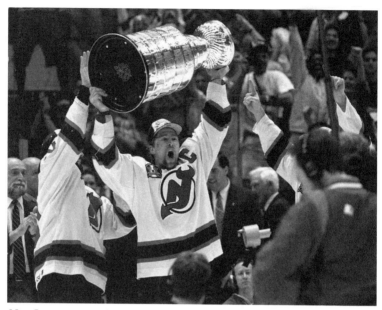

New Jersey captain Scott Stevens holds up the Stanley Cup after his Devils defeated the Detroit Red Wings in Game 4 of the Finals to sweep the series at the Meadowlands in 1995.

and doing whatever it takes to win, then they'll follow. That's the goal as a leader. At the end of the day, you want your teammates to be behind you just like you're behind them. When that occurs, amazing things can happen.

As far as motivating guys, I was willing to do whatever it took to get through to them. The bottom line for me was that I just hated to lose. If things weren't going well with the team, the best way for me to get a guy's attention was in practice. I was a firm believer that practice was where you developed good habits and where you got prepared for the competition ahead. So, if I felt that one of my teammates wasn't pulling his weight, I might address him in practice. I might get angry and throw some big checks his way or even try to get in there and mix it up with him, so that I could get his attention. That was my job as the captain, to make sure everybody was on the same page and that everybody was pulling his own weight. That was one of the ways I would show my feelings when things were good or when things weren't so good.

I always prided myself in being an extremely physical player. I loved football as a kid and I loved that feeling of just nailing a guy in open space. So I guess I sort of felt it was one way, other than maybe scoring a goal or getting into a fight, that I could influence or change the momentum for my team. Big hits lead to momentum, and that leads to confidence for your teammates. I learned early on that playing physical can turn the tide and set the tone, so I embraced that aspect of the game and really worked hard at perfecting it. It was certainly one of my biggest assets.

I think back to two of the biggest momentum-swinging hits I had over the years, and certainly the two involving Eric Lindros [Philadelphia Flyers] and Viktor Kozlov [Detroit Red Wings] come to mind first and foremost. They were both big games for us en route to our winning the Cup, so for that I am just proud of the fact that I was able to do my part in helping to swing the momentum in our favor. My philosophy was always if every guy did his role, then nothing was going to stop us. Well, big hits were my way of doing my part, I suppose.

One of the statistics I took pride in over the years was the plus-minus. [When your team scores a goal and you're on the ice, you're +1, when the opposing team scores a goal and you're on the ice, you're –1.] I always took great pride in being a "plus player." I never wanted my teammates to feel like I was a liability, so I always felt a big responsibility to play good defense. That was the base of my game, for sure. For me, whenever I was doing the right things in the defensive zone, then things just seemed to come a little easier in the offensive zone. I usually had the responsibility to play against the other team's top player, which presented big challenges for me. That was fun, though, and I loved getting up for those challenges. To be able to shut a guy down by playing physical, or to instill a level of fear and intimidation through a certain style of play, that's just fun for me. What a rush.

I didn't talk a whole lot, but when I did it was usually about strategy or about us making adjustments. I wanted to make sure I spoke up at the right times, maybe between the first and second periods, when guys could still make those adjustments for the second and third periods. If something wasn't going right in my eyes, I wanted to fix it right away, so I tried to facilitate those conversations and get guys communicating in the locker room. That was big. I was real vocal in that regard, and I would like to think effective, as well.

Winning the three Stanley Cups, that's the biggest thing, though. It's all about the team, and in hockey it doesn't get any bigger than that. I'm just proud to have been a member of such an incredible organization and a part of so many great teams. I was just really fortunate to have been able to play alongside so many good players and great teammates who played hard and made sacrifices for us. Those guys definitely made my job easier as captain.

PREFACE

I first wore the C as a bantam back in the early '80s for my hometown Fairmont Cardinals, a sleepy southern Minnesota community just a few miles from the Iowa border. It was a huge honor—no kidding—to be named as team captain. Hey, Ma, I'm a leader! Looking back, though, I'm pretty sure it had very little to do with talent and a lot to do with popularity and self-confidence. Big difference. My coach at the time, Fred Carlson, was so amused by the fact that I could regularly talk my way out of the penalty box that he anointed me as the team leader. It probably went something like this:

ME: Sir. Excuse me, sir, but I would really appreciate it if you would please reconsider assessing me with a slashing penalty.... I might have simply fallen into No. 23 as a result of being pushed from behind. I'm very sorry.

REF: Oh...well, when you put it like that, of course, no problem.

What can I say? I had a way with words, even as a 12-year-old. Freddy was a beauty, I loved the guy. He was also my dentist, so every time I came in for a checkup, we would talk hockey nonstop. His son, Paul, was my linemate, and Freddy got thrust into coaching by default. You see, nobody else wanted the job...

so he would just keep on coaching us at every level. He figured he had to drive his kid to practice and to the games anyway, so why not get out there on skates—at least he'd stay warm moving around out in the cold.

Fairmont was a basketball and wrestling hotbed in the long winter months. Hockey country it wasn't. Nope. No indoor arena, no Zamboni, not even any matching uniforms—nada. It was pretty bleak. Just a few outdoor rinks with some old beat-up boards. Pretty much the polar opposite of northern Minnesota, where in places like Roseau, Warroad, and International Falls they actually pull kids out of the wombs by their skate blades.

All that changed in the winter of 1980, though, when the U.S. Olympic Hockey Team shocked the world in Lake Placid, New York. I wasn't even a hockey fan at the time, but as soon as I started watching those games on TV, I was hooked. Half of the kids were from Minnesota, along with the team's iconic coach, Herb Brooks, so I was invested. Herbie had led the Gophers to three national championships in the mid- to late '70s and was truly an icon in the State of Hockey. Seeing them beat the seemingly invincible Soviets, arguably the greatest hockey team ever assembled, was simply magical. Then to watch them rally back to beat the Finns two days later to win the gold medal, it truly was a "Miracle on Ice." For me, that was it…I wanted in. I immediately went out to our local Coast to Coast Hardware store in the downtown plaza and bought a used pair of Bauer Hugger skates. Beyond that, they had a few Christian Brothers sticks and some tape. To get the rest of my armor, we had to drive an hour north to Mankato.

I immediately started playing shinny with my buddies behind our house on Hall Lake. It was so much fun, we'd head out there after school and stay until we couldn't see the puck anymore. We'd come in for dinner and then head out to the rink at Cardinal Park, which had lights, until our parents made us come home to finish our homework and go to bed. A few months later, I found out that Herb Brooks was putting on a summer hockey camp in nearby Faribault, at the Shattuck School. I begged my parents to let me sign up, and they reluctantly agreed. I think they were just happy to get rid of me for a week, but we'll never know.

Once I got there, I was just blown away by how good the other kids were. The talent level between me and the Iron Rangers from up north was almost indescribable. Most of these kids had been playing on traveling teams since they were three or four years old. I, on the other hand, was what you would call an "ankle bender." You know, one of those slugs who could barely stand up. I will never forget the day Herb came over to offer me a few words of encouragement. He could see I was getting frustrated and wanted to build up my confidence. He said, "Way to go, Ross, you're a really hard worker. Keep it up, pal!" Wow, he knew my name! I had completely forgotten that "ROSS" was written in huge letters on white tape across the front of my helmet. Oh, well, I just remember being in awe of the guy.

In 1981 I got my first taste of Stanley Cup hockey when my beloved North Stars made a Cinderella run through the playoffs and all the way to the Finals. Mayhem and bedlam would ensue as Cup fever hit Minnesota hard. Seemingly everybody had jumped on the bandwagon, myself included. Bobby Smith, Steve Payne, Al MacAdam, Brad Maxwell, Craig Hartsburg, Dino Ciccarelli, Brad Palmer, Don Beaupre, and Gilles Meloche had suddenly become household names. For my buddies and me, however, it was all about Neal Broten—the former University of Minnesota Golden Gopher and 1980 Olympian who had joined the team just prior to the playoffs. He was *our* guy. I think we all had serious man-crushes on him, bad mullet and all—but I digress. You'll hear from Neal and Bobby Smith later in the book, both had really interesting insights on what it meant to wear the C.

The Stars lost to the defending champion New York Islanders in five games, but it was a marvelous run that did wonders for the growth and popularity of hockey in the upper Midwest. New York was in the midst of winning what would turn out to be four straight Stanley Cup titles, firmly establishing themselves as one of the game's all-time great dynasties. Clark Gillies, Denis Potvin, and Bryan Trottier all talk about that incredible run in the book, as well.

As Stars fans, we just figured our squad would be going back to the Finals every year, because as fans we're eternal optimists. Well, it would take us another 11 years to get back to the Finals, where this time we got beat by the Pittsburgh Penguins—who were led by one of the game's greatest all-time captains in Mario Lemieux. Sadly, two years later the team got hijacked down to Dallas by a disgruntled owner who still remains enemy No. 1 up here in the great north woods all these years later. One of the young guns on that North Stars team was Mike Modano, who would go on to wear the C for many years with the franchise in Texas. You'll hear from Mike later in the book, too—great guy, a true professional.

Now, as for organized hockey in Fairmont during the early to late '80s? Not so much. The local school didn't sponsor us or even recognize us, for that matter, so it was up to the parents to get things done. Youth hockey programs in places like Fairmont were completely grassroots operations. We had just the bare necessities: an outdoor rink, a warming house, and a couple of shovels to keep us busy between periods. Everybody pitched in as volunteers: dads shoveled and moms sold brownies at the concession stand. It was old-school.

I remember sticking around after practices late at night to help flood the rink out in the bitter cold. Some of my fondest childhood memories would take place out there, though, at old Cardinal Park, with my teammates and pals—some of whom remain my closest friends even to this day. My parents would drop me off out there on Saturday and Sunday mornings and then pick me up late at night. I loved it. Sure, it was freezing, but we didn't care. We came inside only to warm up our toes and to snag a piece of Jake's Pizza, if one of my buddies' moms was nice enough to bring some over for us.

Believe it or not, I actually wound up starting as a freshman on the varsity squad. No, it's not what you're thinking. I didn't get really good over that time and emerge as some hotshot phenom. Remember, this was Fairmont, and there was a serious need for warm bodies. I had a pulse, which apparently more than qualified me to play as the team's first-line left defenseman. Go figure. Big games for us were against other southern Minnesota powerhouses such as Windom, Sleepy Eye, Luverne, and Worthington. Occasionally, we would play larger schools like Mankato, Rochester, or Austin, and that would usually result in a tough lesson in humility, followed by a long ride home.

We didn't even have school jerseys. In fact, Domino's Pizza sponsored us instead. Nice. In fact, the team captain didn't even get the C sewn into his jersey. Because we passed down the jerseys every year to the next crop of kids, we apparently couldn't risk "ruining" one by stitching a C onto it. So we had elastic arm bands for our leaders instead. I know, classy. There were no locker rooms or fancy buses, either, just the bathroom at McDonald's on the way home. The key was to get a ride with one of the players whose parents owned a van (farmers love vans), where you could stretch out on the way home. Sleeping was tough, though, because you had the chain-smoking parents in the front and the nuclear hockey equipment smell in the back—it was like a perfect storm of horrific odors. That was *way* better than getting stuck in a pickup truck, though, because that meant you would have to spend at least 15 minutes thawing out your frozen skates with a hair dryer when you got to the game.

Road trips were always an adventure. I remember one time when I was probably around 12 or 13 and we were playing in Luverne. A big blizzard hit during the game, and we were all snowed in. Each kid got paired up with a host family for the night for an impromptu sleepover. Nope, no hotels in Luverne, just a bunch of chicken farms and hog barns. Anyway, I wound up staying with a kid by the name of Paul Schmuck. Once we got back to the Schmuck home, I called my parents to let them know I was staying over. She asked me for the phone number there, in case she needed to get hold of me.

"Sure, no problem," I said.

"Hey, Schmuck, what's your phone number?"

Before he could answer, my mom screams into the phone in a very disgusted tone, "Ross! Oh my goodness, that is so rude!"

Figuring she wanted me to ask his mother for their number instead, I politely said, "Excuse me, Mrs. Schmuck, may I please have your telephone number?"

My mom just about had a heart attack at this point, screaming at the top of her lungs, "Ross! What in the world has gotten into you!? You apologize to Paul's mom immediately, you're grounded for a week!"

Completely perplexed at this point, my mother then proceeded to explain to me just what the word *schmuck* meant… in Yiddish. You see, we were the only Jewish family in southern Minnesota, and the extent of my cultural knowledge was "limited," to say the least. In fact, other than *tuchas* and bagels, I didn't know a whole lot. And I certainly didn't know that *schmuck* was a filthy word back in the old country. Oh well, lesson learned, I suppose.

I played through high school and had a blast. Not many wins, but tons of amazing memories and friendships. My friends and I used to love to sit in our basement and watch Gophers hockey. It was the best. We loved the Gophers. In those days they truly were the "Minnesota Gophers" because to make the team you had to be from the state of Minnesota. Sometimes Mom and Dad would even buy us a couple of cases of frozen White Castle hamburgers up in Minneapolis and then bring them home for the playoffs. We would nuke them and then sit around watching our Gophs beat up the Wisconsin Badgers while drinking copious amounts of Mountain Dew. We had bad mullets and thought we were so cool. It was awesome.

After graduating in 1987, I went on to attend the University of Minnesota. I had offers to play small college football, but I wanted to be a Gopher. My entire family had gone to the U, and I was so excited to be moving to the "Cities" (Minneapolis/ St. Paul). One of the first things I did was to sign up for Gophers hockey season tickets with a bunch of my new fraternity brothers. The games were amazing, and I absolutely fell in love with the Maroon and Gold. Some of the captains in those days were guys like Tom Chorske, Dave Snuggerud, and Todd Richards— all future NHLers.

Shortly thereafter I wound up taking "Introduction to Ice Hockey 101." It was a one-credit introductory physical education class, and the best part about it was that we got to skate for an hour three days a week at Mariucci Arena, the home of the Golden Gophers. I remember gliding out on that big beautiful sheet of ice for the first time—it was surreal. What a feeling. I will never forget it. "The Barn," as it was known, was an old, two-sided arena full of character and oddities. It was like Wrigley Field, an old dump...but it was *our* dump. There was so much history in that building, and it was full of old hockey ghosts floating around in the rafters.

The instructors of the class were varsity hockey players who would show up about 20 seconds before the class started, say hello, check your name off the attendance roster, and then throw a bunch of pucks out onto the ice. They would then usually say, "Okay, we're gonna scrimmage today, boys!" They would then leave for an hour to do whatever it is varsity hockey players do and then show up again at the end to make sure we put the pucks away. Some schools call it "Underwater Basket-Weaving," but at Minnesota we apparently called it Hockey 101. Needless to say, it was by far my favorite class. In fact, I actually took the course all five years I was in school, no kidding.

Well, over time I became buddies with a few of the varsity players. I would invite them to my fraternity parties, and on occasion they would work with me in hockey class. Eventually, they thought enough of me to encourage me to try out for the team as a walk-on. They figured I was a big defenseman and had a decent shot, why not? I was blown away. *Are you kidding me? Me, "ROSS" from Fairmont, playing for the Gophers?* To say that would be a dream come true would be the understatement of the century. The Gophers were a college hockey powerhouse in those days, perennial favorites to win the national championship year in and year out. Most of the kids were drafted by NHL teams out of high school. They were the best of the best. I was terrified. My buddies on the team said that they would go to bat for me, though, and try to convince the coaches to take pity on me. Nothing ventured, nothing gained, was how I saw it. So I took a leap of faith and just went for it.

It turned out to be a great experience. I pretty much did what I was told and stayed under the radar as a practice pylon. The end came when I tried to impress the coaches by checking one of the team's star players, Todd Richards, who was injured at the time and rehabbing with the junior varsity. (Todd would go on to become the head coach of the NHL's Minnesota Wild and Columbus Blue Jackets.) I remember he was wearing a white jersey with a big red cross on it, and he came skating right toward me with his head down. *Now is my chance to make an impression*, I thought, so I nailed him. It was a great hit, one of my best ever.

At that point things get fuzzy, because shortly thereafter Bill Butters, an assistant coach and former NHL tough-guy, ran me over like road kill. Wham! When I regained consciousness (I literally saw stars, like in the old Road Runner vs. Wile E. Coyote cartoons), I was reminded in no uncertain terms that players with red crosses were injured and not to be touched. (Trust me, in Fairmont we didn't have any fancy jerseys like that—just Domino's.) It was a lesson learned the hard way, unfortunately, because shortly thereafter Coach Woog called me into his office and told me to bring my playbook. Not good. Wooger told me that he loved my passion and my work ethic, but that it just wasn't going to work out. He had to cut me.

I was devastated. My dream of one day hoisting the Stanley Cup had just died. That was the end of the line. After my brief "cup of coffee," however, it came to my attention that there was another position that had become available on the team that might be more suitable to my talents. It wasn't quite as sexy as first-line left defenseman, but it was close. It was for the team mascot, Goldy Gopher. There were two criteria for the job: you had to be a decent skater, and you had to be a complete moron. I apparently fit on both counts and got the gig. Go figure. Goldy had always been a member of the band up until that point, but they were supposedly tired of Bucky the Badger coming over from Wisconsin and kicking Goldy's ass. So my job was going to involve reminding the cheeseheads that rodents are and always have been higher than weasels on the food chain.

School mascot? Hey, why not. I still wanted to be a part of the team, and this was going to be the perfect opportunity to do just that. Technically, I was a cheerleader, which meant I got to hang around with a dozen gorgeous coeds every weekend, which turned out to be an added bonus. Being Goldy was just a blast. I got to be an anonymous entertainer up on an old TV perch under the scoreboard at the Old Barn. The Gophers seldom if ever lost during those days at home, and the collective blood-alcohol level in that joint was about 7.0, which made my job a lot easier. Pretty much anything I did out there was deemed hilarious. Again, go figure.

Needless to say, I got into a lot of trouble. Apparently, it's not okay to throw Kraft cheese singles at the Wisconsin band. Who knew? I got a nasty letter from the dean after that one.

Eventually, a publisher approached me and told me he was interested in writing a book about all of the antics that I had gotten into as a mischievous rodent. I told him I was flattered, but no thanks. I mean, other than my grandmother, who would want to read about this? Then, as I was finishing my last year of school and coming to the realization that Daddy's cash was drying up fast, I reconsidered. I didn't want to work with this guy, though, I wanted to do it myself. I thought, *What if I wrote a book about the program's rich history, but wrote it from Goldy's perspective?* Hey, that's not bad.

I remember calling Mom and Dad to let them know that I had other plans for my graduate school money that they had earmarked for me. You see, my two big brothers had recently gotten their Ivy League MBAs at Dartmouth, and this was the career path that had sort of been laid before me. Dad had worked very hard to save up for my graduate school education, and this was more of an expectation. I was sick of school at this point, though, and needed a break, so I told them that I wanted to write and publish a book about Minnesota hockey instead. There was a very long, awkward pause that ensued, which was followed by the words "failure," "disappointment," and "you're just procrastinating from entering the real world." Oh, and there were also a whole bunch of four-letter expletives mixed in just for good measure. They reminded me that, in addition to having absolutely zero experience in publishing a book, I had barely *read* any books up to that point in my life. Ouch. Okay, sure, I had no business writing a book, but I didn't really care. I was on a mission. Gopher hockey was my passion. I loved it.

So I took a leap of faith and dove in head-first. I bought a tape recorder and just started interviewing current and former Gophers players, coaches, and media personalities. I wasn't going to be winning any Pulitzers, that was for sure, but the Gophers faithful were thrilled that something was finally going to be written about their beloved program. They wanted to read about the behind-the-scenes stuff and then laugh out loud to all of the funny stories. Word spread quickly that I was writing the book, and before long I was getting calls from players who wanted in. They had stories to tell, and by God they were going to tell them.

Then one day I got a call out of the blue from none other than Herb Brooks. Herbie was coaching with the New Jersey Devils in the National Hockey League at the time but still lived in the Twin Cities, so he would come to Mariucci Arena whenever he could to scout Gophers games. He'd seen my shtick and heard about my book and simply wanted to help me out. I was floored. I mean this guy was just larger than life to me, and I couldn't believe he had actually called. I figured he was going to give me a few minutes of his time and pat me on the head. Boy, was I wrong. We wound up getting together the next time he was in town and spent an afternoon together talking hockey. Herb told me he respected the fact that, even though I wasn't good enough to play Gophers hockey, I still wanted to be a part of the team. You see, Herb was all about growing the game, and I think he saw in me a young guy who was ripe to be recruited for his cause. He was right.

Well, after a year of research, nearly 200 interviews, and countless miles on my 1988 charcoal grey four-door Plymouth Horizon, it was done. It was appropriately titled *Gopher Hockey by the Hockey Gopher* and would exceed even my wildest expectations. Within days of the book hitting bookstores, TV and radio stations were calling me, asking me to come on the air to tell stories. Bookstores started calling and asked me to come in for book signings. It was crazy. That Christmas the book was a regional bestseller, and I wound up doing three more printings before it was all said and done. Just like that, I was officially a published author.

Since then I've written nearly 50 sports books and have somehow managed to make my career doing my passion. Along the way, though, I've tried to stay true to many of the life lessons and values I learned from my hero, Herb Brooks. Let me explain. In 2002, shortly after leading Team USA to a silver medal at the Winter Olympics in Salt Lake City, Herbie turned down a multiyear, multimillion-dollar contract to coach the struggling New York Rangers. Herb had coached the Rangers back in the early '80s, shortly after the Miracle on Ice, but he was now 65 years old and wanted to spend the next chapter of his life with his kids and grandkids, something he missed out on a lot of the time the first go-round.

His new plan was to be a full-time grandpa and a part-time motivational speaker. As a speaker, Herb commanded big bucks and was highly sought after by executives from Fortune 500 companies from coast to coast. What he needed, however, were some books to tie into his presentation. Enter Ross the rodent. He told me that there were several big-name writers he had considered for the job, guys from ESPN and the *New York Times*, but that he wanted to go with someone he knew and trusted. He wanted to go with an underdog, a little guy. It was as if God picked up the phone and gave me a call.

We would spend the next six months working on the book. It was intense. He was already working with Disney at that point on the movie *Miracle*, which would feature Kurt Russell as Herb. I knew that when the movie hit the screens that winter, the book sales would take off like wildfire. Every day was a new adventure, and I was having the time of my life. Flash forward to the weekend of August 11, 2003. Herb and I had been asked to play in the U.S. Hockey Hall of Fame Celebrity Golf Classic at Giant's Ridge, on the Iron Range. He was an inductee of the Hall of Fame and was always willing to help them out and do his part to promote the growth of American hockey. We talked about the book and about how we were nearing the finish line. After 11 holes of golf, Herb had to say his good-byes and hit the road. He had a speaking engagement in Chicago with a big pharmaceutical company in the morning and had to drive back to the Twin Cities.

I finished out the round, attended the awards banquet, and then headed over to my in-laws' place on nearby Lake Nichols, where I spent the rest of the afternoon with my wife and daughter. Then, after packing up and saying good-bye, we got into our car for the trip back to the Twin Cities. As we pulled away, I turned on the radio. Immediately I could tell that something pretty big had happened, because every station was in talk mode, and there were some pretty somber discussions going on. Then, I looked at my cell phone and could see that it was maxed out with messages. Something was going on, something big. Finally, after a few minutes of listening to the radio, we figured out what had happened. Herbie didn't make it home. He'd been killed in a car accident. I was beyond shocked. For hockey fans, this was sort of like remembering where you were on that exact moment when John F. Kennedy was shot. It's just seared into your memory, forever. August 11, 2003, that's the date.

I pulled over, hugged my wife and daughter, and just cried. I even hugged my dog, Herbie, who I had named in honor of my friend and mentor. For the next three hours, we listened to caller after caller talk about what Herb Brooks had meant to them. People laughed, they cried, they told funny stories, and they all remembered Herbie. They talked about what a hockey game back in 1980 had meant to them and to their families.

Finally, we came upon the crash site just north of the Twin Cities. Police cars and satellite news vans were still there, as were helicopters, which were hovering overhead. It was a huge story, CNN even carried it live. Traffic was slowed to a crawl by that point, too, as onlookers came to pay their respects to a real American hero. As we drove by, we saw a makeshift memorial that someone had made along the side of the road out of two hockey sticks in the shape of a cross, which was then draped with a Gophers jersey. I broke down and just sobbed.

It was right then and there that I decided I wanted to do my part to continue his legacy for the next generation of hockey fans. I thought about what I could do, and the first thing that came to mind was to finish our book that we had started, only turning it into a tribute to his life instead. And that is exactly what I did.

I called it *Remembering Herbie: Celebrating the Life and Times of Hockey Legend Herb Brooks*, and proceeds benefited the newly created Herb Brooks Foundation. Later came *America's Coach: A Biographical Journey of the Late Hockey Icon Herb Brooks*. Today I serve as the president of the board of that wonderful organization, and I couldn't be prouder to be able to give back to a cause that's so near and dear to my heart. Now proceeds from all of my books benefit the cause—which is all about growing hockey and giving the game back to the kids. That was Herbie's passion, to get everybody drinking his Kool-Aid and grow this beautiful game—from the base of the pyramid up. Our mission is to get the kids back outside, where they can have fun and not have to worry about all the parents screaming and yelling at them about Triple A traveling teams and full-ride scholarships. Here's a scary Cliff Clavin tidbit: nearly 50 percent of 11-year-olds quit hockey in Minnesota today because they're simply burned out or don't want to deal with the politics of hockey, which has become big business. How crazy is that? Herbie used to joke that his dream team would be a team of orphans…no parents to screw things up! If you want to help the cause, please visit www. herbbrooksfoundation.org—thank you for your support!

I learned a great deal about leadership from Herbie, and hopefully you will enjoy reading about some of his life lessons as told by a handful of his former captains. His captains were extremely important to him, and we talked about them often. Guys like Bill Butters, Mike Polich, Joe Micheletti, and Mike Eruzione—you'll hear from all of them in the book about what it meant to wear the C for one of the most iconic coaches in hockey history. Herbie had different captains for different teams, and each had a different skill set. When you read about Bill Butters, Herbie's first-ever captain, you'll cringe when you listen to him talk about the take-it-or-leave-it role Herbie had for him. Herb's philosophies on leadership were profound, to say the least.

Looking back, the Miracle on Ice truly changed my life and showed me that you can be anything you want to be as long as you have a dream and a passion. What started as a demotion for me, becoming Goldy the Gopher after getting cut from the University of Minnesota hockey team, turned into a making-lemonade-out-of-lemons story. Today I'm lucky enough to be able to make my career doing something I absolutely love. I get to watch lots of hockey, write books about hockey, travel the globe speaking to corporations about the life lessons I learn from writing about hockey, and from the proceeds I make doing all of that hockey-related business—you guessed it—I get to relax and have fun by taking my wife and daughter to hockey games. Yes, I really do believe in miracles!

It's the Captain's Privilege to Hoist the Cup First...

There is a protocol for what a player is supposed to do immediately after he wins the Stanley Cup. It goes something like this: First, he cries as the clock ticks to zero and then tosses his equipment yard-sale style all over the ice. From there, he leaps on top of his goalie in utter bedlam, hugs his teammates, and then celebrates like a rock star. After a few minutes of that, he will get in line, single file, to do the customary handshake at center ice with his teammates. He will be respectful of his devastated opponent and try not to act too excited. Next he will stand around laughing and smiling with his teammates as he waits for the commissioner to come out with the Cup. In the meantime, he will compare playoff beards, see who has the most stitches and/or missing teeth, and even maybe sing a few verses of "We Are the Champions" along with the fans— assuming he clinched at home. If not, he hums it to himself in his head. Either way, he's singin'.

Then, after the Cup keeper rolls out Stanley and the commissioner congratulates the other guys for coming in second, he waits patiently for his turn to touch the Cup. The commissioner will first hand it to the team captain and then awkwardly pause for a photo of the two while trying to prevent the captain from ripping it out of his hands in excitement. Once the captain frees the Cup from the commissioner's clutches, he hoists it proudly for all to see. He will then have the choice of doing a victory lap around the rink, all the while cautiously watching for TV cords and confetti, or he will pass it off to a teammate of his choice.

Whom he decides to hand it to is always the $1 million question. It's one of the most exciting moments for diehard hockey fans. Will he go for seniority and give it to the oldest guy on the team? Or will he give it to his buddy who he has been to war with and feels is most deserving? Who will he honor? Nobody knows. One thing is for sure, though, nobody can talk about the said pecking order. No way. That would jinx it. It can be thought of ahead of time, but never discussed openly. Ever. Once the handoff is made to the second player, however, it now becomes that guy's choice as to who he will hand it to. He will then choose whom to pass it to and so on and so on, until everybody has had their turn raising Stanley.

Eventually, the management gets involved—you know, the suits—and the best part about that is watching to see who will fall flat on their back after raising the heavier-than-expected 35-pound Cup on slippery ice while sporting leather wingtips.

Later, they will all pose for an on-ice photo at the faceoff circle. All the players will smoosh together on top of each other with the Cup in the middle. Stars up front, role players in the back. Everybody holds up his index finger to let the world know "We're No. 1!" This tradition, by the way, was started in 1988 with Edmonton and then continued when Calgary repeated it in 1989. Now it's *the* moment everybody waits for afterward. Players don't want to be doing a random TV interview when this is going on because this is the photo that will hang in their office or bathroom until they are 90. It's the "money shot" of the best memory of their life.

The tradition of the on-ice passing of the Cup is wonderful for the fans, but it certainly hasn't always been that way. Looking back, it's widely believed that the first time that the Cup was awarded out on the ice as opposed to in the locker room was in 1932, with the Toronto Maple Leafs, but the practice did not become a tradition until years later. Over the ensuing years, it was common for the commissioner to place the Cup on a table that was brought out onto the ice after the game. He would hand it to the captain, and then the players would come by and pose for pictures standing next to the Cup on the table. Nobody hoisted it until they got back to the locker room.

In 1950, however, Detroit's Ted Lindsay became the first captain to hoist the Cup over his head and then to add a twist, he skated around the rink. According to Lindsay, he did so as a courtesy to the fans who wanted to have a better view of the Cup. It wasn't a victory lap per se—that tradition wouldn't come until 1971—when Montreal Canadiens captain Jean Beliveau skated around the ice at the Chicago Stadium with the Cup held high and his teammates following behind. The reason he did it wasn't to draw attention to himself, though, it was to say good-bye to the fans as the 40-year-old promptly retired following the game.

There are many poignant stories about whom the captain has chosen to hand the Cup to over the years. In 1997, after the Red Wings won the Cup, they gathered for a golf outing that summer. Afterward, defenseman Vladimir Konstantinov and team masseur Sergei Mnatsakanov were going home in a limousine that they had arranged for. Sadly, on the way home, the driver got into a terrible accident after falling asleep at the wheel. Both men suffered brain injuries, and just like that, Konstantinov's career was over. The next year the team beat

Washington to repeat as champions, and when team captain Steve Yzerman got the Cup from Commissioner Bettman, he skipped the traditional victory lap and instead skated straight over and handed it to Konstantinov, who was sitting proudly in his wheelchair. The team had dedicated the season to him, and there weren't too many dry eyes in the house that night.

In 2007, after the Anaheim Ducks won the Cup, it was all about the Niedermayer brothers, Rob and Scott. Rob had played the good younger brother on three prior occasions by going home to Cranbrook, British Columbia, to celebrate when Scott had won the Cup. Rob had been to a pair of Finals over his career but had lost both times. They had even faced off against each other in 2003 when Scott's Devils beat Rob's Ducks. Their mom openly admitted that she was rooting for Rob in 2003 because she so desperately wanted him to share the experience that Scott had. So, when they finally won it together in '07, Scott, the team captain, chose to hand it to Rob first—in what he would later call the "highlight of his career." To celebrate, the two brothers chartered a helicopter on their day with the Cup and partied on top of a nearby glacier in the Canadian Rockies—standing literally and figuratively on top of the world.

Lastly, when the Pittsburgh Penguins beat the Red Wings to win the championship in 2009, Sidney Crosby handed the trophy to Billy Guerin. Eventually, after all the players had their turns, the Cup reached team owner Mario Lemieux, who then returned it to Sid, symbolizing a passing of the championship torch from one generation to the next, from one captain to another. The fans went crazy.

INTRODUCTION

Welcome to *Wearing the C*, my latest hockey book, which cele-brates the science, art, and act of leadership. I spent over a year researching and interviewing more than 100 players for it, and I couldn't be prouder of the final product. I had one simple cri-teria for the subjects I interviewed: they had to have been a cap-tain at some point in their careers. At first I was going to limit my interviewees to only players who wore the C, but I decided to also add players who wore the A. Assistants, or alternates, are certainly captains, as well, and they are very much a part of the leadership dynamic on any team. I also talked to a handful of coaches and general managers, because I wanted to find out how they selected their captains and why.

The how and the why are really what this book is about. I wanted to find out how players lead, and why they do what they do in order to be effective leaders. Along the way, I saw trends, patterns, and common denominators develop. I also recognized that there are many ways to lead, but not necessarily any one *right* way. Rather, it was more about how that individual chose to lead *his* way for the good of that particular team. He might be a fiery leader, loud, in your face, with no fear of calling out players in the locker room. Or he might be a quiet, lead-by-example kind of a captain, who lets his actions do the talking for him. Either way, he finds a way to get the job done—because if he doesn't, he isn't go-ing to have that letter sewn onto his jersey for very long.

With regard to how the book came together, it was a puzzle. One of the biggest issues I faced was just trying to figure out which players had worn letters. It was an extremely difficult process to track everybody down, but it all came together in the end. As for my methodology, I wanted to capture a diverse mix of superstars, role players, enforcers, and grinders—each with his own unique story to tell. Americans, Canadians, Russians, Czechs, Slovakians, Swedes—they're all in there. The only guys I didn't talk to were goalies, because they don't wear the C. Okay, Roberto Luongo wore it in Vancouver a few years ago, but that was the only guy in, like, 50 years to do so. The bottom line was that I didn't just want to hear from the same old people who get quoted all the time, I wanted to go off the grid and get some unique perspectives from guys of all different eras. And I didn't just limit myself to NHL captains, either. Some guys wore it in the minors, or in college, or on an Olympic or international team. Pretty much every player who's good enough to play in the NHL wore a letter at some point along the way—so I tried to capture their stories, life lessons, and wisdom—regardless of where it was.

There are the old-school guys: Phil Esposito, Ab McDonald, and Lou Nanne; the young guns: Zach Parise, Eric Staal, and Kyle Okposo; the icons: Wayne Gretzky, Joe Sakic, and Steve Yzerman. The lead-by-example locker-room guys: Scott Stevens, Brett Hull, and Mike Modano; the foreigners: Zdeno Chara, Mikko Koivu, and Igor Larionov; the coaches and GMs: Scotty Bowman, Glen Sonmor, and Larry Pleau; the father-son combos: JP and Zach Parise, and Pat and Erik Westrum; the siblings: the Hatcher boys—Derian and Kevin, as well as the Hankinson brothers—Peter, Ben, and Casey; and the grinders who wore it as a reward for doing the dirty work: Lance Pitlick, Mike Peluso, and Marty McSorley. Oh, and I included my buddy Natalie Darwitz, too, captain of the 2010 U.S. Women's Olympic team—because we had to have a female perspective. It's an eclectic yet wonderfully diverse assortment of individuals, and their insights are fascinating. Their stories, memories, and life lessons will not only make you think about how you lead others, they will hopefully inspire you to reach heights you never dreamed possible.

I have chosen to give you their stories and answers in the form of anecdotal quotes, too, directly from them and not rewritten in *my* words only to be regurgitated back to you. Hopefully, you will enjoy the format and appreciate it in its simplest and purest form. Some guys I spoke with for two hours, others for 15 minutes. Some I met with in person, other interviews took place over the phone. No, I didn't just turn on my tape recorder and transcribe the conversations, either, it's *much* deeper than that. An entire hour-long interview might be whittled down and condensed into three paragraphs. I wanted to sift through most of the noise and get to the good stuff, and hopefully I have succeeded in that goal. Either way, I didn't want to pollute their quotes with a bunch of filler. So I didn't.

My caveat to you is this: please be understanding with regard to the fact that there are a *lot* of players in the book with ties to Minnesota. Why? Well...I'm from Minnesota and I'm an unabashed and unapologetic homer. Not only did I have access to them, I am friends with them. I still play hockey with many of them in fat-guy beer leagues. Plus I'm a 10-plus-year working member of the media with the NHL's Minnesota Wild, so I had extraordinary behind-the-scenes access to the players in the locker room and in the press box. The bottom line, though, is that, whether it's a guy who played with the Wild, North Stars, or Gophers, he wouldn't be in here if he didn't have something interesting, poignant, or insightful to say. Look, if you're from Minnesota, you'll enjoy the memories. If not, hopefully you'll... enjoy the memories. Either way...just try to relax and enjoy the memories! Nuff said.

In chapter 1 you will read about what it meant for the players to not only wear the C or the A, but also about the deeper significance of how that achievement has affected or changed their lives. I wanted to find out how they led, their style. In chapter 2 you'll read about which captains the players looked up to along the way. I wanted to learn about whom their influences were and how they inspired their own leadership styles. I tried to capture stories of courage, of epic sacrifices in dramatic Game 7s, and of what it felt like to lead a team of grown men to a Stanley Cup title. I wanted it all. I found that the guys really opened up when they were able to talk about somebody else other than themselves. Yes, as you will see, one of the most common denominators of natural leaders is that they're incredibly humble—many of whom *hate* to talk about themselves. For them, it's all about the team. Luckily, they opened up when they were asked to talk about their role models and on-ice heroes.

Chapter 3 delves into how coaches actually go about the process of choosing their captains. It was fascinating. Some coaches and general managers insist on appointing "their guy," while others allow the players to do the voting themselves in the locker room. The politics, the closed-door meetings, the drama—that's all a part of it. Chapter 4 will give you a small taste of those enigmatic players-only meetings that we, the fans, only get to hear about. Are they urban myth or the real deal? Ever wonder what's *really* said behind those closed doors? Now you'll know.

Lastly, in chapter 5 you will read about the life lessons they learned from being captains and how they were able to apply that wealth of information to their lives after hockey. I wanted some nuggets of wisdom, some "business takeaways" that you, the reader, can bring into the office and use to become more effective leaders in your own lives. The answers here are profound and sincere. I think you will enjoy them.

Overall, I wanted to capture honest, real, and raw emotions—that's the essence of what this book is all about. I wanted to honor their achievements and chronicle them in a unique and enjoyable format that has never been done before. What an odyssey it was, but I was up for the challenge and I absolutely had a ball in the process. A big thanks to all the players and coaches I interviewed, especially Scott Stevens and Bobby Clarke, for so graciously contributing forewords to the book. I am truly honored and humbled to be able to share this incredible treasure trove of data with you. Thank you for taking this journey with me. Hopefully you will have half as much fun reading about and celebrating this amazing history and information as I did in getting the opportunity to bring it all to life. Cheers!

CHAPTER

1

WHAT DID IT MEAN FOR YOU TO WEAR A LETTER?

"O Captain! my Captain!..."

To get asked to serve as a captain at any level of hockey is an outstanding distinction to have on your résumé, but to be selected to wear it in the National Hockey League—that's a pretty elite fraternity. There are only 30 teams, which means there are only 30 guys who wear the C, along with another 60 who wear the A. That's it. In a league where up to 800 players see time on the ice every season, that says something. It says you're a leader. So to be named as a team leader, to be that liaison between the players and the coaching staff, and to be the face of your franchise both on and off the ice—it's a privilege reserved for only the very best of the best. Yes, to wear the C in the NHL is without question the ultimate honor in all of sports. That's right. You see, in hockey being the captain actually means something. In most sports the captaincy is more about popularity than about leadership. No disrespect to the other sports, but hockey is different, and it's always been that way. Sure, major league baseball catcher Jason Varitek was a leader with the Boston Red Sox, but as the team captain, what did he actually do? And does Eli Manning, quarterback of the NFL's New York Giants, have any official duties as the team captain other than standing there for the pregame ceremonial coin flip?

In hockey, meanwhile, the guys who wear the letters have actual on-ice responsibilities and duties. Yes, they have an official capacity, it's not just for show. During games they're the ones who are appointed to interact with the referees in order to keep their teammates and coaches informed about penalties, infractions, and lineup changes. In fact, the refs and linesmen will only talk to them, nobody else. That's just a tiny piece of what a captain really does, though. Perhaps most importantly, it is he who must serve as the liaison between the players and management. The coaches will devise a game plan and then lean on their guy to make sure it gets executed properly. They can preach to the players all they want to on the ice about X's and O's, but there will be no buy-in until the cap' sells it to the boys in the dressing room. The players *hear* the coaches, but they don't necessarily always *listen* to the coaches—big difference. It's like when your mom asks you to do something you

Did You Know?

Under the "Designation on Uniform" section of the rules, it states: "The letter C or A must be sewn on the jersey of the team captain and alternate captains. The designation is traditionally placed on the left side of the jersey, though the IIHF, NHL, and NCAA rules specify only that it must be in a conspicuous location on the front of the player's jersey." Incidentally, two teams in the NHL have jerseys with the designation on the right side, as the positioning of the crest on the front leaves insufficient space on the left for the letter—the Detroit Red Wings (regular jersey) and the Phoenix Coyotes (third jersey).

Source: http://en.wikipedia.org/wiki/Captain_(ice_hockey)

don't want to do, versus when your best friend's mom asks you to do the same thing. Best friend's mom 1, your mom 0.

That dynamic, of being the conduit between the coaches and players, is a very slippery slope. The captain will be held to a higher standard, and quite frankly, most players can't deal with that kind of stress. That's why there's only one captain. And that's why picking him is such an ordeal for teams to go through. He has to convey their message on a daily basis, while playing spy, constantly reporting back to the enemy camp. It can be tricky, to say the least. Leadership is a bizarre intangible; there's no set guidelines to follow when selecting a captain. Each team has its own rationale for picking their guy to lead the rank and file. And if there's drama brewing within that rank and file, it's up to the captain to convey that intelligence back to the coaches. They need to know about it so that they can address it. Little things lead to big things in locker rooms, and they need a mole on the inside who can keep them up to speed on everything going on. Sound crazy? Welcome to the world of an NHL captain.

And that's just the beginning. In practice captains have to be the ones who set the tone and lead by example. They have to be the hardest-working guys out there, regardless of whether or not they feel good or are injured. The guy with the C outworks everyone else, that's why they call those extra workout sessions during the summer "captains' practices." And if the team's in a slump, it's up to him to figure out a way for them to get out of it. For the captain, it's all about personal sacrifice and putting the needs of others before himself. Translation: it's *all* about the team. Always.

Off the ice, meanwhile, he will have *many* other duties. In the locker room he has to be the glue that holds the team together. He's the guy who has to create and foster team chemistry by making the rookies feel comfortable alongside the grizzled veterans. If a kid fresh up from the minors isn't fitting in, it's

up to the captain to bring him up to speed and build his confidence. If that means staying after practice and working with him
one-on-one shooting pucks for a few hours, or helping him figure out the coach's playbook, or taking him out for a beer if he's
homesick for mommy, then so be it. That's all part of the job.

It's also up to the captain to quell the drama that can and
will occur when you have grown men of all ages bickering and
whining about the amount of ice time they are or aren't getting, or about how much money they are or aren't making. It's
up to them to keep the peace between the Canadians, Russians,
Czechs, Americans, and Finns—all of whom, by the way, want
more ice time and money. Different music choices in the dressing room, different restaurant choices on the road, bed-check
at the hotel, making sure everybody's on the bus on time, figuring out the seating arrangements for the charter flight to
Winnipeg—that *all* falls under his jurisdiction. Trouble at home
with the wife or girlfriend? Go talk to the captain. Unhappy
about getting sent down to the minors? *Ohhh, caaaptain…*

The captain has to make tough, unpopular decisions on a
daily basis, many of which are going to alienate him from his
teammates. He is the one who is going to have to call a player
out who isn't pulling his weight. It is he who must demand accountability in practice every single day. And nobody will listen to him or respect him unless *he* is the hardest working guy
in practice himself. It's up to him to call players-only meetings
when things aren't going well. It's up to him to have the team
over to his house for a barbecue on an off-day, where guys can
get together and let their hair down. It's up to him to coordinate the logistics for the entire team to meet off the grid at an
out-of-the-way tavern, where they can all sit in the back room,
drink beer, and let off some steam—without worry or repercus-
sion of the coaching staff punishing them for doing something
wrong.

When the team is winning, the media talks to all the players in the locker room. Everybody'd fat and happy when the team is winning. But when things go south and the team heads into the tank—and they all do—it's the captain whom the media want to talk to. And they want answers. As the face of the franchise, like it or not, that's *his* responsibility. All of this and *so* much more falls on the captain's shoulders. Oh, and on top of all that, he still has to do his job as a first-line player and put up points. Everybody is counting on him to lead the team to victory, no matter what. Talk about pressure!

For all of these reasons and *so* many more, finding the *right* captain to lead your team is a *huge* deal. The captain isn't necessarily your best player, he's your most respected player. He's a guy who's liked and admired yet can still have difficult conversations with his teammates when need be. He sacrifices his body by blocking shots, and you'd better believe he won't take a bad penalty or a selfish penalty that will put the opposition on the power play. No way. The DNA of the prototypical captain can embody many different characteristics. He's humble, hard-working, dynamic, strong, fearless, selfless, courageous, sensitive, and above all else... he *leads by example.* (You will hear that phrase way too many times in this book, and for that I pre-apologize.) In a nutshell, he's the team's conscience—always putting what he feels is best for the team above all else. The top officers in the military are taught to care for their soldiers' needs before their own, and the same is true for the man who wears the C. To him, the C stands for character.

Again, it's up to the coaches and general managers to find the *right* captain for their particular team. That's the key. If it's an older, veteran-laden team, then maybe they need a quiet captain who just says the right things and sets a positive tone. If it's a young team full of rookies or foreign players, then maybe you need a vocal leader who's going to get after guys with fire and brimstone. Either way, it takes just the right blend of leadership, athletic ability, and likability to make a good captain.

Great NHL captains are synonymous with their teams. Even casual hockey fans know that the "Great One," Wayne Gretzky, led his Edmonton Oilers to four Stanley Cup titles in the mid-'80s; that "Stevey Y" (Yzerman) was the heart and soul of his Detroit Red Wings squad for more than two decades; that "Super Mario" (Lemieux) overcame injuries and cancer to lead his Penguins to a pair of titles in the early '90s; and that "Mess" (Mark Messier) was the king of Gotham City after delivering on his personal guarantee that his Rangers would end their 54-year Cup drought in '94. You just can't make this stuff up, folks. And they know today that "Sid the Kid" (Crosby) wears the C in Pittsburgh, that "Ovie" (Alexander Ovechkin) is the other commander-in-chief of our nation's capital, that the "Z-Man" (Zdeno Chara) towers above all others in Bean Town, and that "Captain Serious" (Jonathan Toews) quietly leads the way in the Windy City.

Like mythical figures, they become the proverbial "face of the franchise" that the fans identify with. In the new digital age, they truly transcend the game in ways Gordie Howe, Rocket Richard, and Bobby Hull could have never imagined. And it goes far beyond marketing—they are icons whose jerseys are sold by the truckload to every diehard fan who cheers for them. Loyal fans take genuine pride in their leader. After all, he's *their* guy. And, yes, that loyalty sells tickets—lots of tickets, and beer, and parking, and corporate signage on the dasher boards, and luxury suites, and on and on...*cha-ching!* Branding is everything in today's game, and usually your captain's jersey is the No. 1 seller. He'd better be good.

The best captains possess certain intangibles that can only be described as extraordinary. The have the ability to rise to the occasion. It's in their blood. When the game is on the line, that's when the captain plays bigger than everybody else. That's when he earns his paycheck—in crunch-time, in the clutch. He's the guy with icewater in his veins, in overtime of Game 7 of

Did You Know?

NHL teams don't need to designate the same player as captain from game to game, though most do. For instance, in 1985, when Boston Bruins' captain Terry O'Reilly retired, Ray Bourque and Rick Middleton were named as co-captains of the team. Middleton wore the C during home games and Bourque for road games during the season's first half, and then the two switched for the second half. This arrangement continued until Middleton retired in 1988 and Bourque became the sole captain. Some teams name two (such as the Buffalo Sabres during the 2005–2006 and 2006–2007 NHL seasons) or three (such as the Vancouver Canucks during the 1990–1991 NHL season) captains for a season. Some teams rotate captains rather than keep one for an extended period of time (the Minnesota Wild rotated captaincy every one or two months until the 2009–2010 season, when Mikko Koivu was named the first permanent captain since the franchise began). During each NHL game, however, only one player can officially be designated as captain.

Source: http://en.wikipedia.org/wiki/Captain_(ice_hockey)

the Stanley Cup playoffs. Need a big goal, a game-winner? He's your guy. If he can't make an end-to-end rush capped off by the perfect toe-drag, top-shelf, back-handed wrister, then he'll deflect it in form the point with his teeth. That's his role. He's a two-way player who's not afraid to go into the corners or stand in front of the cage. And if someone messes with one of his teammates, he's the first guy there to drop the mitts and start throwin' hands. He's the leader, the protector...no matter what. Nobody puts Baby in a corner!

I wrote a book a few years ago titled *The Code: The Unwritten Rules of Fighting and Retaliation in the NHL* and, in so doing, learned all about the sacred honor code that governs when, where, why, and how players can fight. The code says heavyweights fight heavyweights, lightweights fight lightweights, goalies fight goalies, and yes...captains fight captains. In the 2012 Stanley Cup semifinals between Phoenix and Los Angeles, this code got put to the test when Kings captain Dustin Brown laid out Coyotes defenseman Rostislav Klesla. Phoenix's longtime captain Shane Doan, wanting to protect his teammate's honor, immediately challenged Brown to a fight, and the gloves came off. That's how you earn respect in the National Hockey League. Doan, the face of the Coyotes franchise—having been with the team since its days in Winnipeg—is one of the most respected players in the game today because of the way he leads by example and stands up for his teammates.

The captain is the guy who's there when things get tough. He remains calm and cool through adversity, and you can always count on him to be right there by your side. He's your biggest cheerleader, as well as the first guy to go over to his goalie to offer words of encouragement after he lets in a soft goal. After the game he's the first guy in line to shake hands, looking guys in the eye, giving them a firm grip, congratulating them on their victory. He wins with class and loses with dignity. He's the leader, yet he doesn't relish the spotlight. He's humble. He gives 110 percent every day and always leaves everything out on the ice. When the team doesn't play well, he points to himself first with humility and says, "Boys, I have to be better." And he will be, because he's the captain. And so will everybody else, because they trust him and they believe in him. He's their leader. With grit and tenacity, he inspires those around him to be greater together than they could be individually. That's what great leaders do, they get everybody rowing the boat in the same direction—all focused on a common goal.

The captain rises to the occasion and inspires greatness from all who follow. That's his job. If he does it the right way, he is adored, beloved, cherished, and put upon a pedestal. His legacy will only grow over time. If not, he's either demoted or, in all likelihood, traded away so that they can give the C to someone else and try it all over again. There may not be a tougher, more stressful role in all of sports than that of an NHL captain. Yet it's the most rewarding job in all of hockey. Heck, it's the most coveted role on the team that nearly every player who pulls on an NHL sweater aspires to reach at some point in his career. They may not say that publicly, but deep down they want the C. *Everybody* wants the C. When that big C gets sewn onto his jersey, it gives him confidence, courage, and strength. It's as if he transforms into Superman the moment old Clark puts on that cape—it gives him super powers us lowly mortals can only dream of. Got it?

Here's what some of those superheroes had to say about what it meant for them to don the C...

Adrian Aucoin

It was extremely special to wear the C in Chicago because of all the history with that franchise. A real honor. Just knowing the guys who wore it before me—Chris Chelios and Dirk Graham, whom I had a lot of respect for—made it even more meaningful to me. I know that you don't always need a letter on your jersey to be a team leader, but it says a lot about the kind of person you are and about the level of hard work that you've put in.

There are different types of captains for different types of teams, I think. When I was in Chicago [2005–2007], we were a really young team—so I kind of took on more of a teaching role. We knew that we were in a transition at that point and that we probably weren't going to be competing for the Cup, so we worked really hard on getting better every day. That became our focus—what we could do to continually improve and come together as a team. When you become your team's captain, you sort of wind up becoming a father figure to the other guys, like it or not. That's just a part of the job. You have to be able to steer them in the right direction if they get off course. When they're not too sure which way to go, and which choices to make, then you need to step in and show them the way. The *right* way. Eventually, that team went on to win it all, so I took a lot of pride in knowing that I had played a small part in the development of some of those younger players.

David Backes

Being the captain, it's a big honor. With it comes a lot of responsibility, though. It means making decisions that aren't necessarily what's best for yourself, but what's best for the team. It means you have to be the hardest working, most committed guy out there—every day, no matter what. Your work ethic sets the tone. It's up to you to set an example for the rest of the team and to hold everybody accountable to that. There's no excuses when you wear the C, the buck stops with you. That's your job, that's the deal.

Leading by example means having self-control. It means knowing when to choose your spots. When the other team's biggest guy punches you in the face, you've got a decision to make. Is this my chance to show how tough I am, where I can take a stand and prove myself, and show those guys that we're not going to be intimidated? Or is this my chance to show my toughness by being disciplined, by showing my dedication to my teammates by taking that punch and not retaliating? If we score on the ensuing power play, then I am vindicated. That's a tough, heat-of-the-moment decision—but one you find yourself having to make more often than not in this game. When you master those situations and get a grasp of when each response is best, that's when you know you've come a long way in being a good leader.

Keith Ballard

No matter what level you are at in hockey, wearing a letter is a huge honor. Being a captain recognizes and reinforces the fact that you are doing some things right. As such, when you get that letter sewn onto your jersey, you gain the responsibility and understanding that you are now being relied on and looked to a little bit more by your organization, as well as by your teammates. As far as I'm concerned, though, it shouldn't matter whether or not you wear a letter. Being a captain shouldn't change how you go about your business—how you prepare, how you practice, and how you play the game.

Wearing a letter for a Canadian franchise, especially, can be tough. It's a ton of pressure. That guy has to be able to stand up and face the music every day with the media, which is way more intense up here than in the States. Way more. He's got to be able to talk about what went well and what didn't, continuously, over an eight-month season. It can be a real grind. I saw a situation come about this season with Dion Phaneuf over in Toronto where a member of the media had called him out, essentially, questioning his leadership. Dion's a guy who plays extremely hard every night. He's an emotional player who leads by example and really wears his heart on his sleeve. So to have to answer questions from a guy like that, who's pretty far from the game and pretty far from the locker room, that's the burden that comes with wearing the C. When the group doesn't do well, it first reflects poorly on you and then just works its way down from there. It's the same with general managers, coaches, assistant coaches, and on to the players—starting at the top and going down the pyramid.

Brian Bellows

I wore the C with the North Stars and then the A with a few different teams in the NHL throughout my career. It meant a lot, sure. It's an honor that comes with a lot of responsibility. The main thing is that you have to put your teammates first. Sometimes that means sacrificing your own personal statistics and glory for the betterment of the team. Everything becomes about the team. On the flip side, though, that attitude really helped my game in critical times. Being the team leader means you have to be able to think clearly and calmly. If you're the captain, then guys will be looking toward you to see how to react. I coach youth hockey today, and I've always found that the kids who are the best leaders are the ones who are the calmest under pressure.

Ray Bourque

I broke in with the Bruins back in 1979 and learned a ton from our captain at the time, Wayne Cashman. Terry O'Reilly took over for Wayne a few years later, and he was incredible as a leader. I sort of grew up watching and learning from those two what it meant to be a professional. So when I was later asked to wear the C for a team like Boston with such a rich history and tradition, at first I was scared to death. I embraced it, though, and considered it to be a huge honor and privilege. I wore that C with a lot of pride for 14 years. It was an incredible experience.

For me, leading by example meant being prepared, being dedicated, and being a great teammate. Those were natural instincts that I had and were things that I tried to pass on to other teammates. It wasn't always easy wearing the C, though. Sure, when you're winning it's great, but when times are tough—you're the guy everyone turns to. I learned pretty quickly that you have to be able to bring people together when things aren't going well. You have to

Ray Bourque hoists the Stanley Cup after the Colorado Avalanche won the 2001 Finals. The championship—his first—capped a 22-year career.

step up and try to find solutions to problems on a daily ba-sis. It took me a while to grow into the role, but I eventually got it figured out and became very comfortable with it.

Rod Brind'Amour

It's a huge honor to be named captain, especially in the sport of hockey where it really means something. Hockey is the ultimate team sport, in my opinion, so to be recognized as the leader by your coaches and peers is pretty special. I took it very seriously. My goal was to be the hardest-working player every day. I wanted to lead by example and hope that everybody else just followed along. I think to be a great leader you have to be yourself, that's the key. You can pattern yourself after someone who you like and admire, but at the end of the day, you have to be real. People will see right through phoniness and they won't follow you. The big thing for me, too, was just the concept of the team. I was just one guy, so I really relied on my teammates—espe-cially the veterans who'd been through it before. I wanted to embrace and empower those guys. When we won the Cup in Carolina in '06, yes, I wore the C...but we had a lot of great leaders on that team. You can't just do it with one guy, you need a core group of guys who are all going to set the tone and hold everybody accountable in order to be successful.

Neal Broten

What did it mean to me? It meant that I had to lead by example and work hard every night. It meant that I had to spend more time working with the younger guys and sort of mentor them whenever I could. It meant that I had a few more responsibilities out on the ice. It meant that I had to communicate what the players wanted to say to the coaches and sort of be that go-between guy. And it meant that I had to deal with the media after games and whatnot. Other than that, it didn't really mean that much to me, to be honest. It was just a part of my job. I will say this, though: it means a lot more to be chosen as one of the captains by your teammates, as opposed to being named by your coach.

Andrew Brunette

I wore the C in Minnesota and then wore the A in both Atlanta and Colorado. The C is the ultimate prize, though. To wear it is just a huge honor. You grow up as a kid idolizing those guys wearing the C because they're the team leaders. As a hockey player, other than winning the Stanley Cup, I honestly don't know if there's anything more meaningful than when your coaches or teammates honor you that way—it's a huge pride thing, no question.

As for my leadership style, I just tried to be myself. You can't pretend to be anybody else out on the ice or in the locker room—your teammates will see right through it, and it will backfire on you. Look, you don't necessarily need a letter on your jersey to be a team leader. Different players have different leadership attributes. Leaders take things upon themselves at different times during the game, whatever and whenever they feel necessary. There's no right way or wrong way to be a leader, it's just about finding *your* way. It all starts with work ethic, though, because you really do have to lead by example—otherwise nobody will respect you as a player. There's all sorts of ways you can lead. It might be fighting the other team's biggest guy, setting the tone early in the game with a big body check, or simply working harder than everybody else in practice—that's all leadership.

Bill Butters

I wore the C at the University of Minnesota for coach Herb Brooks. It was Herbie's first year coaching, and the program had just come off its worst season of all-time. We had nowhere to go but up; things were pretty bad. Well, Herbie thought that the team had become too soft and had lost its purpose. He knew that he needed to change the climate. So he came to me and told me that he wanted me to be his captain. Now I was not a big goal scorer by any stretch of the imagination, I was more of what you might call a role player. Herbie understood that.

He took me aside and told me that he wanted me to play really tough in practice. Really tough. He told me that he wanted me to hit guys, hard, and that if they wanted to challenge me, that it was even all right to go ahead and fight them right then and there. I couldn't believe my ears. I told him that these guys were my teammates, my best friends. He said, "Bill, our team isn't very good. We need to get tougher and in a hurry. This is the role I have for you, either accept it or move on." Needless to say, I decided to accept it. And, as a result, a bunch of our top players, guys like John Harris and Mike Polich, suffered the wrath of that decision. Herbie wanted our guys to toughen up, and that was what I helped him to do. It wasn't a very popular move, but I knew that what I was doing was ultimately helping the team. The team doubled its win total that season and then went on to win the national championship the following year. So, even though it was difficult to have to play like that and do those sorts of things to help my teammates, in the end we were all much better off for it. The only downside is that, even today, whenever John Harris sees me coming toward him, he flinches!

Personally, it was just really neat to be able to work with Herbie like that, sort of behind the scenes. I was almost like his assistant coach during that time. He would share with me his strategy on what he wanted to do and how he wanted to do it. That was Herbie, he always had a plan. He asked me if I would participate in being a part of the solution to a problem, and in retrospect I'm very happy that I did. Today I make my living as a hockey coach, and I certainly learned a great deal about leadership from Herbie. Herbie was smart enough to realize that you needed different types of captains for different types of teams. Sometimes you need gritty character guys who are the heart and soul of the team, other times you need your best skill players. It just so happened that I fit the right skill set and mentality for what he felt was right for that particular team. Either way, it was a huge honor to be Herb Brooks' first captain.

Ryan Carter

I wore the C in junior with the Green Bay Gamblers, and I take great pride in that. Hopefully, I'll wear it one day in the NHL, too. I'm still young, but that's something I'll certainly be working toward. Being the captain isn't about being the best player, it's a lot more than that. When they pick the captain, they are looking at how that person conducts himself both on and off the ice, first and foremost. Captains are the guys up in the weight room after practice, when everybody else has left for the day. Captains are unselfish, they have good character traits, and they are usually the most respected guys in the locker room. So, as a player, it's a huge honor anytime you're chosen to be a team leader among your peers. To be selected to wear the C, it's the ultimate reward, really.

Keith Ballard on Emotion and Leadership

I remember my first year in Florida, and it was game No. 81 of the regular season against Atlanta, a must-win for us. We were tied for eighth place and literally had to win that night or else we were out of the playoffs and the season was over. Our captain, Brian McCabe, had just come back from having surgery, which forced him to sit out for a couple games. He had taken a puck in the face, and it was pretty bad. He suffered a broken nose, a broken orbital bone, and had a whole bunch of stitches. His face was a mess, but he insisted on playing. Well, Atlanta was playing really well and we just couldn't get anything going. Late in the game Caber decided to get us fired up, so he dropped the gloves with their star player, Ilya Kovalchuk. They went at it pretty good, and we couldn't believe it. To see your captain at that point, fresh out of surgery, showing that kind of emotion and leadership—it was epic. We fed off of his sacrifice, and it was a huge spark for us. In fact, we rallied and wound up winning the game. It was just awesome to see how one guy could have such an effect on an entire team, I'll never forget it.

Zdeno Chara

It's a huge honor to be selected as your team's captain, a true privilege. You don't demand others to serve you, you have to be there to serve others. You have to be there for your teammates no matter what. You have to have a feel for what they need and when they need it. It's a lot of responsibility, and I have never taken that for granted. You have to be a good leader not only in good times, but also in bad ones—which can be tough. I just try to be there for my teammates and try not to act differently than anybody else. Just because I wear the C doesn't mean I am any better than anybody else, it just means I am expected to lead by example and do the right things on and off the ice to represent my organization. I take great pride in that and will never take that for granted.

As for my style? I try to lead by example. I also try to be a good listener to my teammates, so I can be there for them. Sometimes I get emotional in the locker room, but only if I feel it's important. Otherwise I am probably more reserved overall. I'm quiet most of the time, but I can certainly get loud when I need to. I'm a big guy, too, so when I get loud…it's loud! I also want my teammates to know that I will always stand up for them, even if that means dropping the gloves and fighting. Sometimes you need to step outside your comfort zone and do that, whether it's to protect your teammate or just to change the momentum of a game. You have to be willing to do that as a team leader. I expect them to do the same for me, as well. That's what being teammates is all about. We have each other's backs at all times, no matter what. I think the most important thing for leaders is for them to just be themselves. You can't copy anybody; it won't work. You have to find your style and go with it. If it works, people will follow you and listen to you. If not, you're probably not going to be a leader for very long.

The highlight of my career, without a doubt, was winning the Stanley Cup in 2011. Winning the Cup was such a special moment for me, I mean, that's why we play this game. To get it from the commissioner and be the first to raise it, what an incredible honor. As captain, it's your right to accept it first and then you get to decide who gets it next. For me the choice was obvious, I handed it right to Mark Recchi. I knew that he was going to retire after the game and that was it for him, so I couldn't have been more excited for him at that moment.

The highlight of that entire moment for me happened right before I got to hoist it. I remember skating toward the commissioner and turning around to look at my teammates. They were all cheering so loudly with their hands up in the air and could hardly wait for me to get to touch it. They were genuinely excited for me, and it was very emotional. I pointed at all of them to acknowledge them and to let them know that it was all about the team at that moment. It took all of us to get there, and I was so proud of them. That was the best moment for me, right then and there. Every captain wants to have that personal connection with his teammates, that's what it's all about. Those guys, they were my brothers. You have to make a lot of tough decisions, some unpopular decisions, to get to that point, but once you get there it's all worth it. I get goosebumps just thinking about it.

Kelly Chase

I'd worn the C all the way up until I got to the NHL. But then, when I settled in, I realized that I was more of a role player versus an every-other-shift kind of a guy. It's harder to give a guy like that a letter because he's on the bench most of the time. I wound up getting it on occasion, though, when guys were injured or when they rotated it, and it meant a lot to me. It was a real accomplishment, in my eyes. I took great pride in it because it meant that the people in charge had the confidence in me to lead my teammates. It meant that the coaches trusted me to compete hard every shift and lead by example. So it was a big reward for a guy like me to wear it.

I think, more than anything, wearing a letter pushed me

to hold myself to a higher standard. Whenever I looked down and saw that letter on my jersey, it forced me to be more accountable. I wasn't a very good player, so I had to make sure that my work ethic was in check at all times. Even outside the rink, it made me think twice about my actions. It constantly pushed me and motivated me to continuously get better. I just did whatever I could to help my team win. Even the little things, like helping the younger guys and working with them to get them more confidence. Leadership to me is making sure all of the different personalities are included and feel like they're a part of the team. When guys start going a little bit sideways, you just bump them back into the middle with the rest of the group and away you go. That's it.

My role was to protect my teammates and make sure that they had confidence out on the ice. I did the dirty work that a lot of players couldn't do or wouldn't do. I remember one time when I was wearing the A in St. Louis and I really wanted to feel like I was contributing. I didn't get a lot of minutes out on the ice, so I had to make the most of whatever ice time I got out there. We were playing Dallas, and a bunch of their guys were running around, including their captain, Derian Hatcher, who was just pounding on two of our star players, Brett Hull and Pavol Demitra. That's a big no-no, so I challenged him to a fight. He said that he couldn't fight me because his coach would fine him if he did. I felt really handcuffed on what I could do at that point, so the next shift I got out there, I skated over to the Dallas bench and announced to their entire team that because Derian wouldn't fight me, I was going to beat the shit out of one of their star players, Benoit Hogue. I actually wound up breaking his jaw, which I felt bad about, but I needed to make a point to their team that what they were doing was simply unacceptable. Things settled down after that, which was what I had hoped for. That was how I showed leadership, I protected my teammates and gave them the confidence to do their jobs without the fear of being taken advantage of. Teams knew that if they wanted to take liberties with them, then they were going to have to deal with me.

Tom Chorske

I wore the A in Ottawa and with the Islanders, and it was a huge honor. Just to think about who those guys were who wore letters before me is so humbling. I always had so much respect for the opposing captains that I played against. To line up against a guy like Mark Messier or Joe Sakic or Scott Stevens—those guys are not only Hall of Fame players, they are just unbelievable leaders. Those guys have integrity and are the ultimate professional athletes, in my opinion. They've reached the pinnacle, as far as I'm concerned. Even though I never had a chance, I always strived to be like those guys.

The responsibility of being a leader on an NHL team is a pretty important one. It shows that the coach feels that you've got some qualities and characteristics that matter to him and that he feels can help the team. There's a lot of pressure on that guy wearing the C, though. They deal with the critics and with the media and with management and with ownership and with the fans—not to mention their own teammates. These are the things that captains and leaders of teams do. That's their job. They shoulder the load.

As for my style, I was never a real vocal guy in the locker room or anything like that. Sure, I'd speak up every now and then if we were struggling, but I was more effective as a leader by helping guys on a one-on-one basis. I would try to help my teammates individually, maybe after practice or during the off-season. If they were struggling or in a slump or going through a hard time, I wanted to be there for them—especially the younger guys. I wanted to help them build their confidence, so I would stay late and work with them on whatever it was that I could. I enjoyed taking those guys under my wing a little bit and giving them some helpful advice to make them better players. When they played better, the team played better—that was the bottom line for me.

I wanted to do whatever I could to make my team better. Sometimes coaches leave those players alone to let them either sink or swim, but I was never a big fan of that approach. I'd rather take that guy aside and encourage him to work harder. If the coach wasn't happy with his effort, then I'd tell that guy that, as well…constructively and positively, so he didn't lose his confidence. Sometimes I would just try to get the guy to laugh a little bit to try to get him to relax. I remember one time when I was in Ottawa, I sat next to this kid named Bruce Gardener. He was really having a hard time scoring, so I told him that he had to get his stick's attention. I told him that it wasn't performing properly for him, so he needed to take it into the bathroom and dunk it in the toilet. He looked at me like I was crazy, and then just went and did it. Sure enough, he scored a goal that

Rod Brind'amour on the Perks That Come with Wearing the C

The best memory I have from my time with the Cup actually came the night we won [for Carolina in 2006]. Being the captain, they let me bring it home after the game. I will never forget getting home about 5:00 in the morning and putting it in my kids' bedroom. Then to see their reaction when they woke up next to the Stanley Cup was just priceless.

night, and afterward we just laughed about it. It was like that hilarious scene in the movie *Major League*, when Pedro Cerrano had to make a sacrifice for his possessed bat, "Jobu!" Who knew a swirly could have such a profound effect on a guy's performance? For me, lightening the mood and getting guys to just chill out a little bit, sometimes that's all it takes to find your way out of a slump. It was a story that some veteran had told me when I was a rookie and now I was able to pass it on myself.

Wendel Clark

If you can show up on time all the time, work hard day or night, and get along with everybody, that's pretty much your qualities right there. You don't have to be the best player or the best anything, but you have to know how to get all the guys to get along, going in the same direction, and just play the game. (Source: "Some of Hockey's Best Leaders Tell Us What It Takes," by Paul Grant, ESPN.com, November 12, 2007.)

Bill Clement

I wore the C for the Washington Capitals and it was a privilege, for sure. But it also amounted to a great degree of responsibility that I'm not sure I was ready for at the time. I had just won back-to-back Stanley Cups with the Flyers when I found out I had been dealt to the Capitals in 1975. They were only in their second year of existence at that point and had just set the league record for futility the year before, so this was not a good situation to be coming into. I was only 24 years old, and to be honest I'm not sure my maturity level was significant enough to be an effective captain, especially for a team that was so woefully deficient. I ended up being the leader of the "nowhere gang." As in, we were going nowhere. We lost a ton of hockey games, which was tough. I had just come from an organization that had incredibly high expectations for winning, and now I was on a team that had exceedingly low expectations. It was extremely difficult to stay positive, so I just worked as hard as I could and tried to lead by example. I was a workaholic, and my goal was to get the guys to follow my lead. That was all I could do. Looking back, though, being named as the captain of a young team like that meant a great deal to me. Knowing that they had traded for me and wanted me to wear the C was a huge honor.

Ben Clymer

I wore the A in Washington during the latter part of the '06 season. A couple veterans got traded, and I got asked to wear it, which was a big deal for me. I'd just won a Stanley Cup with Tampa Bay, and I think they saw some leadership qualities in me, which made me feel really good. I'm not going to lie, I was certainly very proud to wear it. It's an honor to wear a letter in the National Hockey League, they don't just give those things to everybody. Along with the honor, though, came a lot of added responsibility and pressure. It kind of heightens your sense of further accountability to your teammates. Once you put that letter, on you're expected to lead by example and put the team first. You have to work harder and do the right things all the time, no matter what. There are people watching you now and you can't screw it up.

It really means something to be the captain in the NHL. I mean, in other sports it's a paper captaincy. The thing that's unique about hockey is that it doesn't have to be your star player who wears it, like the quarterback in football. Sure, it's often one of your better players, but it could be anybody

Did You Know?

Jean Beliveau played 18 seasons with the Montreal Canadiens, captaining the Habs for a decade—longer than any other player in team history—en route to leading the team to five Stanley Cup titles. So respected was Beliveau that the NHL waived the customary three-year waiting period and immediately inducted him into the Hall of Fame.

who best exemplifies leadership. There's no one right type of personality for the job. The key is that they have to be themselves, they have to be authentic. Because, if they're not, the guys will see right through that. A quiet guy can't all of a sudden become a big rah-rah guy in the locker room; it just won't work. The bottom line is that guy just has to work harder than everybody else and do the right things. If he does, everybody will follow.

The guy wearing the C is the guy everybody turns to and can count on when the chips are down. That's the guy who's going to lead through the fire and be there by your side when you go into battle. In a sport like hockey, where it's a constant physical grind night in and night out, players tend to rally behind their leader maybe more so than in other sports. So great captains, who are trusted and respected, and whom others genuinely believe in, they have a ton of influence on the direction of the team. Guys will follow them with their hearts and souls. Great leaders can get the most out of guys and get them to play better than they thought they could. In the playoffs, it's not necessarily the best teams that win, it's the teams that work the best together. Individual talent only gets you so far in this game, you have to have great leadership and great team chemistry—that's way more important, in my opinion.

Matt Cullen

I've been very fortunate to have been able to wear the A in Minnesota, with my hometown Wild. What a dream come true. Seeing my jersey hanging in my stall the first time with that big beautiful A sewn onto it, that was one of the proudest moments of my career. It was so cool. My dad was my coach growing up, and we'd talked about leadership together on so many occasions. When I saw that jersey, the first thing I thought of was him, and how proud I knew he was going to feel the first time he saw me playing in it. I couldn't have done it without him, no way. Other than winning the Stanley Cup, which I was very fortunate to do a few years ago, getting a letter is the next highest honor I've had as a professional.

To be thought of as a leader in your chosen profession means a lot, it really does. And to be singled out as a leader among a room full of leaders, how humbling is that? You put your heart and soul into being the best at your craft as a professional, so when your peers recognize your hard work and acknowledge it, that's a real honor. When you're a captain, you not only represent yourself and your team-mates, you also represent your fans, your organization, and your entire community. So it's a big deal. Guys might downplay it to be modest, but trust me, it means more than people think. I know it does to me.

Ken Daneyko

I wore the A off and on over my career, and obviously you take pride in it. It's nice to be counted on a little more for leadership, although I never felt like you needed to wear a letter to be a team leader. But certainly when you get it, you wear it with pride, knowing that management trusts you to represent the team. As for my style as a leader, I was pretty vocal and talked a lot in the locker room. I tried to get guys fired up and motivated by either telling jokes and keeping them loose, or simply by my intensity. I was more emotional than Scotty [Stevens], and that was my role, to ease the tension in the room and keep the guys relaxed—especially in the playoffs—so that they could do their jobs out on the ice.

Natalie Darwitz

The first time I wore the C was back when I was a peewee. Ironically, I was the only girl on the team, which was pretty cool. That was my first experience as a team leader, and to be honest, I really liked it. I wore it again in high school and then went on to wear it for Team USA in international competition. I wore it several years for our U.S. National teams, and then the highlight was wearing it at the 2010 Olympics in Vancouver. To be named as the leader of your country's team for an Olympic Games is almost indescribable. It's probably one of the highest honors that can be bestowed upon you. To know that the coaches had that level of confidence in me and that they felt that way about me as a leader, it meant the world to me. It was so humbling. I wanted it, though, and was definitely ready for the challenge.

Being the captain is certainly not an easy job. You've got big personalities, big egos, and the potential for big drama. Sometimes it's no fun at all. You're usually not making very popular decisions, instead you're making the "right" decisions—which are usually quite different. It's a daily battle of what's right versus what's popular. At times you are going to upset some of your teammates, which is 100 percent inevitable. One group wants one thing and another group wants another, so what do you do? You just have to listen and try to make the choice that you think is best for the overall good of the team.

There's a lot that goes on behind the scenes when you're the captain. A lot. Like it or not, you're sort of like the glue that has to hold everything together. There's a magnifying glass on you at all times, and there's just a ton of pressure that comes with it. You're being watched at all times, both on and off the ice, and people are constantly judging how you carry yourself. It's ultimately your responsibility to get the team going in the right direction and to set the tone. If things go well, it's the team's success. But then if things don't go well, everybody is going to turn to you, the captain, for answers. It all falls on your shoulders. That's why not everybody is cut out to be the captain, because you have to have that sort of selfless attitude. When the team wins, you might get a pat on the back, but when the team loses, it's *all* on you. Not everyone can deal with that, and it certainly took me a while to get used to it.

Every one of my teammates on that Olympic roster had been a captain on either her high school or college team prior to joining the team, so I just tried to work hard and lead by example. I know that's cliché, but that was my approach. I mean, what was I going to teach them about leadership that they didn't already know? My goal was to get everybody else to do the same, because I knew that if that happened, then the team was going to have success. With 20 strong and opinionated females all vying to be leaders, I just tried to make sure that everybody had a voice and felt included. I tried to focus on everybody's strengths and put them into positions where they could have success.

I also delegated quite a bit because I knew I could trust them. They knew what I was going through, they'd all been there. They saw my approach and how I did my job, and they had confidence in me, which in the end felt really good. I became a more effective captain, or leader, over time. As I gained more and more respect by doing the right things and making the right decisions, I continually earned more and more of their trust. Trust is huge in any position of leadership, it really is.

Shane Doan

Being the captain of the Phoenix Coyotes is a huge honor. As a player, it's the ultimate acknowledgment, I think, from your peers as well as your coaches, to be named as the team leader. It's very humbling when you think about who the guys were who wore it before you. I have so much respect for the guys I followed here in Phoenix: Kris King, Keith Tkachuc, and Teppo Numminen. They were all very different in their approach, but all tremendous leaders in their own ways. They were all very, very good captains, and I was really fortunate to have been able to learn as much as I did from each of them. There are little bits and pieces of each of those guys that have rubbed off on my own style and approach to the game. As for my style? I'd like to feel like I'm everybody's biggest cheerleader. That's the biggest thing for me, to make sure my teammates know that I'm on their side. I don't care if guys make mistakes as long as the effort is there. They know as long as they work hard and do their jobs, that I'll do whatever I can for them in order for our team to succeed. The bottom line when you wear the C is that you have to be a servant to your teammates. And you have to be willing to do whatever it takes to help your team win. Once they see you leading by example, then everybody else just follows along. Eventually, when you work hard enough and long enough, good things will happen for you.

Jim Dowd

My first time wearing the C was for Jacques Lemaire. I got to play for him in New Jersey and then again in Minnesota. To be the captain of a team coached by one of the game's all-time greats, a guy who is one of the most well-respected players and coaches in the history of the game, it was a dream come true. It doesn't get any better than that. I had so much respect for him not only as a coach but as a human being. He was the guy who gave me a shot when nobody else really would, so I would have done anything for him. As for my style as captain, I just worked hard. That's what leadership is in my opinion, hard work and doing the right things. That's it.

Mike Eruzione

To be asked to wear the C for the 1980 U.S. Olympic team was one of my proudest moments as a hockey player. To be the captain of that team, a captain among captains, was truly an incredible honor. We had an entire locker room of leaders, though. Nearly every one of the guys on that team had been his team's captain in high school and college. That was no coincidence, either. That was really important to Herbie, he wanted guys with leadership characteristics.

I was a little older than most of the guys and had previously played on some international teams, so I had some solid experience under my belt as a player. I, too, had been the captain of my high school and college teams, so I definitely felt prepared for the job. For me, it was all about being true to yourself and who you are. I think Herb saw in me someone who was going to be himself, and not change when he got the C sewn on his jersey. Being a good captain means you'll do anything for your teammates. It means that you'll

Mike Eruzione (21), captain of Team USA, in action against the Soviets in the 1980 Winter Olympics. Photo courtesy of Getty Images

show them the ultimate respect both on and off the ice.

One of the things I really tried to do with that team was to keep everybody together. After practice I would organize outings for all of us to go to dinner or to a bar or to just hang out or whatever. Great teams, historically, are full of guys who genuinely like each other. So I wanted to make sure that we were all friends and that we got along. That can be tough on teams like that, where everyone came together from all across the country for a short period of time. One of the things that I'm most proud of is the fact that we became a very close-knit group. Everybody respected each other and trusted each other, and that translated into success for us out on the ice.

Phil Esposito

What did it mean for me to wear the C? Not a fucking thing! I wore it in New York at the end of my career, and it didn't mean a damn thing. And that's the truth. I don't know what else I can say about it. I think it's a bunch of shit! It only means something to you fucking guys in the press because you need something to write about! Guys say it's an honor to wear it? My ass. I don't think it means a fucking thing.

I'm not a fan of being a captain whatsoever. I could care less whether I was a captain or not. Hell, I never asked to be the captain, they [management] told me I was the captain. To me, the captain of the team was the guy who organized the parties. That was it. In fact, nobody wore the C in Boston from the late '60s to early '70s. Instead Johnny Bucyk and I each wore the A. He was the unofficial captain, though, because he was the oldest guy on the team. So when we won the Stanley Cup in 1970, he was the guy who got to hoist it first at the Garden, out of respect. Bobby Orr, one of the all-time greats, never even wore the C there. Yet *he* was the leader of our team, not me.

I tell you what. I don't even believe in having a captain on a team, no kidding. Only because they say you have to have something, I'd have three assistants…that's it. Hell, even when I was the GM in Tampa, I held out as long as I could. We didn't have a guy wearing a C there until '96, when my coach insisted upon it. He said, "We gotta have one!" I reluctantly agreed, which was stupid, but later felt vindicated when the whole thing blew up in his face. He chose Paul Ysebaert as captain, and about 20 games later he was benched. How the hell do you bench your captain?! You just can't do that. The media went crazy over it, too, which was a big distraction for the rest of the team. So I don't believe in having a captain, I never have.

Tom Gilbert

I wore the A in Edmonton, and it was a great compliment. To know that your teammates and coaches have chosen you to represent them as a leader, that's pretty humbling. As a player, that gives you a boost of confidence because it just reinforces the fact that you're doing something right. For me, to wear it in Edmonton, it was even more of an honor when you look at the long list of guys who wore letters there before me. It's a great accomplishment, for sure, but it also means that you have to work twice as hard as everybody else to sort of back it up. You really have to push yourself once you get to that level, it's like there's no going back. You have to work your ass off every single day, especially in practice. And during games you have to do all the little things, like back-checking, and diving for loose pucks, and finishing checks—because your effort is contagious to everyone else. Once you agree to have that letter sewn into your sweater, it's not about you as an individual anymore, it's all about the team. It's about getting the rest of your teammates to all rally around one common goal.

Curt Giles

It's a huge honor, especially if you are picked by your teammates. It might even be the biggest honor you can ever accomplish career-wise, in my opinion, when the people who you work with on a daily basis choose you to serve as the team leader. I wore the C with the North Stars, and it meant a great deal to me. I just tried to do my best and lead by example every day, that was it. I tried to focus on my work ethic in practices and in games, that's where I knew I could earn the respect of my teammates. I remember a guy telling me one time about what it was like to play with Mark Messier, and about how he worked so hard in practice that it was almost embarrassing for the other players because they simply couldn't keep up with him. Guys like that elevate everybody else around them and just make them better.

Beyond that, I really tried to make the younger players feel comfortable and let them know that they were a part of the team. That's so important in hockey. Being captain is not for everyone, though. For some guys, it's just unnatural for them to be singled out as a leader. I was pretty good at separating myself from being friends with my teammates if I had to say or do something that was unpopular. It's never easy to have to call someone out, but as the team leader, sometimes that's what you have to do. It's extremely difficult to do, but if something someone is doing is being disruptive to the team, then you have to do what you think is right.

Clark Gillies

I was very young when I got named captain in New York. Eddie Westfall was the captain at the time, and I thought he was doing a great job. He'd really helped me early on in my career when I first got to the team, and I really appreciated that. But some of the older veterans on the team wanted to make a change and go with a young guy. So myself and Bryan Trottier were nominated as the finalists, and the team voted. I got the most votes and wound up wearing the C. It was a huge honor to be selected by my teammates, yet it was sort of bittersweet in that I sort of took it away from Eddie. I loved Eddie, so that was tough. I was excited about the new opportunity, though. I'd always been one of the captains of my junior and midget teams coming up, but to wear the C on my sweater for an NHL team, I took a lot of pride in that. As for my role as a player, being captain didn't change me too much. I was always going to try to be a leader and I was always going to do whatever I could to help the team win. I never felt like I was any more important or special than anybody else. As far as I was concerned, there were any number of guys who could've or should've worn it.

I enjoyed being a team leader and liked the responsibility, but eventually I got tired of all the bullshit. I got tired of dealing with the media after losses and getting blamed for stuff I had no control over. I got tired of being the go-between between the coaches and the referees, too. I mean, every time there was penalty or a discrepancy I seemed to be running back and forth between the penalty box and the bench, chasing down the referee to ask him what the hell was going on. I just got sick of it. A big role of the captain is kind of being the social chair, and while I did enjoy that part of the job, eventually it, too, got old. It's the captain's job to coordinate off-ice activities, like getting the guys together for lunch when we're on the road. To build good chemistry and to become more than just a team on the ice, but a team off the ice, you have to organize stuff like that. It can be fun doing that stuff, but it consumes a lot of your

Mark Messier on Winning the Cup in Edmonton without Gretzky

"This one's for you, Gretz!" —To honor his former teammate and good friend, Wayne Gretzky, who had been traded to the L.A. Kings the season prior, this was what Captain Mark Messier declared when NHL president John Ziegler presented him with the Stanley Cup after his Edmonton Oilers beat the Boston Bruins to win the championship in 1990.

Source: "Legends of Hockey—Spotlight—One on One with Mark Messier"
(http://www.hhof.com/htmlSpotlight)

time. I eventually came to the conclusion that there were guys better suited for it than me.

So in 1979, after two years of being the captain, I went to Al [head coach Al Arbour] and told him I was ready to hand it over to the next guy. I missed the freedom of being able to just come to the rink and do what I do best, play hockey. I told him that I needed to concentrate more on what I was supposed to be doing out on the ice and not worrying so much about all that other stuff. I essentially gave him my resignation, and he accepted it. Good teams have 10 guys who could wear the C, and that was how I felt about my teammates.

Shortly thereafter, Dennis Potvin took over as the team captain and did a great job. He was reluctant at first to take it from me, but I assured him that I wanted him to have it. To be honest, it was *so* liberating. Ironically, we won the Cup the next year, and there was Denny, front and center when the commissioner presented him with the Stanley Cup. Was I bitter? Not at all, I was happy as hell! In fact, I skated over to him as fast as I could and ripped it out of his hands and did a victory lap!

Wayne Gretzky

It doesn't matter if you're elected captain by the players or appointed by management, the honor is equal. Either way, you have people who are trying to accomplish the same thing as you—winning Stanley—putting their confidence in you and basically telling you they trust you to lead them there. It's about respect and trust, as well as leadership. I don't think you can become a captain without earning respect first.

Bill Guerin

I'd worn the A for about 12 seasons in the NHL but never got to wear the C until I was 36 years old, when I was with the Islanders. So it was a big deal for me. It sort of validates you and all the work you've put in over the years. I had signed there as a free agent and found out at my press conference when [GM] Garth Snow announced it. I was shocked, I really was, totally blown away by the gesture. My whole family was there, and I'll never forget it. It was one of the proudest moments of my career. I mean, it's one of the biggest honors you can get in hockey. Just huge. I'll never forget seeing that big C sewn into my jersey for the first time, I almost lost it. No kidding. When you wear the C, you're a representative of your teammates and of your organization. To know that they value the way you perform on the ice and the type of person you are, that's an incredible feeling.

Ben Hankinson

I had a very uneventful seven-year pro career but was fortunate to have been able to wear a letter on a few teams along the way. It's a huge honor anytime you're chosen to be a team leader. Looking back, it's kinda weird, but wearing a letter means more to me now than it did back then. I appreciate it now a lot more. I wore the C in college at the University of Minnesota, so I was used to it. I certainly didn't take it for granted, but I think it was more of an expectation I had for myself to be put in that role as a team leader. For me, it was sort of a light bulb that went on in my head every time I hit the ice, constantly reminding me that I had to act a little more responsibly than I usually liked to. Even off the ice, as the team captain you were held to a higher standard. You had to lead by example and make good choices all the time, or else there were consequences. You had to be a little more careful about what you said and what you did. You just knew that people were watching you a little bit closer. It kept you honest, if that makes sense. It was tough because my nature was usually to act first and then think about it later, so wearing the C sort of straightened me out. Being a captain, you put the team and winning at the forefront. Period. Your personal achievements—goals and assists—those are secondary. No matter how good you are, if you aren't a team player who's willing to make sacrifices on a daily basis for the betterment of the team, you're not going to wear the C for very long. And you had better work twice as hard as everybody else, too. That's just a part of the job. It's not expected; it's demanded. The best captains, the guys who ooze character and heart, they just come about these qualities naturally. You can't fake it or try to be it, you either are or you aren't.

Casey Hankinson

What does it mean? Well, it depends on where you are, I suppose. When I wore the C in college at the University of Minnesota, it was an unbelievable honor. I was a two-time captain, and it meant that my coaches thought I was a good leader. Fast forward a few years, however, and the next time I wore it was in the minor leagues with the Cincinnati Mighty Ducks—Anaheim's farm team. Big difference. Being a captain in the minors can actually be the kiss of death because it means you've been there too long. Sure, it's always nice to be recognized as a team leader, but if your goal is to make it in the NHL, you don't want to get too comfortable playing down there or you'll never get called up. I mean, when you're the captain, you sort of have to be willing to sacrifice your personal goals and stats in order to focus instead on the overall success of the team. When you wear the C, the team comes before the individual. So if you are the captain at this level, you probably aren't going to have the stats necessary to get that call-up. It can certainly be a double-edged sword.

Being a captain forces you to evolve as a player as well as a person. I remember in college taking it way too seriously. I took every single loss personally and just absorbed all the weight of the team on myself. By the time I was in Cincinnati, I had really matured, and my leadership style had transformed, too. At that point my perspective had totally changed. When things would come up, you would sort of pick your spots. You stood up for what you thought was right and what you believed in, whether people agreed with you or not. Sometimes that's what makes a good captain, the ability to make a tough decision and then stand by it. Being a good leader is all about making unpopular decisions. You realize that you don't do things based on popularity, you do them based on what you feel is right—because that's the reason you were chosen to be the captain in the first place. If you, as the team leader, did it and led by example, then eventually everybody would jump on board.

The most fun I ever had being captain, believe it or not, was during the lockout year of 2005. I had gotten called up to Anaheim briefly the year before and was really excited about finally getting out of the minors. Well, that next year was the lockout, which killed the entire season and totally sucked. I opted not to re-sign with Anaheim because I didn't want to get sent down to the minors again. So I was sitting out, like most guys, waiting and wondering. Then I got a call from one of the coaches in Cincinnati, Dan Bylsma— who is now the head coach of the Penguins—and he basically told me that they really needed me to come back. He said that they had this really talented group of young guns, but no veteran leaders to help them along. Anyway, he kept calling and calling, so finally that December I agreed to come back and rejoin the team. They put the C on me right away, too, which was a very classy move. When I got there, I was shocked. They had this group of kids who were just incredible, guys like Ryan Getzlaf, Chris Kunitz, Dustin Penner, Ilya Bryzgalov, Kurtis Foster, Shane O'Brien, Joffrey Lupul, Aaron Rome, and Tim Brent—all of whom would go on to play in the NHL. So I was the oldest guy on the team, at the whopping age of 28, with all of these young guys—and I had a ball. It was my worst statistical season, but for sure the most fun because I was the leader of this group of guys who were so talented and just eager to listen and learn. They just soaked everything in like sponges. That's where being a captain is pretty cool, in situations like that, with good young players who respect you and are willing to do whatever you ask them to do. Looking back, that was probably the most rewarding season of hockey I ever had.

Communication is the key. As a team leader you have to be able to effectively communicate with everyone. Well, for me, that was tough sometimes because I was usually the guy who was cracking jokes and having fun. Whenever I needed to get everybody's attention, though, I would just get real serious. Funny story. Dan Bylsma, my old coach with Cincinnati, and I had become good friends over the years. Recently I was doing some business in Pittsburgh, so he invited me down to the locker room to meet some of the guys. So we were sitting there with Sidney Crosby, and Dan said, "Sid, this is Serious Hank, the guy who I have been telling you about." We shook hands and talked for a few minutes, nothing crazy. Then after he left, I asked Dan

why he introduced me as "Serious Hank." He then proceeded to tell me that he had been using me as an example
for Sid. He told him how, even though I was the captain
in Cincinnati, I was able to still be a practical joker and
prankster. He talked about how the guys liked me, yet I was
still able to get them focused and serious when I had to—
which he really thought was effective. He had explained to
Sid how I did that by turning down the music in the locker
room and getting dead serious. He told him that when I got
serious, then everybody else knew that they too had to be
serious. So he had been using me as some sort of motivational tool for the greatest hockey player on the planet,
unbeknownst to me, as my alter ego "Serious Hank." How
crazy is that?! Too funny, whenever Dan wants Sid to get
everybody dialed in, he channels "Serious Hank." I think it
freaked out Sid to actually meet me. He probably figured I
was a figment of Dan's imagination. Hilarious.

The bottom line with being captain is that it's all about the
team and all about making sure everybody's rowing the
boat in the same direction. I tried to get everybody to be
proud of their role, whether they were a first-liner or a
fourth-liner, it didn't matter. I wanted everyone to feel valued and that they were a part of the team. That was really
important to me. I never took my role for granted; it was a
huge honor. I knew that there were a lot of other guys on
the team who could've or even should've been the captain—it's a big deal. Guys might say that they don't care if
they don't get picked to be captain, but they do. Trust me.
Heck, I can vividly remember all these years later not getting chosen to be the captain for my squirt team. *My squirt
team!* Yes, it *still* bugs me! So don't kid yourself, it matters.
It's a huge honor because it basically validates you as a
team leader. So I never took it for granted, ever.

Casey Hankinson on Stepping Up

I remember one time when I was playing in the minors with the Cincinnati Mighty Ducks. It was the last game of the year against Milwaukee, and I knew that we were going to be playing them again right away in the playoffs. We had lost the year before to them, and I knew that we needed a little wake-up call. It was a tight game, and they were trying to intimidate us. Shane O'Brien was the only tough guy on our team, and he was in the penalty box. Wanting to capitalize on this, Jordin Tootoo, Milwaukee's tough guy, skates over to our bench and starts taunting us—calling us all a bunch of pussies. As the team captain, I knew that we couldn't allow this to go on, so I just jumped over the bench to stand up for my teammates. In hindsight, I probably showed a little bit too much respect for him by turning him around and letting him know I was coming. I should have just jumped him if I wanted to even have a chance against this guy. He just absolutely crushed me. He cut me for 13 stitches and left me bleeding all over the ice like a stuck pig. That guy is so packed, just a beast. It was awful. Anyway, afterward in the locker room, every single guy came over and thanked me. That meant a lot, it really did. Sure enough, we wound up beating them in the playoffs. I'm not sure if my attempt to be a goon helped or not, but I'd like to think it did. Sometimes as the leader you just have to step up and lead by example, even if that means taking a beating every now and then. In this instance, the guys fed off of that sacrifice, and it got the momentum and energy rolling in our favor. Mission accomplished.

Did You Know?

• Minnesota's Brian Bellows became the youngest NHL captain of all-time (19 years and 131 days) on January 3, 1984, when he took over from an injured Craig Hartsburg.

• Pittsburgh's Sidney Crosby, the youngest permanent captain in NHL history at 20 years old, became the youngest captain to win the Stanley Cup on June 12, 2009.

• Chicago's Charlie Gardiner was the first NHL captain born in Europe (Scotland) to lead his team to a Stanley Cup title (1934).

• Winnipeg's Lars-Erik Sjoberg was the first NHL captain born and trained in Europe (Sweden).

• Dallas' Derian Hatcher became the first American-born captain to win the Stanley Cup (1999).

• Daniel Alfredsson was the first European-born (Sweden) and trained captain to lead an NHL team to the Stanley Cup Finals.

• Detroit's Nicklas Lidstrom was the first captain born and trained in Europe (Sweden) to lead an NHL team to a Stanley Cup title (2008).

• The first two minority captains in NHL history were Dirk Graham, when he was named captain of the Chicago Blackhawks in 1989, followed by Jarome Iginla, who became captain of the Calgary Flames in 2003.

Source: http://en.wikipedia.org/wiki/Captain_(ice_hockey)

Peter Hankinson

I wore the C in college at the University of Minnesota, which meant a lot, and that was pretty much it—except for *one* game when I was playing professionally in the minors with the San Diego Gulls. I had played with the Fort Wayne

Comets the year before, but things obviously didn't work
out for me there, which was why I was in San Diego. Early
in the season we headed to Indiana to play them, and I
was anxious to see some of my old teammates. Now in
San Diego we had a bunch of former NHLers on the team,
mostly older veterans who were on their way out but still
wanted to play competitively. Lots of former Buffalo guys,
including Lindy Ruff—who would later go on to become
the Sabres head coach. We also had Keith Gretzky on the
team, Wayne's brother. Kinda funny, we used to call him the
"Good One." Anyway, I was heading into the locker room
to get dressed before the game and I saw my jersey hanging in the stall with a big A sewn onto it. At first I thought
somebody was messing with me, but then Lindy came over
and told me that this was a tradition that the older guys
liked to do. He said that whenever a guy would play his
former team on the road, they always made him a captain
for that night—just to piss off his former coaches. They figured if the player's former coaches saw him wearing a letter
on his new team, they would freak out for letting a potential
"diamond in the rough" go to another team. They figured it
would help that guy look better to the ladies in the crowd,
too, in case he had any former girlfriends in the stands that
night. So that was it, my one and only time being captain. I
definitely got some interesting looks from my old teammates
during warm-ups, it was hilarious!

Derian Hatcher

Wearing the C is an honor and a privilege, and that's how
it has to be treated. Bob Gainey was the guy who put the
C on me in Dallas, and I think for him it was a statement
about our team identity. He obviously knew my reputation as a player who wasn't afraid to mix it up, and I think

he wanted us to go that direction and get tougher as a group. He wanted us to be a hard team to play against on a nightly basis. I was very proud of that and took that very seriously.

Wearing the C is like a fine wine—the longer you wear it, the better you get. I wore the C for nearly a decade, and I think I was a much better captain at the end of my career than I was at the beginning. I just always had an open mind with regards to learning new things and taking advice about how to become a better leader. We had a lot of strong leaders on our team in those days, and I wanted to include their input into as much as I could. A lot of people thought I was a quiet leader, but I was actually pretty vocal in the locker room. I wasn't necessarily a rah-rah guy, but when things needed to be said, I had no problem saying them.

As for my style, I played hard and tried to lead by example. How you stand and hold yourself says a lot about a you, so I just tried to do the right things on and off the ice. For me, it was all about the team, whatever I could do to help us win was what I was going to do. I didn't care about much else than that, to be honest. We had great success during that time. We won six division titles in seven years and of course won the Stanley Cup in '99. That was the ultimate. I mean, that's why we play the game. That was a hell of a run. So, to be a part of that and to get to hoist the Cup, that's something I'll never forget. It was definitely the highlight of my career. I later wore the C in Philadelphia, and that was a huge honor, as well. It was a different experience for me but a very gratifying one nevertheless to play for an organization with such a rich history.

Kevin Hatcher

For me, it was an extra special honor to wear the C in the nation's capital, Washington. I had a great mentors there in Rod Langway, Scott Stevens, and Larry Murphy, who were all just tremendous leaders. What I learned from those guys is that it's important to lead by example and to treat everybody with respect. That was how I tried to lead when I was given the opportunity to do so, and hopefully that attitude and work ethic carried over to my teammates.

Brett Hedican

I wore the A in Vancouver, Florida, and Carolina, and it meant a great deal to me. To wear a letter at any level is a big deal. As players we all strive to be recognized as leaders, so it's a big honor. It means you're respected by your teammates, so I took a lot of pride in it. That letter serves as a constant reminder of the level of responsibility you assume when you agree to wear it. As for my style, I was definitely a lead-by-example kind of guy. I worked hard and tried to do the right things, especially in practice. Leadership isn't something you turn on and off. It's an attitude, a way of life, a level of professionalism that reflects the way you live your life on a daily basis. It's what you did to prepare for the upcoming season during the off-season. It's how you act when no one's looking. When nobody else wants to go to the gym, it means going to the gym. Alone. It means working hard to get better every day because you owe it to your teammates. Beyond that I just tried to be there for my teammates as best as I could and to try to pick them up when they were down.

Darby Hendrickson

I wore the C briefly with the Minnesota Wild, and it was truly one of the biggest highlights of my career. When the coaching staff and management puts it on your jersey, it says something. It says that you're the guy they want to represent the team, which is a huge honor. The C is the ultimate symbol of leadership, in my opinion. It means you're respected, you're valued by the organization. Respect is something you have to earn every day in the National Hockey League, and getting the captaincy sort of validates you. In Minnesota Jacques Lemaire had a rotating C, where each month a different player got to wear it based on his performance. So it meant something different to everyone who got to wear it. For me, it really motivated me in a way I'd never experienced before. It made me want to prove them right, if that makes sense. I wanted to reinforce their decision and make it very hard for them to take it off of me. Once you get it, it's like a drug—you crave it and don't want to give it up. It's totally unique, like it has mystical powers!

Phil Housley

I first wore the A in Buffalo, my sixth year in the league, and then wore it pretty much for the next 15 years I played in the NHL—including with Calgary and Chicago. I also wore the C for several years in the early '90s in Winnipeg. The only place where I didn't wear a letter was late in my career in Washington, because they already had a bunch of veteran leaders on the team—including Dale Hunter, who had worn the C there forever. At that point I didn't really feel like I needed to wear a letter to be a captain, though. And that goes for a lot of teams. Sure, it's an honor to be recognized, but when you've played 20-plus seasons, it's pretty much understood that you're a leader—regardless of whether or not you have a letter on your jersey.

I really enjoyed being a captain over the years. The accountability piece really drove me. I was never going to ask someone to do anything that I wasn't willing to do myself. Good leaders back up what they say. If I had to get on a guy to work harder in practice, then I took it upon myself to be the hardest-working guy in practice. That was just how I saw it. Overall, though, it's an honor because it means you're regarded by your coaching staff as one of the leaders on the team. You essentially become an extension of the coaching staff; you become their voice in the locker room. It can be tough at times, too, because you're not always going to agree with everything that the coaches want to do. They put their trust in you to fulfill the team's obligations, so it forces you to have to make some tough decisions that maybe aren't the most popular ones with your teammates, personally. I always thought of myself as more of a players' captain, though, in that I was more concerned with what the players needed as opposed to the other way around. I made it a two-way street as much as I could, and I think the coaches I worked with respected that about me. As the captain, you have to be able to effectively communicate back and forth, like a go-between, for all sorts of issues that come up. It definitely added another dimension to my job, though, without a doubt.

As for my style, I was a rah-rah guy. I liked getting guys up for games. I knew how important it was for guys to play with emotion, because everybody feeds off of that. As the captain, I always took it upon myself to make sure the team chemistry was good. When you have a locker room full of guys who not only like each other but trust each other and bond with each other, that's when great things can occur.

You know, in hockey you're on the road a ton. It's charter flight to bus to hotel to arena, over and over again. It gets lonely and you get into a rut. So it's important that when you're on the road, away from your friends and family, you get out with your teammates.

I remember one time when I was with Buffalo, we had just gotten beat in St. Louis and the guys were pretty down. We were on a road trip and were going through a slump, so I thought I would try to shake things up by getting a bunch of the guys out for some food and drinks. It was still early in the season, and I knew how important it was for them to bond together, especially the younger players. Our coach, Rick Dudley, had given us an 11:30 curfew to be back in our rooms, but as one of the team captains, I thought it was more important for us to stay out late and really do some team bonding. I wanted the guys to get to know each other and tear down the cliques between the foreign players and the American and Canadian players, and become friends—that's so important in hockey. I could see the guys talking to each other, letting their hair down a little bit, and I didn't want to kill the vibe. It wasn't like we were getting rowdy or anything, either. We were all hanging out and talking about the team. It was very positive.

The next morning we had a team meeting, and the coaches asked us if we had been out past curfew. A few players who weren't with us also wanted to know why we got to stay out later than everybody else. I immediately stood up and told everyone that it was me who kept the guys out late and that I took full responsibility for it. I wanted to stand up for those guys and take the bullet, regardless of the punishment. Then I explained why I did so, and afterward Coach Dudley told me that I had done the right thing. He knew that as one of the captains, it was important for the team to come together—regardless of whether or not I broke the team rules. He took it as a positive and said it was good leadership on my part. I really appreciated that.

Gordie Howe

I worked extremely hard and gave it everything I had every time I went out on the ice. I always figured that if you went out and gave 100 percent, then you could feel good about yourself at the end of the day, win or lose. I was proud of the fact that I always stood up for myself as well as for my teammates, too, that was important. I never wanted anyone taking liberties with me or my teammates, and I was willing to stand up for them, no matter what, even if that meant dropping the gloves every now and then. The way I saw it, you were never going to win any Stanley Cups if other teams knew that they could push you around. Heck, I had eight siblings growing up as a kid in Saskatoon, so it seemed like I was always fighting!

Brett Hull

It's so hard for me to put into words what it meant, to be honest. Because what it means to me is different than "what it means." I went from being the star player of the team, the guy who could go about his business and be a little loose and have fun, to the guy who has to now lead by example and do all the right things. I gotta be honest, that was a tough transition for me. Wearing the C forces you to take the responsibility for your teammates to another level, if that makes sense. When they put that C on your jersey, it can no longer just be about you, it's now about everybody else. It's *all* about the team.

Dallas Stars right wing Brett Hull takes the puck against the Edmonton Oilers during a game in February 1999.

There's lots of different versions of captains. There are vocal captains, silent captains, captains who just lead by example on the ice; there are captains who love to get the guys and their wives together outside the rink to build team chemistry and captains who love to be that liaison between the players and management—there'a just a myriad of different ways to do it. I've see 'em all over the years, and in the end it just comes down to being yourself. You can't fake it;

guys will see through you in a heartbeat. Hey, my way was unorthodox, but it worked for me.

You can really tell a smart organization by who's wearing the C. Without a doubt. Hell, a lot of times the captain isn't even really the captain. A lot of times they just give it to the best veteran player. The players know who the real, true captain is, though, the real leader. Anybody else is just a figurehead. Meanwhile, there could be a second-year kid sitting on the other end of the locker room who could develop into the heart and soul of the franchise if only he was given a chance to lead. Good teams recognize that and slap the C on that kid. So you never know. The guys like Steve Yzerman, who just do it all, they're rare. When you find 'em, you have to keep 'em.

Sometimes coaches will give the C to a player to try to change him, thinking it will turn him into a leader. It doesn't work. Trust me. To be honest, I think that's why I was given the C. I think they said, "Hey, Hull's got lots of talent, but we need to rein him in and make him a little more disciplined and responsible." They didn't give me the C because I was the best leader, they gave it to me because I was the best player. Big difference. Did it change me? A little bit. I had to evolve and grow up some, sure. But it didn't change me as a player.

Nope. Being the captain didn't change me as a player. I didn't block more shots or check more guys or even score more goals. It just forced me to rethink how I played the game. It takes being a teammate to a whole new level. It's not for everybody, that's for sure. Some guys gave it up because they couldn't handle it. It was a love-hate kind of a relationship I had with the C. I was a rebel and I insisted on doing things my own way. No matter what, I was going to stick up for my teammates, regardless of the consequences.

When push came to shove and I had to choose between my teammates and the organization, those were the guys I cared about. So I got in my fair share of trouble over the years, and as a result I had the C taken away from me on a few occasions. What can I say? I was a rebel!

There's a lot of extra work that goes into it above and beyond just doing your job as a player. It's a grind. As the captain, you have to come in early and you have to stay late. You have to be on time, all the time. You have to be in meetings with coaches on a regular basis. You have to help out the young guys and get them on board so they feel like they're a part of it. You have to deal with the media, a lot. You're looked at differently and under the microscope at all times. When the coaches came up with a game plan that they had devised to win a playoff series, *you* were the guy who had to make sure the plan got not only properly communicated to the other players, but above all else got executed. Whether you thought it was right or not, you had to sell it to everybody else. That's your job. The coaches, the GM, they're all looking at you to do this for them. They know the other players are following you, as the team leader. So it was a *lot* of pressure!

I always enjoyed playing on Olympic teams because it was a room full of captains. It was like there was no pressure. You never felt uncomfortable speaking. Everybody understood the role because they, too, had worn the C, so there was no drama. You could say whatever you wanted to with no fear of pissing anybody off. It was great. You see that with teams that win the Stanley Cup, too. They have a handful of guys who were either captains previously or could be captains if the situation was right. Either way, they're the locker room leaders who are well respected and keep everybody in line.

But again, back to my original statement about "what it means"—it's not really what it meant to *me*, it's what it meant to everybody else in the organization. They look at you in a different light when you wear the C, it's a *big* responsibility. At first, it was tough for me, but then once I embraced the role and everything that came along with it, I was okay with it. It was certainly an honor, and I was very humbled by it.

Mikko Koivu

Wearing the C for an NHL team is an honor, for sure. In Minnesota I'm the franchise's first full-time captain, and that certainly means a great deal to me. [The Wild rotated captains monthly under Jacques Lemaire from 2000 to 2009.] It also brings a lot of responsibility with it. I know that the spotlight is on me at all times as the captain, so I have to make sure I do the right things and lead by my example on and off the ice, each and every day. It's easy to lead when things are going good, but when things aren't going good, it can be tough. Each situation is different, so I just try to listen and respond accordingly. I try to keep an even keel, too, never too low and never too high. Hockey is a long season, and there are going to be a lot of ups and downs along the way. When things are going poorly, I want the guys to hang in there and stay positive. Then, when things are going good, I want them to enjoy it—that's really important, I think.

As for my style, I just try to be myself. If I try to do more than that, it doesn't work. A lot of people try to compare me to my brother [Saku], who's also an NHL captain, but we're very different people. I just try to be open-minded and learn as much as I can from my teammates. I make mistakes like everybody else, but I really try to learn from them in order to get better and grow as a person. That's what it's all about for me, just getting better every day, every week, every month, every year. If others follow that example, then that's great, because in the end it will only make our team stronger.

Chris Kunitz

I wore the A in Anaheim in '08 briefly, the year after we won the Stanley Cup. I was young, just a few years into the league at that point, but I think the coaches thought I played the right way and could emerge as a team leader. Incidentally, that was the year that Scott Niedermayer retired and then decided to come back early in the season. Well, once he returned I gladly gave up my A for him, which I think he really appreciated. I went and told the coach that it was an honor to wear it but out of respect to Scotty it should rightly go to the guy who'd worn the C the year before. I just felt like it was the right thing to do. Incidentally, Chris Pronger wound up wearing the C that season, despite the fact that Scotty had come back and rejoined the team. We had some great leaders on our team that season, and I learned a ton from guys like Chris, as well as from Scott and Rob Niedermayer, and Teemu Selanne. All of those guys really led by example and were a huge part of why we won the Cup the year before. I wound up getting traded to Pittsburgh the following season and have since worn the A there on a few occasions, as well…usually when a guy is out or on the shelf, though— which is okay, I'll take it whenever I can get it!

Jamie Langenbrunner

I wore the C in New Jersey, and it meant a great deal to me, no question. Anytime your organization asks you to represent the team as its leader, it's obviously a huge honor. As for my style, I just try to lead by example. I'm not super loud in the dressing room or anything like that, I just try to work hard and do my job. Hopefully, that rubs off on everybody else. If there's an optional practice, then you need to be there. Stuff like that. One of the biggest things nowadays that I find myself doing is picking up my teammates when they are struggling. The coaches and management are on guys these days more often than not, so a big part of my job is to pick them back up and make them feel like they are a part of the team. There are times when you need to put a little pressure on guys, and there are other times when you just need to pat them on the back. Bringing everybody together as a team is the ultimate outcome, though, always. Finding that balance and being there for your teammates is what being a leader is all about.

I also got to wear the C with Team USA at the 2010 Olympics in Vancouver. That was probably the single greatest honor I've ever had in my career. Winning the Stanley Cup is incredible, but to represent your country in that way is almost beyond words. So it meant a great deal to me. That locker room was full of captains, so it wasn't like I was going to say anything that they hadn't already heard or even said before themselves. So my message to them was basically: the sooner we all check our egos at the door and come together as a team, the sooner we can focus on what it's going to take to win the gold medal. I just worked hard and tried to lead by example, nothing crazy. I made sure that we all communicated a lot, too, which was important. I also tried to make sure that the guys on the fourth line felt just as important as the first-liners. That's tough, because everybody wants to get as much ice time as possible in those types of situations, but there's only so much to go around. Those fourth-liners were used to playing 30 minutes a night for their teams, and here they were getting six or seven minutes, which I'm sure was tough. The guys were great, though, and I couldn't have been any prouder of them. Unfortunately, we didn't bring home the gold, but we performed well, and I thought we really represented our country the right way.

Dave Langevin

I was very fortunate to have been a member of the Islanders when we won four straight Stanley Cups back in the early '80s. Dennis Potvin was our captain, and Bryan Trottier was the assistant in those days, and both were outstanding leaders. I was more of a role player on those teams and never dreamed of wearing the C. My job was to hit people and stir it up out there, not to be the team leader. It happened, though, believe it or not, when Dennis got injured. I will never forget walking into the locker room and seeing all the guys sort of grinning at me as I passed by. I didn't know what was up until I saw my jersey hanging in my stall with a big C sewn onto it. I almost fell over when I saw it! There were so many great leaders on those teams, so I felt completely unworthy of wearing it. No kidding. But Al [Arbour, head coach] wanted to reward my hard work and sacrifice by letting me wear it, and it was something I'll never forget. For him to choose me like that, heck, it was one of the biggest honors of my entire career. Heck, we had 20 captains on that team, but it was still a classy gesture. When you skate around with that thing on you, it changes you. It's like it somehow gives you powers you never knew you had. I played harder and had more confidence, that was for sure. It forces you to skate just a little bit harder every single shift. It's like everybody is watching you when you wear it, looking at your example. You don't want to let anybody down, either, so you play like it's the last game of the season every single night. I just tried to bust my ass and not embarrass myself, to be honest. Looking back, to be the leader of one of the most iconic Stanley Cup teams in NHL history, even for a short while, was the thrill of a lifetime for me.

Igor Larionov

I got to wear the C for the Russian Olympic team in Salt Lake City, and it was just an incredible honor. To represent my country, what could be better than that? And to be named as the team leader by our coaches, that was one of the highlights of my career. Being the captain means being a professional. It means leading by example. It means doing anything in order to help your team win.

Reed Larson

I wore the C in Detroit back in the early '80s. Being a captain means more to some people than others. To me I took it as a very prestigious honor, but at the same time I *never* thought of myself as any better than anyone else on my team. I didn't like being singled out and being seen as special or anything like that, so in that regard it was awkward for me. If anything, it humbled me more than anything else. It forced me to be more responsible and to think about others before myself. I wasn't really a cheerleader in the locker room or anything like that, I just worked hard and tried to be positive. I think I was well respected by my teammates because I wasn't a prima donna. I was willing to drop the gloves and fight guys in order to stick up for my teammates and I was always game for going out for beers after the game. Stuff like that goes a long way in a locker room, I think.

You know, it's easy to be the captain when your team is full of thoroughbreds and you're winning. Not so easy and not much fun when you're not winning, though. I look back at my team pictures from those days in Detroit and think we had more than a dozen different coaches in the nine years I was there. That's usually not a very good sign as to how things are going! So, when things aren't going too well, the media looks to the guy wearing the C for answers. Like I said, when things aren't going too well, those are never easy conversations.

Sometimes management just wants to go in a different direction, and that was the case for me after wearing the C for a few years with the Red Wings. Things were going fine, or so I thought, and then they pulled off a pretty big trade with Buffalo. We sent them four young, high draft picks in exchange for four veterans, one of whom was Danny Gare. The coach came in one day and told me that they wanted to shake things up and that they were giving the C to Danny. He'd been in the league for quite a while and was a well-respected player, so honestly I didn't have a problem with it. Sure, I was bummed out, but this is a business, and unless you're winning Stanley Cups every season, there's obviously always going to be room for improvement. Hey, being a good leader sometimes means doing what's best for the team, so I was very supportive of what management wanted to do. Turned out Danny and I wound up becoming pretty good friends, too, so it all worked out in the end.

It's been an interesting evolution as to how teams have chosen captains over the years, especially since I played. If a team picks a good captain, everybody's happy and nobody says too much. But if they pick a bad one it can have a negative ripple effect throughout the entire organization. Captains used to be chosen in the locker room by the players. I always thought that was the best way, because then the real team leader is selected and the players work hard for their guy. When management appoints the captain, it can cause drama and jealousy among the players. Whom you pick to wear it says a lot. Is it your best player, your leader, your hardest-working guy, your most dedicated guy, the smartest guy, or your most popular teammate? You may not want to go with your top two or three scorers because maybe they're young and don't have the respect of the guys in the locker room.

Sometimes your best players maybe aren't your best leaders, or maybe they don't want the responsibility. Bobby Orr certainly could've worn the C in Boston but never did. Back in the day, a lot of teams used to go with the guy who would keep everybody else in line and make sure they weren't out too late drinkin' to much—like Philadelphia did when they gave the C to Bobby Clarke. Bobby was a tough, scrappy, solid leader who was an extremely hard worker, but he wasn't the best player on that team. Now, was he the most respected? Absolutely. Other guys can just do it all, like Guy LaFleur up in Montreal. Was there anybody better at stepping up and scoring big goals at big times in big games? Not in my book, and that's why he was one of the all-time great captains.

On a side note, and I feel sort of weird saying this, but one of the things I was actually most proud of when I got the C in Detroit was the fact that I think I was either the first or one of the first Americans ever to wear it there. For an Original Six franchise with so much history and tradition, that says a lot. It was sort of like getting past racism, in a very small way, in that we got to a point where we were beyond the whole "American vs. Canadian" issue. There just weren't a ton of American-born players in the league when I got there, so that was significant to me. I know most people don't think about that stuff very often, but for me it meant a lot. Not only was I accepted by management as a leader, but also by my teammates—the vast majority of whom were from north of the border.

Jordan Leopold

I've been playing in the NHL for about a decade now but have only worn the A in preseason games, and sadly that doesn't count! I did get to wear it in college, though, at the University of Minnesota, which meant a great deal to me. What made it so special was the fact that the players voted, not the coaches. That made it even more of an honor, in my opinion, because my teammates elected me to be their team leader. We won a national championship my last year there, too, which is definitely one of the highlights of my career.

Troy Loney

My story with wearing the C is kind of neat in that I was the first-ever captain for the expansion Mighty Ducks of Anaheim. It meant a great deal to me. In hockey, especially, it was a big deal to be named as the team captain. You're expected to lead by example on the ice and in the locker room, and you have to be that liaison between the players and the coaches. You have to constantly keep the coach on tap with the temperature of the team and let him know what's going well and what isn't. It's a lot of responsibility. Not only do you have to go out and play well, you have to do so many other things for the good of the team.

As for why I was chosen to wear the C in Anaheim? Well, I was certainly no superstar, that was for sure! I'd just won a couple of Stanley Cups in Pittsburgh, though, and I think they wanted a veteran leader who'd tasted the fruits of success and who could ultimately be a good influence on the younger guys. They knew that I'd been through the battles and that I understood what it took to win. They figured I knew how to prepare for the grind of a long season, too, and about what it meant to play consistently on a nightly basis. Paul Kariya would join the team the following season and would emerge as the team's first superstar. A lot of teams want *that* guy to be the face of the franchise, much like Mario Lemieux was in Pittsburgh. Needless to say, Paul would wear the C for many years to follow with the Ducks.

As for my style? We had a young team in Anaheim, so the coaches wanted me to lead by example on and off the ice. Unlike a lot of captains, I was pretty vocal in the locker room. I wasn't a screamer or yeller, I just wanted to make sure the guys were ready to play every night. If there was something to be said and I felt the time was appropriate, I was never shy about saying what needed to be said. There were three captains, not to mention other team leaders on that roster—so there were a lot of voices on that team. As the guy wearing the C, I was there to make sure the team was heading in the right direction. In the end we had a pretty good run that expansion season. I thought we could have made the playoffs but we came up short in the end, which was actually pretty disappointing.

Norm Maciver

I wore the A in Ottawa, and it was obviously a big honor. Very humbling. It was the only time in my NHL career that I had gotten to wear a letter, so it was a huge thrill for me. I didn't take it lightly, either, I knew that it was a big responsibility and treated it as such. It forced me to step up my game. I knew that as a team leader others would be looking to me to see how I went about my business, so I definitely worked a lot harder in practices and tried to do whatever I could to help the team win. I came in early and stayed late, all of that stuff. That's what leading by example is all about. I was never going to be an emotional rah-rah guy, so that was my way of showing leadership. Beyond that, I just focused on treating my teammates with respect. If I wanted to earn their respect, I was going to have to do the same to them.

John MacLean

I wore the A with New Jersey when we won the Stanley Cup in '95, and that meant a lot to me. While it's nice to be recognized with stuff like this, to me, it was more about the team. Wearing a letter doesn't change who you are, it's more of a recognition thing. It would mean more to me if you could put Cs on every team leader, not just the select few whom the coaches deem worthy. The key to being a good captain is not changing who you are. You have to be yourself, you have to be genuine and stay true to who you are. You can't fake being a leader, you either are or you aren't. If you try too hard, the guys will see through that, and it just won't work. Now that I'm in coaching, I see it from the other side, and it still rings true—you have to be yourself. Guys will respect you if you lead by example and work hard every day. There's no secret, it's just doing the right things every day and being yourself.

Todd Marchant

It's a tremendous honor to be looked upon not only by your teammates, but by your organization as a team leader. I

Wore the A in Edmonton, Columbus, and Anaheim, and anytime you get that letter on your jersey, it's a huge honor. Leaders come in all shapes and sizes; there's no one right way to lead. Some guys are very talkative and boisterous, whereas other guys are more quiet and tend to sit back and just let their actions speak for them. As for me, I just tried to lead by example and never get too high or too low. The bottom line with being a good captain, in my eyes, is the ability to step up your game when it matters most. Great captains rise to the occasion in the playoffs or in the final minutes of big games. I'll never forget when Kelly Buchberger scored the overtime game-winner when I was with Edmonton to beat Dallas in the '97 playoffs. Or when Scott Niedermayer scored the game-tying goal for us in Anaheim in the last minute of Game 5 in the '07 playoffs against Detroit on the road. We wound up carrying that momentum into overtime and won it and then took the series in Game 6. It was huge. Great captains rise to the occasion, they are catalysts. They can elevate their game in crucial times, and quite frankly, those are things you just can't teach. A player either has that ability or he doesn't. Plain and simple. There are great regular season players and there are great playoff players. Captains are both, but they rise to the occasion in the postseason. That's the difference. They're special people, no kidding.

Paul Martin

I've been fortunate to have been able to wear the A in both New Jersey and Pittsburgh over my career. It's the ultimate recognition. To be recognized by your coaches for your hard work and commitment to the team, that pretty much says it all. In that regard, it's the highest honor you can have in hockey, other than winning a Stanley Cup. Just to know that the other guys in the locker room believe in you and trust you, that makes all the sacrifice worth it. As for my style, I just try to work hard and set a good example and then hope it rubs off on everybody else. My team-mates are professionals, otherwise they wouldn't be here, so I don't feel like I need to show them the way or anything like that. For me, it's consistently doing the right things, like communicating with everyone effectively and being

Did You Know?

In 1948 goaltender Bill Durnan served as the co-captain of the Montreal Canadiens, sharing the honor with Toe Blake. The league ruled against netminders serving as captains after that, although the Vancouver Canucks decided to buck the trend and name Roberto Luongo as their captain in 2008. To stay within the rules, however, Luongo was not able to wear the captain's C on his jersey. Luongo, who replaced Markus Naslund as the captain, held the distinction for two seasons before giving it up. Said Luongo of the controversial experience: "I was fighting with the idea the whole way because I loved being captain. I enjoyed the experience. It was fun. I took a lot of pride in it, and that was one of the main reasons it was tough for me to come to this decision. Being captain in a Canadian city for a team with such passionate fans is a privilege and an experience I will always take pride in. It was a very precarious position to be in. As a goaltender you have a lot of jobs to do on the ice as far as a focusing for 60 minutes, and you don't want to have other stuff creeping inside your head and maybe causing a little bit of distraction."

Source: "Luongo Steps Down as Captain," by Chris Iorfida, CBC Sports, September 13, 2010

positive. Beyond that, it's just being there for my teammates and doing whatever they need me to do in order to help the team win.

Ab McDonald

It's quite an honor to be asked to be the leader in whatever you're doing in life. So I certainly enjoyed my time as captain over the years, you bet. When you look down and see that big C sewn into your sweater, it gives you a little more confidence out there. It reinforces the fact that you are a leader and that you have a job to do. I was actually the first-ever captain for both Pittsburgh and Winnipeg, when they started their franchises, and that was very humbling, as well. I'd been on some pretty good teams in Chicago and Montreal prior to that, and I suppose they figured I would be a good leader for the younger players. It was certainly an honor, but at the same time those were some challenging times to be involved with brand new organizations that were just getting started. Being in Winnipeg was special, though, in that it was my hometown. That was an exciting time. It was a thrill that they asked me to wear the C, too. Bobby [Hull] and I had played together in Chicago prior to that, and he couldn't have been more supportive of the decision, which meant a lot.

As far as doing the job, it's a lot of responsibility but very gratifying at the same time. It was never a chore. You have to be the liaison between the players and management, which could be tough. I always found that as long as I was honest and direct, then everything would work out just fine. I tried to be a good listener off the ice and work hard on the ice. That was how you earned the respect of your teammates, I found.

Basil McRae

I wore the A with the North Stars for a brief period of time, and it meant a great deal to me because I wasn't a superstar by any stretch of the imagination. I wasn't good enough to make it in the NHL on talent alone, so I had to work extra hard and do things that a lot of other guys wouldn't do. It was all about the team for me, though. I'd do anything to help my teammates. We went through three different head coaches in the six years I was in Minnesota, so it was a tough stretch for the franchise. Whenever you have that kind of turnover, it becomes pretty tough to get any kind of traction going. It was an honor to be named as one of the team captains, though, absolutely. It was a big responsibility that I took very seriously. Again, I just never wanted to let down my teammates, so knowing that they believed in me and trusted me just drove me to work even harder.

Marty McSorley

I wore the A in Los Angeles, and certainly it was an honor. Being very blunt, however, I think a lot of people put too much credibility on who's actually wearing the letters out on the ice. You know, in most instances management will decide who wears the letters, but in reality the true decider is the locker room. More often than not, the true leaders on your team are guys who don't even wear those letters at all. They're your go-to guys, your veterans who lead by example—the players who command respect. Those are your true leaders, regardless of whether or not they wear an A or a C.

The biggest thing for me was that it didn't matter what anybody said in the locker room, at the end of the day it's what you do on the ice that matters. That's what leading by example is all about. When you play the game hard, the right way, with respect, that's when you gain a level of trust from your teammates. I just tried to work hard and be there for my teammates, that was my role. If there were opportunities where I felt that I could change the momentum or the focus of the game, then certainly I would do that. If that meant delivering a big hit or dropping the gloves, so be it. As you play the game and learn a few things over the years, you realize that there are times when you need to go out and take the game back, so to speak. So that was what I would try to do, little things that would help us execute *our* game plan. I just wanted to do whatever I could to help the team win, plain and simple. If that meant being physical or intimidating, so be it. I wanted to give my teammates confidence out on the ice. I wanted them to know that they could push the envelope out there with no fear, because I had their backs. I challenged them to do that, and I would get in their face from time to time to make sure that they knew that. I wanted them to go all out in order to help the team win; that's why I was willing to sacrifice my body out there. That was how I could be an effective leader.

Joe Micheletti

It's just a great honor to be voted as the team leader by your teammates, especially for such a prominent hockey school like the University of Minnesota. Just to know that we had a whole bunch of other players who could've worn it proudly, it was a special feeling. I took it very seriously. I wanted to do whatever I could to help make the team better. As Herb Brooks' captain, I learned a great deal about leadership from one of the game's great hockey minds. Herbie was always testing us, always. I remember the day I got drafted. I was just a freshman, and he wanted to make sure it didn't go to my head. So he called me in to his office and said very matter-of-factly, "Joe, you've been selected by Montreal in the NHL and Calgary in the WHA. But don't get a big head over it or anything because you'll never play professionally. Not a chance." That was it, a 30-second meeting, and it was just classic Herbie. There it was, another test from the master psychologist, challenging me to prove him wrong.

Herbie understood how to motivate people and how to get the most out of them. He knew that some guys he could yell and scream at, whereas others he needed to pat on the back. There was a method to his madness, though, that I didn't fully appreciate until I was much older and wiser. I remember one time we were playing at Notre Dame. I was a senior, and we had a lot of good freshmen on the team that year—many of whom would go on to star on the 1980 Olympic "Miracle on Ice" hockey team. Herbie saw how much potential they had, so he was working all of us really hard.

One of those young kids was Reed Larson, who would of course go on to play in the NHL for many, many years. Well, we lost the Friday night game, and afterward I told Herbie that we needed to talk about something. As we walked back to the hotel together, I told him that there was a problem brewing. I explained to him that the guys were not real happy about the way he'd been riding all of them so hard, but taking it easy on Reed. It just didn't seem fair. Reed was young and full of talent, but at that stage of his development, he was certainly making his share of mistakes. I told Herbie that it seemed like everybody else was in his doghouse, except for Reed, and that this was becoming an issue with the other players.

Herbie then stopped and said, "Joe, here's the reason why. Reed Larson is full of potential, and he's going to help us win. Period. He's not to the point yet where I can say things to him that I can say to you. Sometimes I scream and yell at you just to get the attention of the other guys on the team. I know you can take it, you're our team leader. But if I got on Reed like I get on you, we'd lose him for the rest of the season, and our team would not get better, it would get worse. I need Reed to gain as much confidence as he can and to develop the way I think he can develop in order for him to help our team win hockey games. That's why I'm taking it easy on him."

Herbie was counting on me, as one of his captains, to reassure the guys that he was doing the right thing. He was counting on me to help nurture Reed at that stage of his development. I didn't totally understand what he was doing back then, but it's certainly clear to me today. Herbie leaned on his veteran leaders to do things that weren't always the most fun or most popular things to do, but in the end you just had to trust him that they were the right things for the good of the team. He was all about the team getting better every day, every season. Hey, three national championships in seven seasons, how can you argue with those results?

Mike Modano

I'm sure everybody says that it's an honor, which it is. But beyond that, it's also a big responsibility. You are the liaison between the players and the coaches. You have to bridge that gap and be able to communicate effectively, which isn't always an easy thing to do. You have to be able to translate what the coach is trying to do as far as implementing a system, and you try to get everybody on board so that they can follow along. I did what I was asked to do by management, and beyond that I just tried to work hard and lead by example. I wanted to be as supportive as I could for my teammates more than anything, that's a huge part of wearing the C. I wasn't a guy who would single someone out in front of everybody. If something needed to be said or done, I would address it with that person in more of a one-on-one scenario. I never wanted to call a guy out like that and risk embarrassing him. I never wanted someone to feel like they weren't a part of the group or that they were being talked down to. I emphasized the fact that we were all teammates and that we were all in this together. No one was bigger than the logo, that was what we all stood for.

Lou Nanne

I wore the C at every level I played at, from peewees to college to the Olympics to the NHL. I loved being a leader and thrived in that role. Anytime you're asked by your coach, management, or your teammates to serve as the captain, it's a real privilege and an honor. It's a lot of responsibility, so I took it very seriously. They're expecting you to be a leader, so you have to lead. And it's not easy, because now you have to make a whole bunch of unpopular decisions that directly affect your friends and teammates.

Joe Nieuwendyk

It's a very prestigious honor. I mean, there are only 30 of them in the world. It's always flattering when the organization puts its trust in you to be an example and to do the right things. When you're fortunate enough to be given the C in any organization, it comes with a lot of added responsibility, though. You're not just one of 23 guys on the team anymore, you have to be a leader, and that's what being a captain is all about.

I think you learn leadership first and foremost from your parents and through the way you were brought up. The qualities and values you have come from them. I was lucky, I had a good head start at home, I think, and that helped me gain confidence—which is a big part of being a leader. There's no one right way to lead, I've found. Some guys are quiet leaders who lead by example, while others are more vocal in the locker room. It just depends on the situation. Either way, it means that you have the necessary qualities that the coaching staff is looking for in order to lead the team.

I was fortunate to have worn letters throughout my career, the C and the A, and it meant a great deal to me. I first wore the C in Calgary, and I was pretty young back then. I had played with guys like Lanny McDonald, Jim Peplinski, and Tim Hunter, all of whom were great leaders. Those guys were big influences on me and certainly helped groom me for the role. They exemplified what being a leader was all about. They taught me how to conduct myself and how to be a professional. That's what great leaders do, they help the next crop of guys to become leaders so that the organization can continue to grow and flourish.

Kyle Okposo

I've been wearing the A for several years with the Islanders, and it's something that I don't take lightly. It's a great honor that's bestowed upon you by your organization and teammates, so it definitely means a lot. It means you're being held to a higher standard. It means you have to come to the rink every day and work as hard as you can. It means being a professional, both on and off the ice. It means your organization is looking to you to be a leader, and you can't let them down. I'm more of a quiet leader, I suppose, not a big rah-rah guy. I'm not afraid to speak up in the locker room, though, that's for sure, and I have no problem saying what needs to be said when it needs to be said. I just try to go out every day, whether that's in practice or in games, and work as hard as I can. I try to let my work ethic do the talking for me.

Joel Otto

I wore the A for several years in Calgary and occasionally wore the C when our captain was on the shelf. Being named as one of the captains was obviously a big honor, especially considering how many great leaders we had on our roster when I played there. So to be singled out in that capacity by my coaches was certainly something I took a lot of pride in. To earn the respect of your teammates, you have to work hard every day and lead by your example. It can be tough though, too, because when you wear a letter, it means you have to hold your teammates accountable.

I've been a coach now for the past six years with a junior club in Alberta, and I understand the role much better as I've gotten older and wiser. The guy who wears your C matters, he really does. You need a guy who's pulling the rope the right way. You need to trust him because he's going to be the guy who's delivering your message to the rest of the team. You need him to be your hardest worker so he can set an example for everybody else. They're not easy to find, that's for sure. As far as choosing them? I let the players vote and then look at the ballots in private to make sure they voted the right way…my way! It's interesting, but my coaching staff and I talk about which guy would make the best leader of the team prior to the vote, and every year we've done this, the players have voted for that guy. So, in all seriousness, we haven't ever needed to change a thing, no kidding. We've done some tinkering with the guys wearing the As, but never with the C.

All of the added responsibilities of wearing the C can definitely take a toll on a guy. Joe Nieuwendyk wore the C in Calgary for several years and was just a class act. He was so well-respected, as a captain he was as good as it gets. I remember him going through all sorts of turmoil during the lockout back in 1994. We had a really close relationship with our ownership group up here, almost like family, and that all got seriously strained after that. Joe was the guy who had to deal with them on all the negotiations between the players' union and the owners, and it got ugly. It was incredibly tough on him, and in the end he wound up taking it very personally. I will never forget talking to him after he had just gotten back from some marathon meetings and he was really down. He felt like he was caught in the middle and just hated it. It took him a while to recover from that; it was just very difficult on him. Sadly, he wound up heading to Dallas after that shortened season, which really bummed me out because I was sad to see him go.

J.P. Parise

I wore the C in Minnesota with the North Stars, and it was an unbelievable honor. I'm extremely proud of the fact that my boy Zach I are the only father and son in history to both captain NHL teams. How neat is that? For me it was especially meaningful because my teammates elected me as the captain. That was really special to me, it meant a great deal knowing that they thought enough of me to honor me that way. I mean, to be given that responsibility of leading your team, it's the ultimate compliment. It's just very humbling. You know, when you accept that role as the team captain, you have an obligation to give those other 19 guys your best—day in and day out—no matter what. That's your job. It's an awesome responsibility, it really is. That means playing hurt, making sacrifices, and doing whatever it takes to help your team get better and ultimately win.

I remember one time when I was the captain in Minnesota and we were playing up in Buffalo. It was a really tight game, and at one point they had a five-on-three, with two of our guys in the penalty box. Well, I was one of those guys in the box. Sure enough, a big fight broke out, and our guys were getting killed. I was by no means one of our tough guys, but nevertheless I couldn't just sit back and do nothing. So I jumped out of the box and raced over to try to rescue one of our guys who was getting pounded on by one of their enforcers. I knew that I was probably going to get my ass kicked, but I felt very strongly that it was the right thing to do. Even if it meant getting a fine and suspension, for leaving the penalty box. In the end, it was worth the risk. That's how you earn the respect of your teammates, by standing up for them no matter what. That's what great leadership is, in my eyes, doing what you think is right—regardless of the consequences—for the good of the team.

Zach Parise

It's pretty cool. I mean there are only 30 captains in the league, so it's an incredible honor to wear the C. It's a lot of responsibility, too, but at the same time it's extremely rewarding. My dad wore the C for the Minnesota North Stars, so it's pretty neat to think about that aspect of it, as well.

Mark Parrish

I wore the C with Minnesota and the A with the Islanders. When a team feels that strongly about you, to put a letter on you, it's just an incredibly amazing honor. I was lucky enough to get to wear a letter during a few stops during my career, and it meant a great deal to me. It's something they can never take away from you, and I took great pride in that. I remember early in my career when I got to wear the A with the Florida Panthers. A bunch of older guys were injured, so they slapped it on me for a game—it was such a thrill. It was the coolest thing ever. It was like I had officially made it! Captains have to be great leaders, both on and off the ice. The captains are the guys who are relied upon to not only do their jobs on the ice but do the extra stuff off the ice. They are they guys who worry about everybody else. They are the right-hand men to the coaches. They are also the sergeants and policemen of the team who look after everybody else, especially your skill players and your younger players. Being the team leader is more than just playing good hockey, though, it's about having a positive attitude. It's about the way that you carry yourself at all times.

I think every player wants to wear the C. They might not admit it, but deep down as a player—you wanted it. It's the ultimate reward for your work ethic and your sacrifice. Sometimes you would get it as a reward for playing well or getting hot. Some coaches would choose the captains, others would let the players decide. Either way, it was a great motivator. You just knew that if you put your nose to the grindstone and worked hard, and things maybe went your way for a month or two, then you might find yourself wearing it. It's a total lead-by-example kind of an honor. The coaches want those guys, the team leaders, to represent the team and set the tone for the younger players. That's how it works.

Michael Peca

It was a tremendous responsibility that I took very seriously, but also one that I loved. I first got to wear the C in Buffalo and later wore it with the Islanders. Maybe the most meaningful time I wore it was in '01 at the world championships for Team Canada. That was pretty amazing. I got to wear the A the following year in the Olympics, too, when we won the gold medal—which was something I'll never forget. It was a great honor and one that I never took for granted. I guess I always approached being a captain in the sense that it wasn't really going to change anything I did or didn't do, though. I think regardless of whether I had the C on my jersey or not, I was still going to play my game and do the right things to help my team win. Wearing it is a proud thing, though, it really is. Especially in a sport like hockey, which demands so much intensity and commitment. When your coaches, or bosses, appoint you to be the team leader, it's a very special feeling.

As for my style, I just worked hard. I wasn't the best player out there, so I had to rely on other aspects of my game that allowed me to show leadership. One of my assets was hitting people, regardless of who they were or how big they were. It was my job to recognize certain points in the game, maybe during a lull, where I could provide a spark. I wound up getting the nickname "Captain Crunch" from some of the open-ice hits I had given, and it sort of stuck. I earned a lot of respect from my teammates over the years for doing that, too. I think they appreciated that, even though I wasn't the biggest guy out there, I was willing to sacrifice my body in order to help my team.

Buffalos Sabres captain Michael Peca sporting some "playoff makeup."

Mike Peluso

I never wore a letter in the NHL, but I was the captain of my college team at the University of Alaska–Anchorage, and it was a huge honor. No question, for a guy like me, a role player, to be considered as a team leader, it just meant a ton.

Pierre Pilote

To be a good captain, you have to be a good leader and a good politician. We had three or four superstars [in Chicago during the '60s], and you had to know how to handle these guys. No matter how good a captain you are, it's just like politics—you have to win a majority. You have to have the guys on your side, but there's always a little bit of dissension, and you're always trying to fix it before it gets too far and gets into the office. If a guy had a beef, we'd talk about it. If it was reasonable, I'd go to the management. I just tried to lead by example (source: http://www.hhof.com/htmlSpotlight).

Lance Pitlick

I wore the C in high school, in college, and in Ottawa for a couple of seasons. Getting to wear it in the NHL was almost beyond my wildest dreams, to be honest. When they put the C on your jersey in high school, it means you're a good player and that you're a popular player. But when they put it on your jersey in the NHL, it means you're a leader. I think it meant even more to me because I wasn't a skill guy. I was a role player, a hitter, a guy who would stand up for my teammates whenever I could. I just tried to be a quiet leader and let my work ethic and actions on the ice do the talking for me. When I did get pissed off, however, the guys listened. I took it very seriously, being captain—it meant something to me. It was a huge honor for a guy like me, and because of that I worked even harder in how I prepared and conducted myself in the locker room. I've never been a great player, so I had to make up for that through hard work. Even in college, at the University of Minnesota, I wound up becoming the team captain despite the fact that I was only given a partial scholarship. I've always had sort of an underdog mentality, and I wore that as a badge of honor. It just drove me.

Probably my proudest moment as a captain came in '99 when we were playing the Rangers. It was Gretzky's final game in Canada and the hoopla leading up to it was just insane. Wayne had made it very clear to the media that he was not going to be signing *anything* whatsoever because he just wanted to enjoy his final game. Everybody was hounding him and his people for signed stuff, but he said no way. So it was late in the game and there had already been numerous standing ovations for him, it was pretty incredible just to be out there. Anyway, all of a sudden there was a penalty called, and as the captain I went over to the ref to get a clarification. I was standing there and I looked next to me, and there was Wayne. It was just the two of us. Realizing this moment would probably never happen again—where I would actually get to talk to the greatest hockey player on the planet—I said to him, "Wayne, I know you're not signing any sticks today and I totally respect that. *But*...if you'd like *me* to sign one of mine for *you*, I'd be happy to bring one over to you after the game." He just looked at me, all serious, and then just blurted out laughing as he skated off. It was hilarious. Hey, sometimes wearing the C has its perks!

Larry Pleau

I was a captain for the Montreal Junior Canadiens back in the late '60s and later wore the A with the Hartford Whalers in the '70s. As far as what it meant to me, I always looked at it as a privilege. It was a privilege to be looked at as a leader by not only your organization and your teammates, but also the fans and the media. To know that they are looking to you for leadership, that's a huge responsibility. It's up to that guy to get the group all pointed in the same direction. Later, as a coach and general manager, I got a different perspective on who should wear the C and why. I've seen 'em all over the years, and believe me, there's no one right way to be a captain. Some guys don't have to say a word, and their feelings come out automatically. Some guys are real vocal and loud in the locker room. Some guys let their actions speak for them out on the ice.

Shjon Podein

I wore the C in the minors and then actually got to wear it for *one* game in the NHL. It was a pretty funny story, actually. I was playing in Philly, and it was at the end of the season. We were out of the playoffs and we must have had, like, eight veterans who were either scratched or on the shelf. I remember being in the locker room and seeing that C sewn onto my jersey before the game. All I could do was put my head down and laugh. My teammates were really razzing me about how far the team had gone down the depth chart to finally get to me; it was pretty hilarious. Hey, I wasn't the greatest player out there. So anytime you can be recognized as a team leader, it's an honor.

Nowadays I am coaching high school kids. Whenever I pick my captain, I think back to all of the life lessons I learned along the way and try to make the right choice. What I've had the best success with is picking kids who lead by example first. I listen and I look in the locker room to see which kid the other kids are gravitating to and following. That kid with the strong personality, that's your leader. You can't teach that. But he has to be the *right* leader. Yes, he has to be a solid player, but not necessarily your *best*

Lance Pitlick on Exercising a Little Muscle Every Now and Then

Sometimes as the captain you have to exercise a little muscle every now and then. I remember one time during the lockout [2005], I was wearing the C up in Prince Edward Island. I was the veteran leader of the team and was logging a ton of ice time. In the minors you could play five games in six nights, and I had become pretty wiped out. On top of that, I had a dehydration problem, so I couldn't go out with the guys drinking unless we had a few games off afterward. As a result, I had to try to go to sleep in my hotel room on many occasions when everybody else was partying all night, which really sucked. Anyway, one night I was just exhausted and was trying to get to sleep. We had some new guys who had just gotten called up that day, and they were shit-faced, running around the hotel like idiots. I finally had enough and went out in the hall to politely ask them to please keep it down. One of the rookies looks at me, not knowing who I was, and says, "Fuck you!" There I was, standing there in my boxer shorts, half asleep, and now this. I had two choices. I could smile and go back to bed or I could exercise my authority as the team leader. Needless to say, I pounded the crap out of that kid right there in the hallway. I wasn't sure how it was going to go the next morning, but everything got smoothed over when the kid apologized and bought me breakfast. Lesson learned, I suppose!

player. He has to lead by example every day in practice, though, and he has to make the right choices—both on and off the ice. He has to have the ability to make decisions that are not necessarily popular but are right for the team.

He's got to be all about the team, not all about himself. Once I've found that guy, I've found a heck of a captain. It's tough, though, trust me, they don't make 'em all that way these days!

I have an acronym I use with my kids from the attributes I most admired about the captains I played with over my career, which is SAVE: S for selflessness—they were humble and that it was about the team, never about them; A for attitude—they were always positive and did whatever was best for the group; V for values—they were good people on and off the ice; and E for everyone is always being taken care of—meaning it's all about the team and about making sure everyone was involved and working toward the same goal. If I can get my guys to focus on this, then I know we're on the right track.

Mike Polich

I was a captain with Montreal's minor league team in Nova Scotia and also at the University of Minnesota under legendary coach Herb Brooks. I learned a lot playing with the Canadiens over the years but nothing compared to playing hockey for Herbie. Being one of his captains was always an adventure, let me tell you. Herb was a tough coach, very demanding. If you were one of his captains, he had very high expectations for you as a team leader. I remember playing in a game during my senior year. We were getting beat, and I had just taken what Herbie called a "selfish penalty." In other words, a guy had hit me, and instead of letting it go, I retaliated and hit him back—which resulted in a penalty. To make it worse, they tacked on a misconduct, which resulted in an extra 10 minutes in the penalty box. Herbie was really upset. He would always preach to us about being disciplined, because the refs would never give the penalty to the guy who hit you but rather to the guy who retaliated. Between periods, Herb called me out in the locker room and really let me have it in front of the entire team. He ranted and raved and really laid into me about how I had let the team down by taking a selfish penalty and that it was just unacceptable. Herb was a big team guy, but in this instance he singled me out and went after me. He said, "Polich, you're supposed to be a leader? What, you can't handle taking a hit out there? Guess what? Hockey's a physical game, and apparently you can't handle it. What a prima donna! You really think you can make it in the NHL with that type of undisciplined attitude? Leaving us short-handed like that was unbelievable—you're the most selfish player I've ever seen!" He finally got done screaming at me and then slammed the locker room door behind him. You could've heard a pin drop in there. It was just brutal. I didn't know where to hide. Well, the guys started getting ready and eventually everybody started heading back out onto the ice for the next period. I was usually one of the last guys out of the locker room, so I was in there by myself just before the period started. Just then, Herbie walked in and came over to me. He sort of smiled, put his hand on my shoulder, and said, "Come on, Michael, show these kids what this game is all about. We've got 20 minutes to turn this thing around, show me what kind of leader you are." It was incredible. Here he was screaming at me 10 minutes ago and now he's got his arm around me. That was Herbie, knocking you down one minute and then building you back up the next. He knew that I was the captain and that I could take that sort of abuse, so he used me as an example. Sure enough, we rallied back and were able to use that moment as a positive learning experience. I'll never forget it.

Pat Quinn

There are certain leadership qualities that are very important. The biggest thing I think is you have to have the respect of your teammates, and that starts with showing them respect. I think you're a liaison between coaches and players, so you have to be able to work that relationship well. You have to have empathy for your teammates. You have to be the rock around which they look to for support. On the ice, you've got to be the best worker at practice, you have to lead that way. You have to have humility. (Source: "Some of Hockey's Best Leaders Tell Us What It Takes," by Paul Grant, ESPN.com, November 12, 2007.)

Mike Ramsey

I wore the C in Buffalo. It was a huge honor in knowing that the organization respected me enough to put the C on my jersey. But, personally, it didn't change who I was or my role on the team or my responsibilities—it was just a letter. To be honest, I thought it was more of a media thing than anything else. I certainly never sought it out or asked for it. Nevertheless, it was nice to be recognized my management that way. I was more of a lead-by-example captain; I didn't say a whole lot. That was my style. Captains who are real vocal in the locker room, they have to back that up out on the ice. If you preach hard work or being on time or whatever, and then back it up—that's how you earn the respect of your teammates. My biggest issue with wearing the C was the issue of when the organization chooses to "move in a different direction," that typically meant you were going to get dealt because it's tough to take the C off of your sitting captain. So getting it is a big honor, but it can also signify the end of your career pretty quickly if the team doesn't do very well on your clock.

Tom Reid

To wear the A or the C is certainly an honor for any member of a sports franchise. When they put a letter on your jersey, that tells you something not only about yourself but about how your teammates and bosses feel about you, too. The role of the captain has changed tremendously over the years. The captain's role in my eyes is to be that link between management and the players. To do that is an awesome responsibility, and you don't take it lightly—more so now than ever before. In today's game, there are so many more things going on that require the captain's involvement. Back when I was playing, there were only a handful of reporters and members of the media you had to deal with. Nowadays there is an infinite number of them all demanding your time—especially in the postseason. Hockey is big business now, and in order for the league to not only maintain its stature but grow, the team leaders have to be out there front and center leading the way. Quite frankly, it can be tough for some guys to deal with all of that pressure.

It's critical for teams to pick that *right* guy, the face of the franchise, so to speak. It's important. He has to wear a lot of hats for you, too. I think nowadays the captain is the guy who has to stand up in the dressing room and be able to deliver either an inspirational pep talk or a good kick in the ass that every teem needs once in a while to get your team going. Beyond that, though, his role with the coaching staff and with management has evolved into dealing with all sorts of other off-ice stuff too—some of which can be very distracting. Stuff like travel arrangements, hotels, team meals, tickets for family members, you name it. So this person has a lot more responsibilities than ever, much more so than in our era.

I've been in broadcasting for a number of years now and

have been able to see the game from a different perspective. Some teams really struggle with their captains. I've seen situations where a team will put a letter on a guy in hopes of making him a better player, but rarely does that work. And the other players really resent that, too. You're either a leader or you're not, in my eyes. The C doesn't make you a leader, it just says that the organization feels that you have the qualities to be a leader. Big difference. Look, the players are the ones who really determine who the real leaders are. They're the ones who recognize whether or not the letter is deserved or not. And your leader might not necessarily be your best player, either. You have your on-ice leaders, the guys who wear the letters, and then you have your locker-room leaders—your veterans and lead-by-example guys. The players know who's the leader, regardless of who's wearing a letter.

In Minnesota, where I do radio with the Wild, I watched this first-hand with Jacques Lemaire. He never had a permanent captain for all the years he was here. He wanted to spread it around and let different players get the opportunity to experience that responsibility of wearing a letter. He used it as a reward, so to speak, where he would let guys earn it on a monthly basis. Each month they would choose a new captain based on performance, and it certainly didn't always go to the best players. He mixed it up and let a variety of players get it, which proved to be very popular in the locker room. It actually became a fun tradition for the guys whenever they would announce a new captain. They would all gather at center ice at practice, and then that player would put on his new sweater, with the C sewn on it, and he would do a victory lap around the ice with all his teammates cheering and banging their sticks on the ice. It was great.

Travis Richards

I wore the C for many, many years in the minor leagues with the Grand Rapids Griffins. I had a few cups of coffee in the NHL but was never able to stay up there for whatever the reason. I was pretty much a career minor leaguer, like Kevin Costner's character, Crash Davis, in the movie *Bull Durham*, I suppose. Being the captain was a big deal, though, I really enjoyed it. I would say I was more of a quiet leader who sort of went out and set the tone for everybody else.

Our team is an affiliate of the Detroit Red Wings, so I spent about a decade watching Steve Yzerman up close and personal. I'd go to training camp up in Traverse City and just watch him, the guy was incredible. I played in a handful of exhibition games and was just in awe of the guy. He was about as humble as they come. What a great leader. He did everything the right way. He truly led by example—blocking shots, dropping the gloves, working harder than everybody else in practice—you name it, he did it. The things I learned from watching him, I was able to pass along to our guys back home, which our coaches really appreciated.

I played with the Griffins for 10 seasons and wore the C for most of them. However, toward the end of my career I chose to give it to one of the younger guys who I thought would make a great leader. I gladly passed it on to him in exchange for an A. I was the old veteran guy at that point and was happy to pass the torch. That's what it was all about for me—showing the young guys how to play the game the right way. It was getting out on the ice early and then being the last guy to leave. Stuff like that. It's the extra stuff that gets you where you ultimately want to go in life, and those who are willing to make those personal sacrifices are the ones who will be successful.

Doug Risebrough

I was very fortunate in that I was able to wear the C in Calgary for a number of years. I played in Montreal for many years and saw how revered the captains were there. So it was a great honor, absolutely. Most guys like myself see themselves as players who are just trying to be a part of a team and contribute wherever possible, and then all of a sudden one day management asks you to assume a leadership role. It's very humbling.

In my situation, I was chosen by the head coach. They know who the leaders are and who they can have a rapport with as a liaison to the players. Some teams, however, let the players choose. I've always found that to be a challenging thing for players to do, though. It has the potential to become a popularity contest at that point, and that is certainly not a good situation for any team to be in. Later on, when I became a general manager, I made sure we made those tough decisions behind closed doors. Because today it goes well beyond the ice and what goes on in the locker room. Your captain has to be able to present himself to the media, he has to be able to speak to your corporate partners, and he has to be able to interact with the fans in ways we never imagined years ago. So you need a guy who connects with a whole bunch of various people both on and off the ice. He essentially becomes the face of your franchise, which is a pretty big deal these days.

As far as choosing that guy, it can either be a 30-second conversation or a week-long process—depending on your situation. I think you have to find somebody who reaches a lot of people. Some guys are great players but not necessarily great leaders. Other guys might come across as intimidating to some degree because they might be quiet or maybe they hold a high accountability for themselves. So I think whoever you chose should have the ability to relate to a lot of different players. You also need an everyday player, in my opinion. You need a guy who's going to bring the same level of intensity night in and night out, to set the tone for the rest of the team. He needs to be respected in the locker room by the guys yet still have the ability to be compassionate. That's rare, but all the great captains had those qualities.

Gordie Roberts

I played for a lot of years in the NHL and wore the A briefly from time to time, but never long term. I was more of a role player, I suppose. Certainly as I got older, though, I was looked upon for leadership in other ways. So I just tried to lead by example and be a good teammate. I wanted to contribute and do whatever I could to help my team win, plain and simple.

Brian Rolston

I've been fortunate to have worn a few letters throughout my career—the C in Minnesota and then the A in Boston and now with the Islanders. It means a lot anytime the coaches think enough of you to label you as a team leader. Typically, the team's best players and leaders are the ones who get selected for it, so, more than anything, it sort of reaffirms the fact that you are doing some things right when you get it sewn onto your jersey. To know that you have the respect of your peers does wonders for your confidence, trust me. As a captain, you really do have to lead by example. I know that's a cliché that gets way overused, but it's really at the core of what being a professional is all about. As a leader, you have to show the younger guys how to play the game the right way. You have to show them how to prepare and how to make the right choices on and off the ice.

Joe Sakic

When you're named as a captain, it's obviously a great honor. It means that the coaches have a lot of respect for what you are doing both on and off the ice. It's an honor, but it's also a big responsibility. As captain, you're sort of the mediator between the coaching staff and the players. You spend a lot of time relaying messages back and forth each way, which adds a whole other element to your job in addition to just playing. When they name you the captain, they're doing so for a reason. They like the way you approach the game and what you bring to the table. Every captain is different, and each one has his own style. As for my style, I just tried to be myself. I was more of a quieter kind of a guy, I suppose, probably more of a lead-by-example type of captain. There are times when you need to step up and be that vocal leader and times when you need to sit back and just listen and observe. I was pretty loose in the dressing room, but I would speak out if I thought it was necessary or if the time was right. Overall, though, I never really wanted to say too much or too often…that just wasn't my approach.

Without a doubt, the biggest perk of wearing the C is getting to raise Stanley first. When Commissioner Bettman handed me the Cup in '96, it was such an incredible feeling. I just felt the weight of the world lifted off of my shoulders. I hoisted it proudly and then handed it off to Curtis Leschyshyn, who had been my teammate in Quebec. We had gone through some tough times together, and I wanted to acknowledge him and let him know how much I respected him by handing it to him first. Later, when we won it again in '01, I decided to give it to Ray [Bourque] without raising it first. It was a spur-of-the-moment thing to do, but I just thought it was the right thing to do at the time. As players, we all knew what he meant to the game, and I knew that I wanted to do something special for him. He came back for one more season to try to win it, and it became our focus that season to get it for him, no kidding. He drove us as much as we drove him, it was pretty incredible. He worked so hard that year, and it was extremely gratifying to watch him hoist it, one of the proudest moments of my career.

Nick Schultz

I wore the C and the A in Minnesota, and it was certainly an honor to be thought of as a leader by your coaching staff and teammates. As for what it means? It means you have to be a leader, both on and off the ice. It means making the right choices, even when no one is looking. I'm more of a lead-by-example kind of a guy, I suppose, and probably a little less vocal than some other captains. As I have gotten older and gained more experience, it's been easier for me to speak my mind in the locker room in certain situations, but overall I just try to do whatever I can to support my teammates and to ultimately help my team win. That's always been my attitude. I try to work really hard in practice, that's where it all starts, in my opinion. As a leader, you want to be looked upon as a true professional in every aspect of the game, so that's what I strive for.

Brendan Shanahan

I didn't wear the C very often, but I was fortunate to wear the A for quite a bit of my career. I was usually Robin to somebody's Batman! It's an honor to wear a letter, in my eyes, though, regardless of whether it's a C or an A. Anytime your organization and your teammates recognize you as a leader, it's a big honor. As a captain you have to wear two hats. First and foremost you have to carry your own load out on the ice an do your job. You have to make sure that your game is where it needs to be so that you are productive. But then, at the same time, you have to be the team leader and sort of look after your teammates. It's a balancing act, for sure.

I remember the first time I got asked to wear the C, it was in Hartford. Paul Holmgren was the coach, and after training camp he told me he wanted me to be the team captain. I actually told him that, because I was new to the team, I didn't think I was a good choice. He asked me to think about it and that we would revisit it in a few weeks. Sure enough, a few weeks later I remember flying home from a preseason game in which I had played pretty well, and he called me up to the front of the plane to talk to him. He just looked at me and said, "I don't care what you think, you're the captain." I felt really honored to wear it, but it was a big responsibility. I didn't know if I was up for it at first, because there were so many other great players and leaders on our team, but eventually I settled into the role and embraced it. I never totally felt right about it, though, because there were so many other great leaders on our team who could've worn it.

Even today, you are starting to see more and more teams in the NHL that are going without a captain. They might go a year or two with just a couple assistants, rather than putting a C on a guy who isn't ready for it, or maybe just isn't the right guy for it. If you don't have one, you don't have one. Great leaders are hard to find, they really are. Your best player might not be your best choice as a captain. There's

The Detroit Red Wings' Brendan Shanahan (14) celebrates with Mathieu Dandenault after he scored against the St. Louis Blues in a November 1999 game.

a big difference. If a young guy emerges and fills that role, great. Or if a veteran is up for it, then that can work out, too. But if not, then teams nowadays are willing to wait for the right guy. It's a big deal. The captain is your leader and the face of the franchise. He's the guy the media is going to want to talk to when things aren't going well. You need someone in that role who is capable of representing both the players as well as management. So they have to make sure they get it right.

Neil Sheehy

You don't have to wear a letter to be a leader, but wearing the C is definitely a great honor. It's humbling to see it sewn on your sweater for the first time, no question. I first wore the C for my high school team and then in the minors, followed by a neat experience where I got to wear it in 1992 for Team USA at the world championships in Germany. I later wore the A for a while with the Washington Capitals, as well. To be recognized as a team leader, wherever it is, it's always special. Being a captain means you have to bring your A game each and every night. To be selected to wear it means that the coaches and management see innate qualities in you that they think will benefit the team as a whole. They want you to serve as a role model, so to speak, for the rest of the team. They want the other players to emulate those characteristics in hopes that they will collectively become better. Luckily, I never had any idea of just what exactly those characteristics were when I was playing, or I probably would have focused on them way too much and crumbled under the pressure. [Laughing] I mean, that's sort of daunting when you think about it!

As the team leader, you have to make things happen and you have to lead by example. That's your role. And when things aren't going right, it's up to you to do something that changes the course of the game. For me, I wasn't a goal-scorer, so that meant being more of an emotional rah-rah guy and getting physical. That was how I could lead by example, by hitting guys and trying to swing the momentum that way. If that meant dropping the gloves out there and fighting someone, so be it. I was willing to do whatever it took to lift my teammates, to give them a spark; that was how I demonstrated leadership. It might mean blocking shots, or shadowing the other team's top player to get him off his game, or any number of things. Each player has to find his own way to earn that respect, and for me that was my way. Good leaders find creative ways to get their team-mates to wake up a little bit—that's what it's all about. So that letter on your sweater serves as a constant reminder to let you know that there are people counting on you to make sure you do those things each and every night.

Darryl Sittler

I always tried to believe that you lead by example. You've got to walk the talk, so to speak. If you do that, it's all you can do. Just be who you are. I was fortunate to have guys who had a lot of leadership qualities around me, guys like Lanny McDonald, Tiger Williams, and other players. To me, as a captain, it's nice when you have that support from quality teammates. (Source: "Some of Hockey's Best Leaders Tell Us What It Takes," by Paul Grant, ESPN.com, November 12, 2007.)

Bobby Smith

It's kind of funny, but as I like to say, the only C I ever had on my jersey in the NHL was in Montreal, and it wasn't the little one that stands for *captain*…it was the big one that stood for *Canadiens*! I did, however, get a chance to wear the A on occasion in Montreal when either Larry Robinson or Mats Naslund was out or injured. We had a lot of great leaders on that roster in those days, so it was certainly an honor whenever the coaching staff would ask me to wear a letter and represent the team. When you look back at the Hall of Fame lineup of players who wore the C for this organization, guys like Henri Richard, Jean Beliveau, Yvan Cournoyer, Serge Savard, Bob Gainey, and on and on—it was just a thrill to be out on the same ice that they skated on, to tell you the truth.

My views on captains have evolved since I got into coaching and management. Lately, I've seen teams go in one of two directions when it comes to who wears the C. One school of thought says you go with your leader, a character guy, like Johnny Bucyk in Boston or Serge Savard in Montreal. Another school says you go with your best player, your top goal-scorer. But when the game is on the line come playoff time, it's gonna be Guy LaFleur or Bobby Orr who makes the difference—not Johnny Bucyk. So those are two very different views that teams take, and I see value in both of them.

The captaincy is also an obligation. You wouldn't want Guy LaFleur to say, "You know, I'm really helping out with the leadership and working with the young guys, it's too bad my production has gone from 50 goals down to 20." Right? Guy LaFleur's job with the Montreal Canadiens was to be the offensive spark plug and score goals. Do you want him doing too many other things that take his focus and concentration away from that? That's the question you, as the general manager, have to ask. Some teams ask their captains to be a sort of on-ice coach, where he has to be looking out for his teammates and seeing who's struggling. A guy like Bob Gainey (Montreal), who was a defensive player and didn't have to necessarily worry about scoring 50 goals, played that role extremely well. So you have to decide what's best for your team and make that decision accordingly. It's never an easy decision.

Some guys simply don't want that added pressure and responsibility. I remember when I joined the North Stars in the late '70s. The franchise had just merged with the Cleveland Barons, and in training camp we had players from both teams come together in the merger. We voted on our captain one day after practice, and we all pretty much chose Al MacAdam. Al stood up and, to the disappointment of just about everybody in the room, said, "I don't want to be the captain. It takes too much away from my play. I can be a leader on this team, but it's more important for me to play well and just focus on that aspect of my game." Essentially, he said that the C was too much of a burden for him. He didn't want to have to talk to the media every single day, and he didn't want to have to meet with the coaching staff on a daily basis to discuss certain things. Looking back, I give him a lot of credit for being honest about it. That had to be a tough decision, but I respect him for it. He wound up being a great leader and was a very productive member of our team. I think he scored 90 points the following year, so I think he made the right choice.

The leadership of a hockey team is not one guy's job. When the old Philadelphia Flyers won back-to-back Stanley Cups in the early '70s, I recall reading that something like 15 of the players had worn the C on their junior teams. That's a room full of leaders right there all working toward the same goal. It was the same for me when I was playing in Montreal, I would look around the dressing room in awe sometimes just thinking about the talent that was in the room. When you assemble teams like that, full of leaders, you end up with a character hockey team. So you see those types of intangibles come to the table on draft day, when they are looking at a young prospect's attributes.

Steve Smith

First and foremost, it's an honor anytime you're recognized and singled out as a team leader. Certainly it was a proud day for me when Brian Sutter announced that I would be his captain of the Calgary Flames. Wearing the C adds a level of responsibility to your job that not every player wants to deal with. I enjoyed it, though, and really thrived in that role. For me it was more about leading by example out on the ice as opposed to the words that I spoke. I wanted to let my actions do the talking for the most part, and that was my approach to leadership. Sure, you had to make a lot of unpopular decisions for the good of the team, but that's what being a leader is all about.

Eric Staal

It's something I take a lot of pride in. Being considered a team leader is a huge honor. I've always found that you have to be yourself as a leader. If you do that and you work hard and perform, then others will follow. There were other captains and great leaders I learned from along the way, but at the end of the day you have to do it your own way. For me, in Carolina, it's about doing the right things every day. It's about doing the little things that ultimately help your team be successful. It's about working really hard and leading by your example. I just try to work as hard as I can every practice and every game, that's where it starts and ends for me.

I learned about leadership from my parents and brothers growing up in Thunder Bay. My parents worked extremely hard and raised us with strong values. They really encouraged us to do our best in whatever we did, whether it was in hockey or school or whatever. Being the oldest, you're always kind of thrust into doing everything first. I was always showing my younger brothers the way, so for me being a leader sort of came naturally. Those guys have all done a great job in blazing their own paths as professionals today, and I couldn't be prouder of them. They developed those same characteristics and leadership abilities on their own. Marc and Jordan both wear the A for the Rangers and Penguins, which is pretty neat to see.

Mark Stuart

I currently wear the A in Winnipeg but have worn the C at a few stops along the way, including on the U.S. World Junior Team, which was pretty special. Anytime you wear a letter on your jersey, it means something. It's big. I take great pride in it. Wearing it in the NHL is pretty humbling because it means you have the respect of your coaches and teammates. I take it very seriously, absolutely. Leadership is one of those things where I think you either have it or you don't, you can't force it. It comes natural to some people and each person has their own way of showing it. For me, it's just by working hard and doing my job. Every practice, every game, I think about what that letter means and about what I can do to help my team that day. For me that might mean playing physical or sticking up for one of my teammates. My role on the team isn't like most captains, who are the top skill guys on the team. Every now and then I need to go out there and shake things up. If I feel like someone is taking liberties with one of my teammates or if I feel like the momentum isn't going the right way, then I'll drop the gloves—absolutely.

Regardless of who wears the letters, every team has a leadership group. There's always a small group of veterans, the respected locker room guys, who are the real leaders behind the scenes. They are the guys who set the tone at practice and do the little things, like getting everybody together for dinner on road trips, stuff like that. They don't have a C or an A on their chest, but they're just as important to the team's overall chemistry.

Gary Suter

I wore letters in Calgary and in San Jose toward the end of my career. What it meant was that you had earned the respect of your coaches and teammates. It was a big honor and also a big responsibility. There are all sorts of different ways to lead. Some guys are real vocal. Some are belligerent and will go out and do whatever they can to fire the team up, whether that's a big hit or a fight or whatever. Others are quiet and just lead by example. That might mean how they approach practice or off-season training or what they do when they're out at night. All of that stuff matters when you are a team leader. The bottom line, though, is that there's really no right way. It's about each person finding his own way.

It's a 24-hour deal, though, because you're being watched at all times. It's not only how you play on the ice, it's how you carry yourself as a person. It's about being a professional. Again, it's a lot of responsibility, and quite frankly not everybody wants it. When you're a kid, everybody wants it, and in the end they give it to the best player. But, as you get older, the C goes to not necessarily the best player, but the best leader. Big difference. I've been coaching youth hockey for more than 10 years now, and I really try to pick the right kids for that role. Sometimes your best players are selfish, so in my opinion those guys don't make good leaders. It just sends the wrong message to the rest of the team. He's got to be a great team guy first, that's what leadership is all about.

Darryl Sydor

It's very gratifying to be named as a captain, but to me it was just a letter. I don't want to sound disrespectful or unappreciative, but it wasn't a very big deal to me for the fact that we had so many other leaders on those teams. I mean, we had guys who'd worn the C on other teams in the locker room, and I certainly wasn't any better or a more respected leader than they were. I played in the NHL, and I've just always felt that you don't need a letter on your jersey to be a leader. So, while it was a nice honor to be recognized by my coaches for my hard work, getting a letter honestly didn't matter too much to me.

Bryan Trottier

Wearing a letter, it's an elite fraternity. Every time you face off against an opposing team, they are constantly sizing you up and looking at your leaders. And it's not just who's wearing the C, but also who's wearing the As. Sometimes it's none of those guys, and it's your veteran guys who are leading the charge. They're looking at how those guys conduct themselves under pressure and how they hold themselves accountable when they screw up. I took a lot of pride in it. It's something that, as a player, you take very, very seriously. It's something that reflects not only your style of play, but your conduct, your poise, your composure, your intensity, and your demeanor, as well—both on and off the ice. The captain is a reflection of an organization and even of a community. When I was a captain of the New York Islanders, I was constantly reminded of the fact that I represented not only the Islanders fans, but all of New York. So I took that responsibility very seriously. It was a heavy burden at times, but I was up to it and really enjoyed it. You can never abuse that privilege, you just carry yourself with a sense of confidence and pride. As for the job of being captain, for me it was all about leading by example and about being there for my teammates. Beyond that, I wanted to conduct myself like a professional with the media and the referees, not to mention the fans. When you are a team leader, all eyes are on you. So you have to act with a sense of dignity and you have to make the right choices, even when no one is looking. I wasn't perfect by any stretch of the imagination—I made a lot of mistakes along the way. But I always owned up to them and apologized after the fact. People want their leaders to be accountable, good or bad, they want someone to stand up and be responsible. So that's what I tried to do.

Wes Walz

To wear the C at the highest level of professional hockey, it's almost beyond words. To know that you have the confidence of the coaching staff and of the entire organization, it's a pretty incredible feeling. As a player, it's the ultimate feather in your cap. They believe in you as a player, as a guy for others to look up to, and they admire your work ethic and preparation. It's very humbling. I just tried to work as hard as I could and bust my ass every day. I didn't say a whole lot, instead I just tried to let my actions

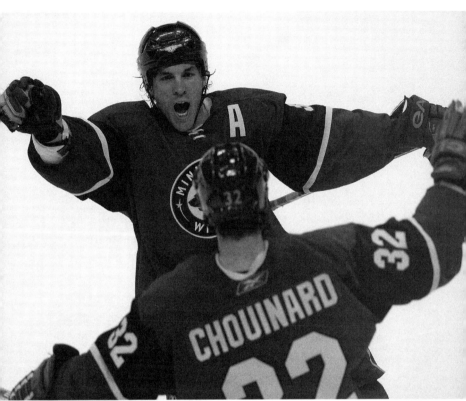

Minnesota Wild centers Wes Walz (wearing the A) and Marc Chouinard (32) celebrate Chouinard's empty-net goal against the Toronto Maple Leafs during a 5–3 Wild victory in January 2006.

do the talking for me. That was it. I wore it in Minnesota under Jacques Lemaire. He used a rotating captain system and would reward guys for their hard work. If you did the right things and played the right way, this was his way of thanking you as well as incentivizing you. I was one of the more permanent captains on the team, in that when I wasn't wearing the C I would quite often wear the A. Either way, it was a huge honor. The funny thing about being on a team with a new captain every month was seeing the new guy with the C trying to lobby the team photographer to get the team photo taken the particular month he was wearing it!

Erik Westrum

I was lucky, I got to wear the C in high school, in college at the University of Minnesota, in the minors with the Houston Aeros and Toronto Marlies, and then over in Europe with a few different teams. I never got to wear it in the NHL, though, which would have really been a thrill. To wear it is big, no doubt about it. In fact, my dad and I are the only father-son combo to wear it at the University of Minnesota, which is pretty neat, too. I've just always had the attitude that when it comes to playing hockey, you play for your teammates. And anytime your peers recognize you as a team leader, that's special. It means you're not only well respected, but also that you're playing the game the right way.

I've always enjoyed the leadership aspect of sports. I always wanted to be that guy who scored the big goal. That was leadership to me. If we were down, I wanted to score. That was how I could help my teammates the most, I always felt. I hated coming off the ice to be honest, I wanted to be out there every second doing whatever I could to help my teammates win. That's just my mentality.

As for my style, I was a lead-by-example kind of a guy—but I could be pretty vocal in the locker room, too. I was probably best at taking the younger guys under my wing. I enjoyed that aspect of the game. Anytime you can help the younger guys and get them to buy into the same systems and philosophies that the older guys believed in, that's pretty rewarding. That's so important in hockey, to get the younger guys on board and feeling like they are a part of it right away. The sooner they feel accepted and included, the better the team is going to do in the long run. As a player, you want to win, first and foremost, but to be a role model and help some guys along the way—that's pretty fulfilling, as well.

Another aspect of being the captain that I really enjoyed was being the team's social chairman. To build chemistry and create those bonds among players, you had to get the guys out and do fun stuff together. So I really enjoyed organizing the team bowling outing or team happy hour or team dinner. Some were with families, some were without— it just depended on the situation and what I felt the team needed. When you're winning, grab the wife and kids. When you're losing, it's just the guys—and we're going to let our hair down.

I'd get it started with a players-only meeting after practice in the afternoon where we'd talk about what we needed to do to get the ship turned around. We'd set some goals and talk about expectations. We'd talk about guys being accountable. Then we'd go out and yuck it up over some beers and just connect, as friends. We'd forget about hockey for the night. It's so important to be able to do that. So, for me to be able to facilitate that and organize it, that was very meaningful to me. Especially if we were in a funk and got it turned around as a result of something we did off the ice that somehow brought everyone together in a positive way.

I tried to use my sense of humor to get guys to relax, too. On the ice I'm super-competitive and serious, but off the ice I'm goofy as hell and am a totally different person. I re- member one time when I was playing in the minors in Utah. We'd just gotten beat pretty badly, and the coach told us to all stick around the locker room after the game for what I assumed was going to be a major ass-chewing. I could tell that the guys were tired and beat up at that moment, and that this was not going to help at all. I asked him to please reconsider having his meeting because I felt really strongly that this wasn't the time for it. He was pissed off and sort of poo-pooed me and blew me off. So I took matters into my own hands and wound up sneaking into this room in the arena where they kept the mascot suits for intermission shows and whatnot. In there was this huge inflatable sumo suit. I threw it on and barged into the locker room. Everybody just about died. I tackled one of our star players and started wrestling him, it was hilarious. The coach could see what I was doing and decided to go along with it. Instead of him bitching at us, he canceled the meeting and told us to all go out for happy hour. The guys had some fun, drank some beer, and kind of chilled out a little bit. They forgot about hockey for the night. Sure enough, guys loosened up, and our season turned around at that point.

My dad, who also played professionally, always reminded me that hockey was a job, and that when the games were over it was important to just leave it all at the rink. Come home and be a husband and a father, you owe that to your family. Have some fun, win or lose, it's important to be able to check out and recharge your batteries. Otherwise you burn out and then you're no good to anybody. He was a sore loser like I am, but it's great advice. I never forgot that.

Pat Westrum

I've been coaching and scouting for many years now, and I can tell you that choosing the right captain is a very important decision. I wore the C in college and then wore the A on a U.S. national team, and in the minors—but

never in the pros. Wearing a letter for me meant that I had
a responsibility to lead by example and just do the best I
could on and off the ice. You have to be able to communicate with the coaching staff, because once you become a
captain you're kind of the voice between your peers and
the higher-ups. It's up to you to keep the peace in the locker
room, too, and to hold your teammates accountable—
which wasn't always easy, because these guys are your
friends. It's needed, though, otherwise little issues grow and
fester into big ones, and then things start going on behind
closed doors. I've seen that, and it can get ugly. Cliques
form, and a few renegade players sort of create a mutiny,
and before you know it, you have a cancer growing. As a
captain you have to get along with everybody and be able
to communicate with them, so you can talk to the guys before stuff like that happens. The bottom line is that you have
to treat people fairly and with respect. If you did that, then
you were going to be all right.

Steve Yzerman

To be the captain of such a great group of hockey players
in such a fine organization like the Detroit Red Wings was
a real honor for me. I just tried to be myself out there and
lead by example. I practiced hard and tried to play well every game, and hopefully that rubbed off on my teammates.
You earn respect in this league by working hard and doing
the right things, on and off the ice. So that's what I tried to
do on a daily basis. Nothing fancy, just hard work. I tried
to step up in big games and just do whatever I could to help
my team win. That's what it's all about.

For me, winning the Stanley Cup was the most important
thing I accomplished in my career. It was a long journey
getting there, too—14 years, to be exact, before we finally

Did You Know?

Steve Yzerman wore the C for a league-record 20 seasons with Detroit and led the Wings to three Stanley Cups. He was considered such an icon to the franchise that, when they retired his number, they put a C right on his banner at Joe Louis Arena. So it will always be known that, even in retirement, Yzerman is the Red Wings' captain.

won it. I went through a lot of tough seasons in Detroit before we were able to eventually get it right. So, to look back now at what it means, I would have to say that it has clearly defined my career. The Cup is so special because it's so hard to win. Those two months of playoff hockey after already going through six months of the regular season really wear on you. So, when you are the last team standing at the end, that means you've survived and that you're the champion. I'm just extremely proud to have played my entire career in Detroit and that I was able to be a part of bringing three Stanley Cups to that great city.

One of the great privileges of being a captain in the NHL is that you get to be the first guy to hoist the Stanley Cup. Usually the captain will then hand it to the assistant captain, or maybe the team's most veteran player. Well, when I won it for the first time in 1997, I decided to hand it to our owner, Mike Ilitch. I skated a lap with it first to let the fans see it but then handed it to Mike, who was sitting in the first row of the stands at the time. We had been through a lot together over the past 14 years leading up to that point, and I thought it would be a fitting gesture. I think he really appreciated it. It was a neat moment.

Jason Zucker

I wore the C for Team USA at the world junior championships, and it was a huge honor. Anytime you get selected to be a team leader, it means a lot, especially in a situation where you're representing your country. Wearing the C doesn't change you as a player, but it changes your perspective with regard to how you approach the game. It means that you have to put the team before yourself. As a captain, you have to lead by your example in practices and in games, as well as off the ice. It means you have to make sure your teammates are doing the right things and then be prepared to hold them accountable if they're not—which is never an easy thing to do. I've never minded that aspect of being a leader, though. If someone was doing something that the coaches felt was wrong, then I would talk to that person. I'd never call them out in front of everyone else or anything like that, but I'd talk to them respectfully about why it was wrong and then about how I could maybe help them to improve. I'm a big fan of constructive criticism if it helps guys get better, because at the end of the day that's what it's all about. I know I appreciate it when guys take me aside to point things out to me and talk to me about getting better. Right away when I got to Minnesota, our captain, Mikko Koivu, took me aside and helped me out with a few things. That meant a lot. I'm just starting out in the NHL as a rookie, but I certainly hope to be in a position one day down the road where the coaches will feel good enough about me as a player and as a person to put the C on my jersey. I have a long way to go, but that's something I'm definitely going to be striving for.

CHAPTER
2

WHO WERE THE CAPTAINS YOU REALLY LOOKED UP TO OR ADMIRED AND WHY?

Getting the players to open up prior to this chapter was difficult at times. It was difficult because, as I learned, captains are very humble and modest people. They don't like to talk about themselves or their achievements, that's just not in their nature. They do, however, enjoy talking about their mentors, heroes, and role models—which is precisely what this chapter is all about. The stories and memories here are straight from the heart. Selfless acts are not only recognized but celebrated by those who witnessed them first-hand. I wanted to know not only *who* their most respected and favorite captains were, but more importantly *why*. And I didn't just want to hear about the characteristics that made someone a great captain per se, I wanted a good story to back it up. So I tried to dig deep and really ask probing questions to get the guys to come out of their shells. Many of them got emotional when talking about their first captain, or the captain who took them under their wing and gave them the confidence they would need to one day wear the C themselves.

Adrian Aucoin

When I first got into the league with Vancouver, I was fortunate enough to play with Trevor Linden. He was just about everything you could ask for in a captain, really respected and truly a great leader. Then Mark Messier came in and took over as the team captain. What a warrior that guy was. Just the way he went about his business, both on the ice as well as off, it was amazing. The game was so important to him, and he was so passionate about the team's success. I learned a great deal from him, no question, he was a true professional. The thing I remember most about Mark was that he never seemed to apologize for anything. Because he was so dedicated and worked so hard, no matter what he did—his intentions to make the team better were just always right. So even if things didn't work out, he wasn't sorry about it. He was just all-in, and if it worked, great; if not, so be it. But he wasn't going to apologize for trying, regardless of what it was. His attitude was, if you were trying hard and playing the game the right way and things didn't work out or you made a mistake along the way, then that was all right. He might not be happy about it, but he was okay in knowing each of us gave it our all for the betterment of the team. It was just all about the team with him, no matter what. From there Markus Naslund took over, and he wound up becoming one of my best friends. I've never met anyone who was more dedicated to trying to play the game the right way. Just a great guy. Then, full circle, to Phoenix with Shane Doan. What can you say about this guy? Incredible. Everybody knows what he brings every night. Everybody knows the type of person he is, his honesty, his dedication, and his leadership. He's pretty much everything you could ever hope your captain could be.

David Backes

I really looked up to Dallas Drake. He was the captain when I first got to St. Louis, and I thought he was just incredible. He was at the tail end of his career at that point, and I was just a kid, but he sort of took me under his wing. I really appreciated that. He'd talk to me in the locker room and in practice, little stuff, but very meaningful. Just to see the respect that he commanded from the other players, it was very inspiring to me. I think the thing I learned the most from him was that you have to respect everybody. He treated everyone right and really cared about his team-mates. He accomplished a lot as a player and was just a great leader. Great guy.

Keith Ballard

Shane Doan was the captain in Phoenix when I was there, and I can't say enough good things about him. He's one of the greatest captains in the NHL, without question. I really looked up to him. Not only was he a great teammate, he's such a good person off the ice—total lead-by-example kind of a guy. Without a doubt, he's always the last guy off the ice every practice. He's always working to get better and to help his teammates get better. As a leader, he never asks anyone to do anything that he's not doing himself. He was the first one to hold himself accountable, yet he was also there to hold everybody else accountable. I just have so much respect for the guy. Look at what that franchise has gone through, both on and off the ice, over the past 10 years. It's insane. It would have been so easy for him on so many occasions to just bail on that franchise. He could've let his contract run out and become a free agent in order to sign somewhere else, or he could've easily asked for a trade. Yet he remains so loyal. He's been with that franchise from the beginning, and in my opinion, he is its heart and soul. What an amazing person. Just first-class, a true professional.

Brian Bellows

I really enjoyed playing with Guy Carbonneau when we were both in Montreal. He was a really good leader and overall just a great captain. What I will always remember about Guy was how calm he was, especially during our biggest games. I'll never forget being in a double overtime playoff game the year we won the Stanley Cup in '93 and his telling us between the extra sessions in the locker room to just stay relaxed. He said, "Play your game and don't get too pumped up, boys, that's all." Sure enough, we won the game. He had this calming effect on us and really got us to keep our composure, even at the most stressful times. That's what great captains do, they calm everybody down and keep them focused on the task at hand.

Rob Blake

I played with Wayne Gretzky for the first six years of my career in L.A., and he was certainly somebody I looked up to a great deal. What I learned from Wayne was how a captain has to handle himself away from the ice. Whether it was media requests or autograph requests or charity involvement or just being in the spotlight that was seemingly always shining on him—he always handled himself with class. I was given the C after he moved on to St. Louis, and let me tell you, those were some pretty big shoes to fill, to say the least.

From there I got traded to Colorado, where I was fortunate to play alongside Joe Sakic. What a great leader he was.

He was very quiet, too, not a yeller or screamer at all—a real lead-by-example kind of guy. Joe's level of play was unbelievable. The bigger the game, the better he played. He just seemed to thrive under pressure.

Later in my career, I was given the opportunity to serve as captain of the San Jose Sharks. I think it was here where I really came into my own as a leader. I learned a ton from our head coach, Todd McLellan. He really helped me understand how important it is to take over the team. His philosophy was that by the end of the season the team is being run by the leaders in the dressing room, not the coaching staff. He knew that the coaches came in with a plan and then that was it—it was up to the leaders to help execute it. So he felt very strongly that the captain had to be the guy who could facilitate that. It was critical. Coming into San Jose, I had already worn the C for 10-plus years, yet he taught me more about what it meant to be a captain than all those years combined in just two seasons. The guy was just incredible.

Ray Bourque

Terry O'Reilly was my captain in Boston when I first broke into the league, and I thought he was an incredible leader. I'd have to say he was the hardest working guy I ever played with. How he practiced, how he prepared, how tough he played, how passionate he was about the game— he was just the ultimate Bruin. I was really in awe of him as a younger player; he taught me so much about how to be a professional both on and off the ice. When your captain is that well liked and respected, everybody just follows his lead.

Dan Boyle

I think what's key about Dave [Andreychuk] is that he's
one of the guys. When he talks, the players listen. We all
respect what he has done on the ice and we all respect him
off the ice. (Source: "A 'C' of Responsibility," by Shawn P.
Roarke, *Impact!* January 2003.)

Rod Brind'Amour

I was fortunate to have played with some pretty amazing
captains over the years. I always enjoyed playing on the
Olympic and World Cup teams because those teams are
basically made up of captains. To sort of watch how the
best leaders in the game come together, it's pretty humbling.
If I had to pick one guy from all my years of playing who
really stood out, I would have to go with Steve Yzerman.
He led by his example on the ice and always handled
himself with such class off the ice—just a true professional.
I remember playing with him on some international teams,
and I was always so impressed by the fact that he would go
back out onto the ice after games to get in extra ice time.
He took his craft so seriously, and I had so much respect
for that. He didn't say a whole lot, but he didn't need to.
I admire leaders like that the most, guys who just let their
actions do the talking for them. I'll follow those guys all day
long. Anybody can get up in front of a room and say the
right things, but to back it up out on the ice is what really
matters. That was Stevey Y to a tee. He backed it up.

Neal Broten

Two guys stand out over the years. First, I thought that Craig
Hartsburg was an excellent captain. We played together
in Minnesota. He was a solid defenseman and a great

Shjon Podein on the Coolest Thing He's Ever Seen a Captain Do

I'll never forget right after we won it in 2001 when Commissioner Bettman handed the Cup to Joe [Sakic]. As the captain, it's his privilege to raise it first, but he selflessly declined to do so and instead handed it directly to Ray [Bourque] so that he could be the first to raise it. Ray had waited nearly two decades to hoist it, and Joe didn't want him to wait a second more. I will never forget that moment for as long as I live. There wasn't a dry eye in the house. We all wore hats that season that read "Mission 16-W," meaning the team needed 16 wins to get Ray his Cup. Ray never took that thing off. I remember that last shift before the final buzzer went off in Game 7. We all wanted Ray to be out on the ice, and it was getting close, so Rob Blake came flying over to the bench to come off and then screamed at an exhausted Ray to get out there for the last few seconds of the game. He hopped over the boards and got to enjoy the moment. It was classic, just classic.

competitor out on the ice. He was just an all-around good guy and someone I certainly looked up to. Scott Stevens was another guy who I really thought did a great job. We played together briefly in New Jersey, and he was just a tremendous competitor. He'd give his left leg for the team if it came down to that; the guy just hated to lose. He was a pretty quiet guy and really let his play do all the talking, which I kind of admired. Good captains can just tell which guys need a kick in the butt or a pat on the back, depending on their personalities, and that's how they would lead. I respected guys like that a whole lot more than the guys who just sit and flap all the time, telling you how to play the game. I didn't particularly care for guys like that too much. That's why I liked Hartsy and Scotty, both were really laidback kind of guys. They definitely earned the right to wear the C in my eyes.

Andrew Brunette

I played for several great captains over my career, but the guy who stands out the most is Joe Sakic. I played alongside Joe for three years in Colorado, and he was just amazing. Aside from being a phenomenal player, he was an incredible leader and a fierce competitor. He was the best, what else can you say about Joe? The guy was incredible, just the ultimate teammate whom you would do anything for. He was such a calming influence on us, always playing at an even keel. He was a quiet leader. Regardless of how bad things were going, you could always count on Joe to just stay the course and set the tone for everyone else… smooth and steady. And he had the ability to step up his game when it really counted. He played his best in our biggest games, which is an incredible attribute. You could just always count on him, no matter what.

It was all about the little things with Joe. I remember after practices, he would be the first guy off the ice. That sounds crazy, because usually the team leader is the last guy off the ice, but that wasn't Joe's deal. He was the *first* guy out there every practice, where he would do his work and get extra time shooting and whatnot. But afterward, he didn't want to make guys feel like they *had* to stay out there. I mean, no one comes off the ice before the captain does, that's just one of those unwritten rules in hockey. Well, Joe didn't want to put that pressure on guys. So he went out early, and then came off on time so that the guys could come off when they chose to. He left it up to them. If they wanted to stay late, no problem, but he didn't want to put that pressure on them to *have* to be out there just because he was. That was a little thing, but it meant a lot to the other guys. He was very thoughtful that way, always thinking about the little things that would ultimately effect the team chemistry and morale.

I remember late in the season with Colorado one year, we were all together watching game film. The coaches were tough on us and were pointing out mistakes; it was brutal. Typically, a lot of coaches are afraid to point to the super-stars on the team for stuff like this and say, "It's your fault." Instead they will point the finger at and put the blame on somebody else. Well, that scenario played out that day, but instead of Joe just sitting back and doing nothing, he stood up and took full responsibility. He said, "No, that's not his fault, that's *my* fault. I gotta be better there, and I'm going to try to get better there. I'm sorry." I was floored. Here was our team leader, the captain, our superstar, just owning it and taking full responsibility. Most guys wouldn't do that, but not Joe. That's accountability right there, and that's why Joe was the most respected guy in the locker room.

Another great captain I played with early in my career with Washington was Dale Hunter, who was great because he was so competitive. That guy just hated to lose. He was a very emotional guy, and his enthusiasm rubbed off on everybody else. You just felt like you had to play to the level he was playing at, otherwise you might be letting him down—which nobody wanted to do.

Lastly, I would add Tom Fitzgerald to that list, as well. We played together in Nashville, and he was a wonderful captain, too. I really looked up to him. He was so principled and really lived by a core set of values. The one thing with him that I will always remember was that it was always about the team, the group, never about him. He worried about everybody on the team and cared more about others than himself. He was very selfless. If he had a bad game, personally, he never let it show. He was always positive, and that rubbed off on the guys, as well.

Ryan Carter

Two guys come to mind. One of them I am currently playing with in New Jersey, Zach Parise, who is such an outstanding captain. What a great guy, on and off the ice, so humble. He's so unselfish, too, for him the team always comes first. The other guy is Scott Niedermayer, who I was fortunate enough to play with in Anaheim. He was just amazing, a true captain in every sense. What amazed me about him was how he always conducted himself in such a professional manner. Day in and day out, he was so consistent that way. Never too high and never too low, and that really rubbed off on the guys. He sort of set the tone and the mood for how we were going to practice and play as a team, it was incredible. He just had a presence in the locker room. He was a very quiet guy, too, he never talked just to talk. When he decided it was time to say something, everybody listened because we knew it was going to carry so much meaning. When Scott Niedermayer spoke, guys paid attention. I remember one time between periods during a big game, our coach came in and was pretty upset with the performance of a certain player. He was kind of yelling at this guy, and after a little while Scotty stood up and said, "Okay, that's enough." The coach respected him enough to back down and leave the room, just like that. It was a pretty surreal moment, I'll never forget it. Then, the next day, the coach even came back in the locker room and apologized to that player publicly. Good coaches let good captains do their job, and for Scott Niedermayer—his job was to lead the team and look after the players. He stuck up for us on and off the ice, and that was why we would do anything for him. As his teammates we just didn't want to let him down. If I'm ever lucky enough to get asked to wear a letter again, that's the guy I will try to emulate. I have so much respect for that guy.

Shawn Chambers

I played with Scott Stevens in New Jersey, and I'd have to say he was one of best captains of all-time. He was mean, gritty, tough, and he just led by example. He was pretty vocal in the locker room, too. I mean, when he spoke, the guys listened. He was just incredibly well-respected.

Zdeno Chara

I tried to learn as much as I could from my teammates, wherever I was playing. Sometimes the best leaders aren't even the captains, they are your veterans who have been around for a long time. When I played in New York [Islanders], there were a couple of great leaders on our team, Kenny Jonsson and Tom Chorske. They were both really good at working with the younger players, and I have a lot of respect for those guys. Then, when I played in Ottawa, I played with Daniel Alfredsson, who was and still is a tremendous captain. I would like to think that little bits and pieces of all of those guys have rubbed off on my own leadership style that I use now as the captain in Boston.

Kelly Chase

From a leadership standpoint in his play, I would have to say Brett Hull was unbelievable. We played together in

Zdeno Chara (33) of the Boston Bruins skates against the New York Islanders in an October 2006 game. Photo courtesy of Getty Images

St. Louis, and I never got tired of watching him score goals. He was a warrior. He complained about everything but never about being hurt. He'd play through so much pain on a nightly basis and never took a night off. I remember talking to some of his teammates from the '99 Dallas team that won the Stanley Cup. They were telling me that he was practically playing on one leg. He didn't say a peep about it, either, he just sucked it up and played hockey. That's the definition of leadership right there, in my eyes. When you see other guys who take nights off because of little bumps and bruises, and you compare them to a superstar like Brett Hull, a captain no less, who plays through unimaginable pain on a nightly basis, it makes you think twice about your level of commitment to the team. Brett was a fantastic captain.

Scotty Stevens was another amazing captain. He was a quiet leader who led by example and was just tougher than hell. He was physically tough and he was mentally tough. Just a warrior. He was so confident as a player, too. It was intimidating to see how confident he was out on the ice.

Lastly, I would have to say Garth Butcher, whom I played with in St. Louis. He was my all-time favorite. Great guy. Garth was my captain during my rookie year, and I will never forget how he just took care of me. I didn't have a nice suit, so he bought me one. From a leadership standpoint, he just took the young guys aside and showed them how to do it. He showed me how to prepare and how to practice. I had no clue, but he showed me the way. Garth was a big part of my career because he let me follow him around and learn from him. He made me feel like I was a part of the group. Gino Cavallini wore the A that year, and I'll never forget how he paid for all my meals on the road because I didn't make very much money. Those are things that you remember and then pay forward as you get older and wiser throughout your career.

I will never forget the time I got suspended for 10 games at the end of the season early in my career in a game against Chicago. I was sticking up for one of my teammates who had gotten cheap shotted and got into this huge fight, which resulted in the suspension. Now, it was just sort of understood in those days that and the team would pay your salary while you were out, but I never got paid for whatever reason. That year Scotty Stevens also got suspended for a couple games, and I later found out that the team paid him for the games he sat out. I was kind of upset because it was a ton of money that I had lost at a time when I wasn't making very much money. Now granted, I was no Scott Stevens, but I thought the organization would still take care of me. Nope. So I went to Garth at the following training camp and told him the story. He just looked at me and said, "Don't worry, Chaser, I'll take care of it." Sure enough, Garth took it upon himself to go around and talk to each guy. He basically said, "Listen, this kid fights for us every night and he lost a pretty good chunk of change, so we need to make it right for him." Each guy chipped in a couple hundred bucks, and he wound up collecting about five grand. He handed me this envelope just stuffed full of cash and said, "Chaser, this is from your teammates, and we want you to know that we appreciate what you do for us. We know the team didn't do the right thing by not paying you, but we need to get past that and move on as a team." I was just blown away. What an unbelievably classy thing to do.

Tom Chorske

I was fortunate to play alongside a handful of great captains over the years, solid hard-working guys who led by example, like Chris Chelios, Scott Stevens, Daniel Alfredsson, and Randy Cunneyworth. Another guy I played with who has gone on to become an incredible captain is Zdeno Chara. He was my roommate when he was a rookie, and I take great pride in the fact that I was sort of able to mentor him a little bit early on in his career. He's a great person, and I couldn't be happier to see the success he's had as the captain of the Bruins. All of those guys were very high-integrity and high-character guys and were cut from the same cloth. I had a lot of respect for all of them, just really good people on and off the ice.

Scott Stevens probably had the biggest impact on me. He was incredible at leading by example. His actions on the ice did all the talking for him. He wasn't a guy who was going to stand up and give a real long fiery dissertation to the guys before the game. That's not to say he wouldn't bark out some choice words in the locker room between periods, though. He was a man of few words, but what words he did choose to say were very meaningful. When he spoke, guys listened. And they acted. He was just incredible at getting everybody on the same page and ready to go to work. He was very demanding, especially in practice, where it was just the expectation that you had better be trying as hard as he was. It didn't matter what your role was or how many minutes you played, he set incredibly high standards and held everybody accountable. Scott was just all about the team. He didn't care about anything else, it was all about the team and about winning hockey games. It was just an incredible, follow-my-lead, jump-on-my-back attitude.

I've seen captains call certain players out before. It's rare, but it happens. If one of your star players isn't playing well, you need a captain who can get that guy to step up his game and bring more effort. He'll just tell him that he owes it to the team and to his teammates. That's tough to do, but the top captains—the respected leaders with a lot of cred-ibility—they can get that kind of stuff done. Scott Stevens was that kind of a guy. No question.

Bill Clement

Playing in Philadelphia when I first got into the league, I was fortunate that I got to play for two very good but very different captains. My first captain was Eddie Van Impe. Eddie was a quiet leader. He was very dedicated to helping anybody who needed help either on or off the ice. He was a leader by example in the sense that he sacrificed his body, and even his personal safety, to help the team win. He didn't speak too much, but he had a real loud voice, so when he said something the guys listened. Everybody respected Eddie. So what I learned about leadership from Eddie, more than anything, is that sometimes less is more.

The guy who replaced Eddie as the Flyers' captain was Bobby Clarke. What a guy. For sure, the most dynamic player I ever played with. I don't think there was a deficient bone in his leadership body. He was so dedicated to the team and to winning, that was what it was all about with him. That was sacred to him. He led by example, no matter what. He would attempt to win at all costs. He was ruthless with opponents and was never afraid to stand up to anybody. As a team leader, he demanded excellence from everybody around him. He was forthright and direct with his teammates and wasn't afraid to be confrontational with them with regards to what he felt was required of them. And, most importantly, he had the ability to have difficult conversations with people, anytime and anywhere. He just wasn't afraid to say things that needed to be said, which was incredible. The bottom line with Bobby Clarke was that he was a winner. Not only was he an outstanding leader, he knew how to win. Bobby was the real deal, just an amazing captain.

I remember in 1974 when we were playing the Rangers in the semifinals of the playoffs. I wound up tearing some ligaments in my knee, and it was pretty bad. We played the Bruins in the Finals, and I really wanted to play. We had three other guys who were all out with injuries and we had been forced to call up some guys from the minors, and they just weren't there talent-wise. I watched the first two games in Boston and was just beside myself. Fearing I would never get the opportunity to play in a Finals again, I asked him to take my cast off so I could try skating on it. He told me that I needed to be in it for at least another 10 days, but reluctantly agreed to let me "test it out" on skates. I went out on the ice to try it out, and it felt just awful, I could barely put any weight on it—it was just too painful. A few hours before the start of Game 4, I was soaking in the hot tub in our dressing room. Bobby came in and saw me in the tub, so he came over to see how I was doing. I told him I couldn't bend it 90 degrees and that starts and stops were pretty much impossible.

He then sat down and proceeded to tell me that he wasn't sure if we could win the Stanley Cup without me that night. He told me how valuable I was to the team and that the team needed me out there. He talked about how good I was at killing penalties, and winning face-offs, and playing tough defense. When he was done, he told me that, if there was any way I could play, he would personally really appreciate it because it would greatly enhance our team's chances of winning the championship. He told me that he didn't want me to jeopardize my career, but then reassured me that even if I was at 60 percent, I was still better than the call-up guys. He then got up to leave and said, "We're ready to welcome you back to the lineup as soon as you can make it back out there with us." I was just blown away. I mean, here I was, a 22-year-old kid, and our team captain—*Bobby Clarke*—was asking me to play so that we could win the Stanley Cup.

As soon as he left, I jumped out of there and grabbed our team trainer. He taped up my leg so tight I could barely bend it, but it worked. I went out there to test it out again, and this time I was determined to rejoin my teammates. I was limping on it pretty badly but found a way to use my good leg to push off and make turns. I remember my trainer looking at me just before the start of the game. He asked me if I could go, and my brain screamed, "Not a chance!" But my lips said, "Yes!" So I played Games 4, 5, and 6 with a great degree of difficulty and pain, but it was all worth it when I got to hoist that beautiful Cup.

Bobby was a great leader and could get guys to play beyond what they thought they were capable of. He asked me to contribute, and I didn't want to let him down. I never would have had the courage to do it without his encouragement. He took me to a whole other level of determination that I didn't even know existed. Looking back, sure it was crazy to play on that knee. But in retrospect, thank goodness I did—because it was such an incredible feeling to have been able to say that I played a small part in our franchise's first-ever Stanley Cup championship. He didn't pressure me, he nurtured me and pulled me into making a decision that I ultimately had to make on my own. That was how he motivated guys, one on one, where he would sort of test you and challenge you. You just didn't want to disappoint Clarky. No way.

Part of being the team captain is being the liaison between the players and the coaching staff. He's the conduit, the go-between, and that's a tough spot to be in a lot of times as a player. What made Bobby so unique was his ability to get along with the players as well as with management. I will never forget the time Clarky skated up to me right before the start of Game 4 of the '75 Stanley Cup Finals up in Buffalo. It was during warm-ups, and he said to me, "You gotta have a good game tonight. They (management) asked me if you should play or (another player who I won't mention), and I told them you. Don't let me down." So they were consulting him on roster spots in the Stanley Cup Finals, that's how much they respected this guy's opinion. Furthermore, Bobby wasn't afraid to come to me to say, "I need you to deliver tonight because I stuck my neck out for you." Talk about motivation! Clarky was a master at stuff like that, getting guys to play big in big games and holding them accountable. What an amazing leader. He was a *huge* part of why that team won back-to-back Stanley Cups, without a doubt.

Ben Clymer

I was very fortunate to have played alongside Dave Andreychuk in Tampa Bay. He was a great captain, just a tremendous leader. He was a veteran guy and really led by example. The defining moment with Dave that I will never forget came in Game 7 of the Stanley Cup Finals the year we beat Calgary to win it in 2004. We were up after two periods and about to head back out onto the ice for the third period. Dave, who was 42 years old at the time and had gone 22 seasons without winning a championship, stood up and said, "Guys, we are *not* fucking losing this game!" It was simple, yet profound. We all wanted to win it for Dave, our captain—our heart and soul. We were so fired up after that. Guys were willing to block shots with their teeth at that point. We all just felt like there was no way we were going to be denied. And we weren't.

Matt Cullen

I'd have to say Rod Brind'Amour, who I played with in Carolina, was the best captain I've ever played with. The way he handled himself and led by example was amazing.

He wasn't a real loud guy in the locker room and didn't say a lot, he just went about his business. When he did say something, though, he really thought it through and made it meaningful. Guys listened when he spoke up in the locker room and had something to say. He was so good at saying the right thing at the right time. He was always so positive, too, never negative.

His teammates respected him so much for the way he went to work every day. It didn't matter if he was tired or injured or whatever, you could always count on him to give 100 percent. No kidding, he was the hardest-working guy in practice every single day. It was incredible. There was just no way you could let up around him. He forced everyone on that team to get better. There was no way you could take a night off when he was around. He made you accountable without saying a word, it was incredible. I learned so much from just watching him prepare every day. He was such a great leader, yet he didn't try to be. That was just his nature, to work hard and do the right things. He epitomized the old adage: leadership isn't what you say, it's what you do. He was a huge part of why we won a Stanley Cup there in 2006. I know this, we wouldn't have won it without him leading the way. I was just so impressed with him, he's such a great guy.

Ken Daneyko

I spent most of my career playing along Scott Stevens in New Jersey, and he was one of the best. Scott was a real lead-by-example type of captain. He was more of a quiet leader in the locker room and really let his play out on the ice do the talking for him. He didn't say too much, but when he did, it was heartfelt, to the point, and meaningful. Guys listened. He could get emotional, but usually all it would take for him to get his point across was a look. Scotty's looks could say a thousand words! When he wasn't happy with the team's performance, sometimes that was all it took to shake things up—the look. His work ethic and preparation were second to none, too. He was always the hardest worker every practice and every game. Everybody just followed his lead. He was incredibly respected, and quite frankly, nobody wanted to ever let him down. Just a heck of a player, one of the best.

Another guy I really looked up to as a captain was Mark Messier. Mark and I grew up together, and he's a dear friend. Although we only played together in one world championship, I learned a ton from him. He taught me so much about what it took to make it in the National Hockey League. I'd have to say he's one of the greatest leaders ever. The guy just commanded so much respect, even as a young man. From the way he carried himself to his work ethic, he was just a natural born leader. Maybe the best of all-time.

Natalie Darwitz

Cammi Granato was certainly somebody I looked up to when I was a younger player. She was the captain of the '98 and '02 U.S. Women's Olympics teams, and she was really a pioneer in this sport. I admired her because, not only was she a great player, she had great values and morals. Regardless of the situation, it always seemed like Cammi made the right decisions. Being the captain means making a lot of unpopular decisions that inevitably disappoint some of the people on the team, but Cammi was somehow always able to keep everybody happy. She made tough choices, a lot, that didn't necessarily benefit herself or her friends on the team, either. She might make a controversial decision about a certain situation and explain it by

Mark Messier celebrates his second-period goal against the Vancouver Canucks on their way to victory in Game 7 of the Stanley Cup Finals at New York's Madison Square Garden in 1994.

telling us that she felt it might not benefit the team today, but a year from now, that's when it would pay dividends. She was just all about the team. The *team* came first. And she would just always stick up for what she thought was right. Regardless of what the other 19 of us felt, she did what she was best for the team at *that* point. She'd listen and she'd value our opinions, but in the end she made those tough

Did You Know?

Mark Messier is the only professional athlete to have captained two different teams to championships, having led the Edmonton Oilers to the Stanley Cup in 1990 and the New York Rangers to the Cup in 1994.

calls. People respected her and trusted her because of that. That takes courage, guts. As a result of that, they were much more willing to go along with what she said and did.

Jim Dowd

I grew up in New Jersey, and in high school I had posters of John MacLean, Bruce Driver, and Kenny Daneyko on my wall. I worshipped those guys. Flash forward five years later, and I was their teammate when we won the Stanley Cup. I still have to pinch myself whenever I think of that. Unbelievable. All three of them were incredible [assistant] captains. Just great, great leaders. Those guys ran the locker room, and whatever they said, went. They worked really hard every single practice and just led by example. They helped the young guys. They treated everybody with respect. They were just great guys. They were a huge reason why that team had success, without a doubt.

Add in a guy like Scott Stevens, who wore the C about as good as any guy in history, and what more could you ask for? Scotty was the epitome of the word *captain*. He didn't way much, but when he did, guys shut up and listened. He let his actions speak for him very loudly. I will never forget Game 2 of the '95 playoffs in Detroit. We were scared shitless of the Red Wings, they were the No. 1 team in the league, and everybody was predicting that they were going to sweep us. Well, we were down by a goal, and the game was really tight. Detroit's Slava Kozlov came skating down though the zone, and Scotty just nailed him. It was nuts, he was seeing stars he hit him so hard. The place was just silent. After that, the Detroit guys thought twice about trying to intimidate us. That was what Scotty had the ability to do, to change the entire atmosphere, the momentum, with one big hit. It was a statement. Scotty gave us confidence. Needless to say, we went on and won the Stanley Cup.

Tom Gilbert

When I was in Edmonton, Shawn Horcoff wore the C and he was a great leader. Unlike a lot of other captains, he was very vocal guy. Whether we were way ahead or way behind, he was still talking on the bench and out on the ice—regardless of if he was having a good game or not. Shawn was all about the team, and that was why he was so respected. He was a selfless player who worked hard, and that's what you're looking for out of a leader.

Curt Giles

A guy who I really admired was Paul Shmyr, who I played with in Minnesota. Shmeersy was a great captain. He really made everybody feel like they were a part of the team, especially the younger guys. He'd go out of his way to welcome them and get them feeling comfortable right away. He would work with them and include them in everything, and that went a long way in not only building up those guys' confidence, but in building the team chemistry. As a leader, he was very outspoken. He had no qualms whatsoever about speaking up against some of the older veteran guys, too. He'd call them out and say what whatever was on his mind. He was just a team-first kind of a guy; everything with Shmeersy was about the team.

Another guy who was just a fantastic leader was Freddy Barrett. When I first got to Minnesota in the early '80s, there were several stories in the local papers about how I was going to be taking Freddy's job. It was really awkward because he was my roommate at the time. I will never forget one night we were playing up in Toronto, and he took me aside to talk to me. He said, "I'm sure you're reading all the same stuff I'm reading, but I just want you to know that, if there's anything I can help you with moving forward, please don't hesitate to ask." I was blown away. I mean here's a guy who I'm supposed to be replacing and he's willing to help me become a better player. What a quality person, just first class. That was the definition of a great leader right there.

Clark Gillies

One of the guys I really respected a great deal was Bobby Clarke. I will never forget playing against Philadelphia one year in the playoffs. Bobby wound up getting a huge gash in his face from a skate blade. It was ugly, from the bottom of his jaw to his check bone, and blood everywhere. Most guys would be done for the night and then some. Not Bobby. He wasn't about to let his teammates down. He wasn't gone more than 10 minutes, if that. He went in and got stitched up and was right back out there, playing just as intense as he was before. There were no helmets in those days, either. It was incredible. He led by example and was not about to let his teammates see him quit. Bobby certainly earned my respect that night, without a doubt.

Wayne Gretzky

I always felt I had the strength to lead because of the players around me. I think every successful captain has had strong lieutenants surrounding him. Personalities deliver messages in different ways, and different styles can help you. Players with incredible work ethic are leaders. Standing up for what's right, that's leadership. Vocal support is really valuable—and guys who dedicate their hearts and souls to winning the Stanley Cup are born hockey leaders. I was blessed to have many of these types of players around me—Mark Messier, Kevin Lowe, and Marty McSorley—without them, I'm not sure our teams would have succeeded.

Bill Guerin

I was fortunate to have played with Scott Stevens in New Jersey early in my career, and he was a fantastic teammate. He was very, very influential on a young player like myself at that time. I learned a ton from just watching him in practice. He wasn't a man of many words, but when he spoke, guys listened. As a player his competitiveness was off the charts. The guy was a warrior. His consistency, his professionalism, the way he carried himself, the way he worked harder than everybody else—those were the qualities that made him one of the greatest captains in NHL history.

Ben Hankinson

I was fortunate that I had a chance to play for a few great captains during my career. Scott Stevens, for starters, what an incredible player. The ultimate warrior. He practiced just as hard as he played, and that attitude rubbed off on everybody. He forced everybody to practice harder and pushed everybody on that team, regardless of who you

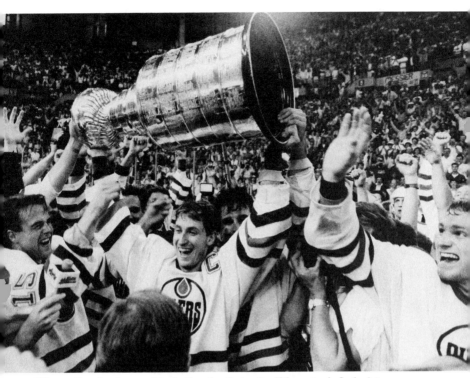

Wayne Gretzky skates with the Stanley Cup after Edmonton's 3–1 victory over Philadelphia in Game 7 of the 1987 Finals. Flanking Gretzky are Kent Nilsson (left) and Marty McSorley (far right).

were. He made everybody better, without a doubt. Just a total lead-by-example kind of a guy, too. Quiet off the ice, but he had a very strong presence and intensity on the ice. His actions spoke much louder than his words. Coaches can say stuff and tell you to do stuff, but it's guys like Scotty who really motivated the rest of the players. What made him so unique was the fact that he was an extension of the coach by the way he led. No doubt about it, captains like Scott Stevens put coaches into the Hall of Fame.

I remember watching him just running guys in practice in order to send a message to the entire team. Talk about a wake-up call! He didn't have to say anything, he just let his actions do all the talking out on the ice, and everybody got the message loud and clear. He'd run veteran players, too, not just the young guys. He wasn't afraid to do stuff like that, and quite frankly, it was really effective. He would call guys out in the locker room, too. He was just all about the team, period. Anybody who wasn't pulling their weight, he got after them and made an example out of them. He demanded that everyone step it up, especially during the

The 15 Greatest Team Captains in NHL History

According to *Bleacher Report* (through 2012)

15. Scott Stevens, New Jersey Devils
14. Jarome Iginla, Calgary Flames
13. Daniel Alfredsson, Ottawa Senators
12. Bobby Clarke, Philadelphia Flyers
11. Denis Potvin, New York Islanders
10. Mats Sundin, Toronto Maple Leafs
9. Pierre Pilote, Chicago Blackhawks
8. George Armstrong, Toronto Maple Leafs
7. Ray Bourque, Boston Bruins
6. Wayne Gretzky, Edmonton Oilers & Los Angeles Kings
5. Steve Yzerman, Detroit Red Wings
4. Mario Lemieux, Pittsburgh Penguins
3. Joe Sakic, Quebec Nordiques/Colorado Avalanche
2. Mark Messier, Edmonton Oilers, New York Rangers & Vancouver Canucks
1. Jean Beliveau, Montreal Canadiens

Source: http://bleacherreport.com/ articles/1096961-15-greatest-team-captains-in-nhl-history

playoffs, and he simply wouldn't accept anything less than your best. The guy was amazing that way.

The second was Mario Lemieux. One of the highlights of my career was when I was with Pittsburgh and I got to play on the same line as Mario during a preseason game. What a thrill. What a presence that guy had. Everybody looked up to him. You just did not want to let him down. His size, his skill, his soft-spoken leadership style—the guy was just the complete package. The things he could do on the ice, just draw-dropping. And the way he was willing to play through pain was epic. He had so many injuries throughout his career, but he never complained. He just sucked it up and played. I remember seeing him when his back was in so much pain that he couldn't even bend over to tie his own skates—somebody else had to do it for him. It was incredible. Hell, I would have tied them for him if the Pens would have kept me around for a little while longer!

Third, I would have to say Lance Pitlick. I'd say Pit was as good if not better than any captain I ever played with. He was like Scotty Stevens in the sense that he, too, was a warrior the way he played. Probably one of the best open-ice hitters to ever lace 'em up, the guy was scary. Opposing players had to keep their heads on a swivel when he was out there, without a doubt. He completely sacrificed his body for the team and would do anything to stand up for his teammates. Teammates would go through a brick wall for him, he just had that kind of aura about him. Guys wanted to play for him, he was an amazing leader. Very, very blue collar, too, just a quiet lead-by-example attitude that rubbed off on everybody else. He didn't have the talent, yet somehow he managed to play eight years in the NHL. I have so much respect for Pit, what a great guy.

Casey Hankinson

The captain I looked up to the most was my old college captain at the University of Minnesota, Scotty Bell. He was a senior when I was a freshman, and I just had so much respect for that guy. He was a freaking walk-on who was such a good leader that eventually they gave him the C. He wasn't the best guy by any stretch, but he outworked everybody and would sacrifice his body for the team on a daily basis. He was a very principled guy. He was one of those guys who just didn't care if it was right, wrong, or indifferent. If he believed in it, he stood up for it. Period. That style really resonated with me. He was so honorable, and you always knew where you stood with him. Like it or not, you had to respect it because he was never wishy-washy about anything.

I'll never forget at the end of the season we had a players-only meeting. We had a decent squad that year, but we knew that it was going to be tough to win the conference title. Well, some of the older guys were talking about sort of shutting it down at the end in order to seal up home-ice advantage for the postseason tournament, and settling for second or third place. Scotty heard that and went nuts. He said, "*Fuck* that! Guys, if that's the attitude you have, then I don't want to be on this team! You guys are a bunch of quitters. We're in this to win the championship, I'm not settling for second place." That was a very impactful moment for me. To see his passion and conviction, it was amazing. You just knew that you could get behind that guy because he was never going to quit. We wound up coming in fourth place, *but*, behind him leading the charge, we did make it to the final four. What you saw was what you got with Scotty. Great guy, great leader.

Derian Hatcher

I always admired Steve Yzerman. The way he played and how hard he played always impressed me. He was a great captain. I was able to play with him for a season in Detroit after I left Dallas, but unfortunately I got injured and missed most of the season. Just to see him lead the way he did, though, it was amazing. He was such a respected player, one of the best of all-time, for sure.

Kevin Hatcher

When I was in Washington, I was really fortunate to have been able to play alongside Rod Langway. I really looked up to him, he was a great player. You knew what you were going to get from him every game. He played the game as hard as anybody. I mean, he was one of the few players at the time who refused to wear a helmet, which says a lot about his toughness. He was old-school. He was a great leader, too, whether it was in the dressing room or on the ice. His work ethic was just second to none.

Brett Hedican

Two guys come to mind: Rod Brind'Amour and Mark Messier. Roddy was a tremendous captain. We won a Stanley Cup together with in '06 with Carolina. I had so much respect for him as a player. He's a consummate professional, a guy who worked so hard every day in practice. Nobody outworked Roddy. Great guy, too, a real positive influence. I've never heard him say a bad word about another player. We became buddies off the ice, and I'm proud to say he's one of my best friends to this day.

Roddy had a very calming influence on the team. As intense and competitive a guy as he was, his style was a little more laid back in the locker room. I will never forget what he said to us right after Game 6 of the Stanley Cup Finals. We'd gone up on Edmonton three games to one only to see them rally back to tie it. We were heading back to Carolina for Game 7 with very little momentum, and the guys were nervous. Roddy, very calmly, just said, "Boys, relax, the work has already been done. If we play our game, we're going to be Stanley Cup champions." It was simple yet profound. He was right. We had trained *so* hard that year, harder than we'd ever trained before. We came in early and we stayed late, every single day. Yes, the work had already been done. Sure enough, we regrouped and went out and took care of business.

Mark Messier is another great captain. I played with Mark in Vancouver, and he was just an unbelievable leader. The way he conducted himself on a daily basis just made guys want to get better. He had that effect on people. As great a player as he was, I think his greatest asset was his ability to bring guys together. He wanted to make sure everybody felt like they were a part of the team—that was really important to him. He'd do little things to make sure every guy felt important. He made sure everybody felt like they were a big piece of the puzzle, whether they played three minutes a night or 30 minutes a night. Once you get to know him, it becomes pretty obvious as to why he's won so many Stanley Cups.

Darby Hendrickson

I played for a few great captains during my career: Mark Messier, Mats Sundin, Doug Gilmour, and Joe Sakic. All of those guys were very high-end players, but each was totally different in their approach to leadership. I played with Mark in Vancouver, and that guy was the ultimate captain. He didn't talk very much, he was more of a quiet leader. It was his wording, though, in how he said things that really made him unique, in my eyes. In my experience with him, that was what was most impressive to me, the way he was able to effectively communicate with each person on the team. Mark wasn't afraid to call guys out; he was tough. It was almost like he was the coach of the team at times. That's what great leaders do, they sort of take over the locker room and get the guys to jump on board. When the team takes over and claims ownership of its own locker room and sort of rises above the coaching staff, it's a special moment. You need a guy who can lead that process, and Mark was that type of dynamic leader.

In Toronto there were a few, including Mats Sundin and Doug Gilmour. Doug was similar to Mess in that he didn't talk much, yet he was *very* intense. He was such a competitor and extremely emotional as a leader. Between periods it wasn't uncommon for him to go off and really get guys fired up yet still remain calm the entire time. Doug had won a Cup and was highly respected by the players. I'll never forget my rookie year in Toronto. I was suiting up for my first-ever playoff game, and he came over to my stall in the locker room to talk to me. We were in the old Chicago Stadium, I'll never forget it. He kneeled down, grabbed me, looked me right in the eyes, and said, "I know you're young, but we need you to step it up tonight." It meant a lot to me that he took me aside to talk to me like that, and made me feel valued. I was just a rookie call-up and wasn't even sure he knew who I was, but I was really pumped up and ready to go after that, let me tell you! Great leaders get everybody on board and make everyone feel like they are a part of it.

Mats, meanwhile, was also very calm. He was just a solid player who led by example. He was very respected and very well liked. To wear the C in Toronto, that takes a special person who can handle all the media scrutiny and everything else. Mats was the right man for the job; he just did and said all the right things. He was the perfect face of the franchise. He was never too flashy, just consistent and solid. A warrior, though, who was a great player and extremely competitive.

Lastly, in Colorado I played with Joe Sakic. What can you say about Joe? The guy was unbelievable. He was successful in everything he did, on or off the ice. As a leader, he was so smooth, I was so impressed with that guy. Guys wanted to follow him because he was just that charismatic. He was the real deal, no question—one of the best of all-time. He wouldn't call guys out, rather he would work with them and then hold them personally accountable. He was constantly reinforcing what it was going to take to win the Stanley Cup. It was all about the team and all about winning championships. When he spoke, guys listened.

Phil Housley

When I first got into the NHL with Buffalo, Gilbert Perreault was our captain, and he was a great leader. Very positive. I really looked up to him and had a lot of respect for the way he played the game. He was more of a lead-by-example kind of guy. He wasn't real vocal, but when he got angry, the players listened. Another guy I admired was Dale Hunter, who I played with in Washington. He wasn't a real rah-rah guy, but he had your back every night. He'd go to battle for you and really was a fierce competitor.

From left: Ted Lindsay, Gordie Howe, and Sid Abel (wearing the C) of the Detroit Red Wings. Photo courtesy of Getty Images

Gordie Howe

I will never forget the advice Sid Abel, our great captain, gave me when I was a young player. He told me that, whenever you scored a goal, you should bow your head to acknowledge and thank the fans. He reminded me that they were paying our salaries, and I never forgot that. We had some wonderful fans in Detroit, and I just appreciated so much all the support they gave us. When we won, it wasn't for us, it was for them. I knew that those fans were paying top dollar to see their home team win, and I wanted to do everything I could to make sure we gave them their money's worth.

Brett Hull

I played with Steve Yzerman in Detroit, and he's about as good as it gets in terms of being the complete captain, in my opinion. The guy was just a fantastic teammate. I will never forget when we won the Cup together in 2002. We were down 2–0 at home in the first round to Vancouver, and I was like, you've got to be kidding. I mean, we had like 10 Hall of Famers on this team, it was ridiculous. The media had already practically anointed us as champions, so anything short of that would've been a complete and utter disappointment. So we came back into the locker room after we lost Game 2, and not one single player took his equipment off. Everybody just sat there quietly, waiting for Stevey to say something. I was waiting for this big rah-rah speech from this iconic guy, but as it turned out, he was the least vocal captain who ever walked the face of the earth. He just stood up very calmly and said, "Hey, relax. We're the better team. We're gonna go there, win both games, and then sweep them. But we just have to stick together and play our game." Everyone just sort of looked around the room, relaxed, and was like, "Oh…okay." It was like Moses on Mount Sinai! If he said it, it must be true! Sure enough, we swept 'em and went on to hoist the Cup. Incredible, I'll always remember that.

Mikko Koivu

I really admired Brian Rolston. He was a great leader and was someone I really admired. We played together in Minnesota, and he helped me a lot, especially when I was younger. Being new to the U.S. from Finland and trying to learn the language and culture and all of that, I really appreciated his help. Brian was a quiet leader but was very respected by all of his teammates. I think he's a great example of what a captain should be.

Chris Kunitz

I played with Scott Niedermayer in Anaheim, and he was a great captain. He showed me that you don't always have to be a rah-rah guy. Instead, you can earn respect by just leading by your actions on the ice and by playing the right way. Great guy. Nowadays, in Pittsburgh, I get to play alongside Sidney Crosby. He's a quiet guy yet wears a lot of emotion on his sleeve. He's a young leader who's embraced everything that hockey has thrown at him, yet he's been able to thrive with all eyes on him. He and Scotty are similar in the sense that, when the game is on the line, they both want to be out there. Both are outstanding leaders and guys I really look up to in the game.

Tom Kurvers

My first captain in the NHL was Bob Gainey, with the Montreal Canadiens. His approach was professional at all times. His desire to improve himself showed in the way he practiced and the way he prepared every day. Everything was about the team with Bob, and that showed in every single thing he did, on or off the ice. He was a quiet leader for the most part but was never afraid to speak his mind in

Dale Hawerchuk on Being Named Captain of the Winnipeg Jets in 1984 at Just 21 Years of Age and Then Going on to Tally 130 Points That Season

It was a little intimidating. But there were guys around to help, like Randy Carlyle was captain in Pittsburgh. They [the Jets] probably thought the captaincy would help me, which it did. I accepted it, and it made me a better player and better person.

Source: http://www.hhof.com/htmlSpotlight

the dressing room. He'd get after us if we weren't pulling our weight or if we were in a slump. Guys respected him a great deal, so when he said something, everyone listened. Strong leaders have that ability to unite groups around a common goal or cause, and he was great at that.

He took care of everyone, too, and made sure that they felt like they were a part of the team. I remember my rookie year, my roommate Chris Chelios and I spent Christmas at the Gaineys' house. How amazing is that? What a classy guy, a real professional. His stature and composure and style were completely first-class, and that's why he's held in such high regard by hockey fans even to this day. To be a part of winning the Stanley Cup that rookie year with the Canadiens was definitely the highlight of my career, and when I think back to the little stories and memories along the way, it just makes it even more special for me.

Another guy I really respected was Lindy Ruff, who I played with in Buffalo. A great leader who, like Bob, went on to become a great coach. Lindy had a real vibrant personality. He was a real sharp guy who worked hard every day and was someone you could always count on. He took the time to get to know people and was very well liked in the locker room. He knew when it was time to put his foot down, though, and when to back off and let things be. I enjoyed playing with him, he was a good guy.

You know, it's easy to follow a good leader—and both of these guys were very good leaders. They were both selfless guys who had a team-first mentality, which I really respected. I now work in management in the NHL, with player personnel, so I can tell you first-hand that having the right captain on your team makes a big difference. Guys like Bob and Lindy don't come around very often, that's for sure.

Jamie Langenbrunner

Playing in Dallas early on in my career was a real blessing because I was able to play alongside so many guys who had worn the C at some point in their careers. Derian Hatcher wore the C when I first got there, but we had an all-star lineup of great leaders on those teams. Joe Nieuwendyk was one of those guys I really looked up to. He'd worn it in Calgary and was just amazing. He sort of took me under his wing and showed me what being a professional was all about. He was just an unbelievable leader, both on the ice and in the dressing room. I tried to pick his brain as much as I could, and he couldn't have been nicer to me. I never forgot that, and I've really tried to pattern my own leadership style after his. Another guy in Dallas I really admired was Guy Carbonneau, who'd worn it in Montreal. The way he conducted himself and prepared himself on a daily basis was incredible. He just worked so hard, whether it was in practice or during games, and that rubbed off on everybody else in such a positive way. Later in my career, I played for New Jersey and was so fortunate to have been able to play alongside Scott Stevens. What can you say about Scotty? The guy is incredible. He was a very quiet leader who led by example in the way he prepared and the way he played every day. He just loved the team and would do anything he could to help the team win.

Dave Langevin

Dennis Potvin was our captain during the four Stanley Cups in New York, and he did a great job for us. We had so many fantastic players on those teams, though, I think there were a lot of different guys who could've worn it, to be honest. Al [Arbour, head coach] sort of set it up that way, too, where a lot of different guys acted as team leaders. When you have a young team, I think the captain is very important because you need him to set the tone and lead. In our situation, however, I think everybody considered themselves to be a leader. I really do. Al encouraged everybody to be a leader, too, that was important to him. Looking back, I think one of the biggest reasons Dennis wore the C was because he was so good with the media. He was a real pro with that stuff, and that was a big part of it, especially being in New York with all the media attention that was constantly on us. He was our spokesman, without a doubt, and he seemingly always said the right things to the press. Clark Gillies had worn the C prior to Dennis taking over, and he gave it up because he didn't want to deal with the media. The pressure of it all was so intense that it affected his play on the ice, so he gave it up. I'll never forget the team meeting where he announced that he was giving it up. Dennis wanted the role, though, and wound up doing a heck of a job for us. As for his style, he was mentally very tough, yet he was the kind of captain you could go talk to if you had a problem. Great player, too, one of the best defensemen in the game in those days—a Norris Trophy winner. Overall, he was the perfect captain, he just did it all on and off the ice.

Igor Larionov

I was very fortunate to have played with Steve Yzerman in Detroit. What can you say about Stevey Y? He's one of the best captains of all-time. Every time he stepped onto the ice, he was ready to go, always leading by example. He was a warrior, always battling no matter what. If he was injured or sick, it didn't matter, you could always count on him. He did it all, he'd block shots, he'd score goals, he'd stick up for his teammates—just an inspiration to everybody on the team. The guy was amazing.

Reed Larson

Two guys come to mind—Dan Maloney and Dennis Hextall—who both wore the C in Detroit when I was there in the late '70s. They weren't the cleanest players, that's for sure, neither was ever going to win the Lady Byng [annual trophy recognizing the most gentlemanly player in the league]! But they looked after me, and I had a lot of respect for those guys. I trusted them and knew that they had my back. They didn't show up in the box score every night, but they worked hard and were great leaders in other ways.

Jordan Leopold

I was really fortunate to have been able to play alongside Joe Sakic for a few years in Colorado. He was by far the best captain I ever played for. Talk about a guy who leads by example, Joe was amazing. Such a hard-working guy and *so* respected by everybody. I think everybody my age who played the game looked up to him as a kid, so to be able to play with him was really a thrill for me.

Troy Loney

I had the opportunity to play alongside Mario Lemieux for most of my career in Pittsburgh, and they don't come much better than that. Mario was a pretty quiet guy and didn't say very much. He just led by example and let his actions speak for him out on the ice. Mario would will the team to victory. I will never forget our two Stanley Cup runs. Mario's back was so bad that he had to have a trainer tie his skates because he literally couldn't bend over. Then to see him score some of the goals he scored during the playoffs, it was incredible. He truly inspired everybody around him through his actions out on the ice. No matter how hurt or dinged up you were, if you saw Mario out there in pain playing at that high of a level—it just forced you to suck it up and give it your all. As a player, you just didn't want to let him down, and that's the ultimate sign of a great leader, in my opinion.

Norm Maciver

I got to play with Mark Messier for a while in Edmonton, and they don't come much better than that. You could feel his presence in the locker room, no kidding. It was like he gave off this aura of confidence around him that sort of filtered throughout the team. His leadership skills were off the charts. I mean, there was absolutely no question as to who the leader of our team was in those days. I can't even really explain it, but just to be around him made you a better player. Mark was a very vocal leader, too, and he wasn't afraid to talk to guys and hold them accountable. He worked extremely hard in practice and expected everybody to do the same.

His gift was his ability to make everybody on the team feel comfortable. And that wasn't just on the ice, it was off the ice, too—which is so important to your team dynamic, your chemistry. Mark was the glue that held us all together, it seemed like. The way he treated you made you feel special, too. It didn't matter if you were a veteran who'd been playing there for 10 years or a rookie who just got called up, he made you feel like you were a part of the group. Even when we were on the road, he made sure to include everyone in the team meal. It doesn't sound like a big deal, but it was, because when you get a bunch of guys all going off in their own directions, it creates cliques. Mark wanted everyone together and made sure to keep us all together. Sure, Mark was the best player on the ice, but his ability to unite the team might have been his greatest quality, in my opinion.

John MacLean

I played with a couple of great captains in New Jersey, starting with Kirk Muller. He was a great leader as a player, and he's a great leader as a coach—today we work together on the same coaching staff here in Carolina. When Kirk left for Montreal, Scott Stevens wore the C, and he was the heart and soul of our team. What a warrior. Scotty's physical play out on the ice could change the momentum of a game. When he ratcheted up the intensity level, it was like, "Watch out!" Both were lead-by-example type of leaders, and both gave their best effort on a nightly basis. Both were great competitors, too, and that's why their teammates really respected them.

Todd Marchant

I played with a few great captains over the years. For starters, Kelly Buchberger was the captain when I was in Edmonton, and he was unbelievable. He was a real lead-by-example kind of guy. He would sacrifice his body and play every game like it was his last. He played that way every single night, regardless of the circumstance—whether you were in the playoffs or out of the playoffs, early in the season or late in the season, early in the game or late in the game. He went out there and played every shift with the same intensity and fearlessness. The guy would just do whatever it took to help his team win. He was amazing. He wasn't our best player, but you could always count on him to give you his best. That's what made him such a good captain, in my eyes.

Doug Weight then wore the C after Kelly left, and his style was very different. He was arguably our best player at the time in Edmonton, and as such, he didn't play with such a reckless abandon, so to speak. What I admired most about Dougy was how he never treated anybody any differently. Whether you were a fourth-line guy who played three or four minutes a night or a first-liner who played 30 minutes, he treated everybody with the same level of respect. The way he was able to get everybody on board and acknowledge their role and contribution, it was awesome.

Another great captain I played with was Luke Richardson, when I was in Columbus. I had played with Luke in Edmonton prior to that and had gotten to know him, but to see him shine as team captain was pretty neat. Luke was a lot like Kelly Buchberger in that he was a lead-by-example kind of guy. He worked hard both on and off the ice and made sure that guys were doing the extra work that needed to be done. If guys needed to get in the weight room or stay after practice to work on something, he'd encourage them to do so for the betterment of the team. And he wouldn't just tell them, he would join them. So when your captain does those things and is that hard of a worker, everyone else is just expected to do the same thing. Great leadership like that is contagious, especially for your younger players.

Lastly, in Anaheim I was fortunate enough to play alongside Scott Niedermayer. Scotty was not a real vocal guy—he didn't say a whole lot in the dressing room. He left that to some of the other guys, guys like myself and Chris Pronger and Teemu Selanne. Scotty was the type of guy who led by the way he played. Plain and simple. He was not only the hardest worker on the team, he was arguably one of the most talented players, as well. His ability to elevate his game when the chips were down, especially in the playoffs, was incredible. There just aren't too many players who are capable of doing that. The guy won at every level he's played at, and after playing with him, you could tell why. He hates to lose and is willing to do whatever it takes to help his team win. Winning is in his blood. I have a ton of respect for Scott Niedermayer.

Montreal Canadiens Hall of Famer Jean Beliveau on the Captain's Duties

A captain has three roles on the team. One, is during a game, when the fans and referees are watching him. Two, his role between management and the players, and to be available to the players at all times, whether it's for hockey reasons or personal reasons. And three, a captain must represent his team and city well.

Source: http://www.hhof.com/htmlSpotlight

Paul Martin

I've been fortunate to have been able to play with a few pretty amazing captains so far in my career—Scott Stevens and Scott Niedermayer in New Jersey, and now Sidney Crosby in Pittsburgh. Each one's got his own style, that's for sure. Scotty Stevens was the epitome of a guy who led by example. He worked extremely hard every day and expected everybody else to do the same. He didn't force you to be accountable, but after watching his work ethic and sacrifice on a daily basis, it just made you want to follow his lead. As a player, he was a warrior out on the ice and was never afraid to stick up for his teammates. That was what it was all about for Scotty: the team. How do you not look up to a guy like that? He was the quintessential captain, in my eyes.

Scott Niedermayer wasn't a rah-rah guy, either, but if something needed to be said, he would definitely say it. His leadership style was more about playing well night-in and night-out, and then expecting guys to follow his lead. He wasn't as intense as Scott Stevens but a tremendous leader in his own right.

As for Sid, I've never seen anyone work as hard as he does. In practice he's an animal, just go-go-go nonstop. He's a perfectionist and constantly trying to perfect his game, too. His knowledge of the game is off the charts. I saw one time where he missed a tip-in that could've been the game-winner for us. He was really upset about it, so the next day in practice he had a guy shoot pucks at him for an hour after practice just so he could get it right. That blows me away. Here is the best player in hockey working on a drill like that over and over and over. But that's his mentality. That work ethic rubs off on the guys, too, when your leader, who's also a superstar, works harder than everybody else. It just forces guys to step up their own games.

Coaches love captains like that because they don't have to say a thing. The peer pressure, so to speak, is far more impactful than any coach yelling and screaming at you.

Sid's also really good at getting the guys to stick together, especially on the road. He'll be the ringleader in getting everyone to go out together, so that guys get to know each other better. That's how you build trust and chemistry, and create a close-knit team, by doing stuff like that. It's so important. Sid got the C when he was really young, which I'm sure was tough for him, but his maturity and poise on and off the ice is as strong as any captain in the league. I mean, look at the guy, he's not even 25 and he's already worn the C for a Stanley Cup championship team as well as an Olympic championship team. How amazing is that?

Ab McDonald

I was very fortunate to have played for some great Montreal Canadiens teams back in the '50s. Rocket Richard was our captain back in those days, and he was something else. What a player. The players really respected him, too. We had a whole bunch of outstanding leaders on those teams—guys like Jean Beliveau, Doug Harvey, and Jacques Plante—and that certainly made the captain's job a whole lot easier. To wear the C for an organization like that, though, especially during that era, that really said something. I was also in Detroit for a couple of years in the mid-'60s and got to play alongside Alex Delvecchio. Needless to say, he was a very fine hockey player. He was more of a quiet leader who led by example, I suppose. He'd taken over the captaincy from Gordie Howe a few years earlier, and that spoke volumes about the type of player and person he was. He was a real gentlemen.

Basil McRae

I played with a whole bunch of great captains over the years, and there were a few who stood out above the rest. I played with Peter Stastny in Quebec, Steve Yzerman in Detroit, Craig Hartsburg in Minnesota, Al MacInnis in St. Louis, Chris Chelios in Chicago. All of those guys were 100 percent great leaders and role models, just very honorable people. The guy who probably stands out the most though is Stevey Y. What an amazing story his is. I was playing with him in Detroit when Jacques Demers went out on a limb and gave him the C. It was a pretty big deal because I think he was only 20 years old at the time. The Wings were in a real transition period at that point and needed an identity. We could all sense that he was going to be a star in the league. You could just tell, he had that "it" factor. None of us were really sure that a 20-year-old kid could handle that type of responsibility, though. After all, this is an Original Six organization with a lot of history and a pretty demanding fan base. Stevey stepped up, though, and embraced the role. He worked his butt off each and every day and really became the face of that franchise. He put the team on his shoulders and gave that team an identity. It was incredible. The way he handled himself in the locker room, he was well beyond his years in terms of maturity. I was a few years older than Stevey at the time, yet he was a great role model for me. I was in awe of him, I really was. I mean here was this young, single guy, who was supposed to be having the time of his life—and now he's going to take on this awesome responsibility. He showed responsibility, maturity, and leadership well beyond his years. To watch him take over as a kid, develop into a leader, and then steer that team to the success it had over the next couple of decades… looking back, all I can do is smile. Wow, what an incredible story. He might just be the greatest captain of all-time.

Marty McSorley

Certainly playing alongside Wayne Gretzky for so many years, that's where I would have to start. Gretz was a great leader. He really tried to lead by example and was just a tremendous competitor. His mentality was that to be an effective leader, you had to do so by your performance and your actions on the ice. And he brought it every single night, no matter what. He made sure to back up whatever he said in the locker room, too, that was very important for him. He didn't like it when guys would say stuff and then do something completely different. He was a quiet leader for the most part, but there were times when he would get angry and get emotional—and that was all part and parcel of his competitiveness. He had such a strong belief that every time he went on the ice he was going to make a difference. There was an aura about him that, whenever he jumped over the boards and hit the ice, everybody on that bench felt very confident. We believed in him. He was our leader. I'd do anything for the guy. Heck, that was my job— to make sure nobody took any liberties with him that would somehow prevent him from doing his job.

I'll never forget the playoff series against Calgary back in '88 when I was with Edmonton. They were our biggest rival in those days and had some tremendous talent on that team. They finished the regular season in first place overall, and we knew that it was going to be a battle against those guys. Gretz and Mess [Mark Messier, the assistant captain] both addressed the team before the first game. Mark was a great captain, too, just so much raw emotion. He told us that it was going to be a hard-fought series and that, in or-der to win, we were going to need absolutely everybody in the locker room to get this done. He really put the emphasis on *everybody*, no matter how many minutes you played, it

Longtime Detroit Captain Ted Lindsay on His Top Three Career Highlights

Winning the Stanley Cup certainly was the highlight of my career. Making an All-Star team was a phenomenal thing. Finally becoming captain of the Detroit Red Wings was a great honor. They were the greatest bunch of players in the world, and to be their captain was very gratifying.

Source: http://www.hhof.com/htmlSpotlight

was going to require every man being 100 percent committed to the goal. He told us that whoever won that series would win the Stanley Cup, and he was right. We wound up sweeping them en route to winning it. I remember Gretz scoring the overtime game-winner in Game 2 on the road, it was just an unbelievable shot past Mike Vernon. That was so huge, it completely swung the momentum our way and took the wind out of their sails. They never recovered, and we just got stronger. We fed off of that goal, collectively, and kept the pressure on. That's what great leaders do, they lead by example and back up what they say.

That was the culture in Edmonton. Our veteran guys were amazing there. When I was a rookie in Pittsburgh, we did not have good veterans on that team. There wasn't any respect for the young guys, in my opinion. It was really fractured. Then, when I came to Edmonton, it was like a cold pail of water being dumped on me as to how they approached the game, it was amazing. It was so refreshing and motivating because they wanted everybody to do well, no matter what. Even if that meant you were going to take somebody's job two or three years down the road. They didn't care. They cheered for everybody in that locker room. The leadership demanded it. There was a level of respect for the young guys that was unprecedented. The only times they would get on anybody was if they felt a) they could handle it, and b) if it was to better their performance or their situation. There was no selfishness in that locker room, it was all about the team. That's why they won all those Stanley Cups up there and became a dynasty, because of that attitude that trickled down from our leaders.

Barry Melrose

I played with Darryl Sittler in Toronto and I had a lot of respect for him. He was a great captain. He played hard, he played with guts, and he played with courage. When Darryl Sittler stood up in the dressing room and said something, everybody shut up and listened. When he told us we had to fight more or hit more or block more shots, we did it. We believed in him because he led by example, literally. I mean, there he was out there dropping the gloves, hitting guys, and sacrificing his body by blocking shots. You trusted a guy like that because he was right there with you in the trenches.

Joe Micheletti

When I was playing in Edmonton, Al Hamilton was our captain and he was a great guy. He was a veteran guy who had been playing for many, many years and was a real solid player. What I will always remember about Al was how he made it a point to spend time with the younger guys like myself. He would have us over for dinner at his place at least once a week, which was such a neat gesture. I really appreciated it so much. That left a mark on me, no kidding. He was very influential on my career in ways he probably never even knew.

Joe Nieuwendyk

There are a few guys I really admired along the way. Lanny McDonald and Jim Peplinski were great leaders when I played with them in Calgary. They showed me how to be a professional, and I will always be grateful for that. I always thought Mats Sundin was a terrific leader. We played together for one season up in Toronto, and I thought he was fantastic. He wore the C in that hockey-crazed market for years and did so with such class. Just the way he carried a lot of the load on his shoulders was pretty impressive, because that's not easy to do. Not a lot of guys can do that, he was unique. Scott Stevens was a real quiet leader in New Jersey, but he led by example in ways most other players simply can't. What a fierce warrior. I got to play with him in New Jersey for a while, and I was so impressed by how he led, he was an extremely well-liked and respected captain. Another guy I thought was great was Joey Mullen, who wore the A in our locker room in Calgary. Man, what a terrific leader that guy was. I bet he didn't say 10 words in the locker room, yet he gave his heart and soul each and every night. And for a little guy, wow, he was tough.

Kyle Okposo

Doug Weight was a guy I really looked up to early in my career. He wore the C in Edmonton before wearing it in New York and was a tremendous leader. I used to pick his brain whenever I could about all sorts of stuff, and he was always willing to help me, which I really appreciated. I learned a lot from just watching him do his job. He was a guy who'd bring it every day. He was so good at talking to the group, just an extremely motivating person. He knew when to be tough on guys and when to back off in order to keep the atmosphere in the locker room loose. I really admired that about him.

Joel Otto

When I first got to Calgary, we had tri-captains, which was kind of unique: Lanny McDonald, Doug Risebrough, and Jim Peplinski. Each one kind of brought his own style of leadership to the mix. Doug was the fiery guy who came in and smashed his stick across the water bottle table to wake us up. He demanded hard work out of all of us and played the role of hardass. Lanny was the calm captain, just old-school in every way. He was the veteran who'd been through the battles and always reassured us that we would be fine if we just took a deep breath and relaxed. Jim, meanwhile, was kind of the thinker of the group, always asking "why?" He always had an answer for how to do it and for which way we should be pulling the rope. Three guys with three very different demeanors, but all very effective leaders in their own way. All three were great, and I learned a ton from them as a young guy.

J.P. Parise

I learned a lot from Teddy Harris, who was the captain before I was in Minnesota. He was superb, really a great leader. The players respected him so much, and that's what made him such a good captain. Great guy, one of the best.

Zach Parise

I was lucky in that I got to learn a lot from being around some pretty amazing captains over the years. One of the most influential was a guy I got to sit next to for four years

New Jersey Devils captain Zach Parise skates against the L.A. Kings in Game 5 of the 2012 Stanley Cup Finals. Photo courtesy of Getty Images

when he was captain for us here in New Jersey, Jamie Langenbrunner. Great guy, great captain. I was able to just observe him do his job on a daily basis, and from that I learned a ton. I wasn't afraid to ask a lot of questions, either, and luckily he was a really good teacher. Another guy I had a lot of respect for was Chris Drury, who was an alternate captain with Team USA at the Olympics. He did a great job for us, he's such a hard worker. Both of those guys had great work ethics and really led by example. They'd played in the big games before and had risen to the occasion. Just the way they carried themselves, on and off the ice, you could just tell that they had been there before. That quiet confidence is contagious, and it spreads throughout the locker room. The guys feed on that, and it becomes a big part of your team chemistry and really your overall success.

Mark Parrish

I was lucky enough to play with some great players who've worn letters over the years, guys like Scott Mellanby, Kirk Muller, Gord Murphy, Bret Hedican, and Dino Ciccarelli, to name a few. They are true professionals, men with great character, unselfish, charismatic…there's almost an aura around them. I watched those guys a lot early on in my career. I just watched the way they prepared and the way they carried themselves, I learned so much from them. To see the way they balanced practice time with family time, those intangibles really stuck with me. Those guys were so passionate, you could just see the joy and love they had for the game. They genuinely cared about everybody in the locker room and would do anything they could to help the team win. That attitude really rubbed off on me, and it's something I've tried to emulate over the years in my own way. Just being around guys like that not only made me a better hockey player, it made me a better person. No kidding, being around guys like that is addicting. You want to be a part of that, it's just an amazing feeling. You almost don't even realize what it is until you play for a team where you don't have that kind of atmosphere. So, for me, whenever I've been honored to wear a letter, I've always tried to get the young guys to feel that same way.

Michael Peca

Early in my career I was blessed in that I was able to learn a great deal about leadership from two absolutely amazing captains, Trevor Linden and Pat LaFontaine. Both were great guys and awesome role models for me, and I was very lucky that they both kind of took me under their wings and helped me along. I really appreciated that and certainly tried to pay it forward with the young guys I played with, as well.

My first two years in the National Hockey League were with Vancouver, where Trevor wore the C. He was a relatively young captain but was extremely well respected by the players. Great player, great teammate. He was a tremendous leader both on and off the ice, which is a really important aspect of being the captain. And with Trevor it wasn't just always about the game, either. He did a lot of great work in the community and for various charities, which I really admired.

Later, when I signed with Buffalo, I got to play alongside Pat—who's one of the greatest captains to ever the play game, in my opinion. Pat led by example each and every day in practice where he was always the hardest-working guy out there. The way he carried himself in the community, too, was just fabulous. You couldn't ask for a better team leader. When Pat got traded, I took over the captaincy, and let me tell you, those were some big shoes to fill. I was only 23 years old at the time, too. I learned a ton from him, though, and I certainly patterned many aspects of my own leadership style after him.

Another guy I really admired was Jason Smith, who I played with in Edmonton late in my career. What an incredible captain he was, just incredible. When you look up "sacrificing your body" in the dictionary, a picture of Jason Smith comes up. That guy was unbelievable. He played with broken bones in his feet and in his hands, pulled groins, stitches—it didn't matter. He never wanted to let his teammates down so just sucked it up and played, regardless of the injury or how much pain he was in at the time. He gave everything he had for his team. He was fearless, too, never afraid to block shots from guys who shot the puck as hard as anybody in our league. He didn't get much glam and glitter, but he was one of the most respected guys I ever played with. So, when I think of a captain who really embodies leadership from a personal sacrifice perspective, there's no one better in my opinion that Jason.

Mike Peluso

I played with a handful of great captains over the years. For starters, I would have to put Dirk Graham right at the top of the list. He was without a doubt the best leader I ever played with. The best in the business. Truly an incredible captain, that's all I can say. It didn't come easy for him, either. He came up through a tough, tough era of hockey. There were many, many times where Dirk stood up for the team and put himself on the line. He was really good at maintaining the team chemistry and was able to keep everybody on an even keel. He was able to work with our coach, Mike Keenan, very effectively. He mentored a very young Jeremy Roenick when he was a rookie All-Star. He kept our goalie, Eddie Belfour, at the top of his game. He was a great manager of people and personalities, many of whom were larger than life. But that was his gift, to lead the entire team toward a common goal.

Scott Stevens would be right up there, too. He was such a great leader. We played together in New Jersey for several years, and I think the world of that guy. Scotty led by example. He wasn't a real vocal leader, but when he spoke, the guys listened. He was a very, very competitive guy. He hated to lose and was willing to do whatever it took to make sure his team won. He was just all about the team. He was so tough, too, one of the best open-ice hitters of all-time, he was like a linebacker on skates. Just incredible.

Another guy I really admired was Scott Niedermayer. He was more of a quiet leader, as well, but what made him unique in my eyes was the fact that he was so incredibly positive. You would never hear him say one bad thing about another player. It's easy to point fingers when the team's not playing well, but he would never put the blame on other people. He was a really strong leader, great guy.

Chris Chelios was also a great leader. Again, another guy who led by example out on the ice. He was kind of a quiet guy but really commanded respect from his teammates. He would always put the team ahead of himself, too. He was

Mark Messier on Trust

Your players have to trust you. They have to be able to look at you and know that you're consistent in your approach and your philosophy and what you believe in. Establishing a relationship where they can trust you is very important.

Source: "Some of Hockey's Best Leaders Tell Us What It Takes," by Paul Grant, ESPN.com, November 12, 2007.

always there to back up a teammate and was never afraid to jump in and lend a helping hand in a tough situation.

Another guy I have the utmost respect for is Steve Smith. He was never afraid to step in and back up one of his teammates, regardless of who was throwing punches on the other end. Man, that guy was so tough. I remember more than a few line brawls where he was the first guy in there, fists flying, ready to protect his guys. I learned a great deal from him about what it meant to be a good teammate.

Funny story with Steve. I remember one time when I was playing with Chicago during my rookie season. I had just gotten called up from Indianapolis and was going to be joining the team for our western road trip—L.A., Edmonton, Calgary, and Vancouver. The circus was in town using the [Chicago] Stadium, and we were going to be on the road for a pretty good stretch, I was really excited about it. Mike Keenan [Blackhawks head coach] had called me and told me to join the team as soon as I could, so I went right from a three-game road trip to the airport. I didn't have very much stuff with me, and I certainly didn't have any fancy suits or anything, either. Hell, I was making $27,000 a year at that point and was pretty much broke. All I had was this one white suit, and it was pretty ugly. It was one of those deals where if you buy the jacket the pants come for free! I wore that thing every night, it was all I had. Well, we won like four of five on this trip, and on the last night in Edmonton, all the guys went out to celebrate. Mike threw a bunch of money in the pot for us and told us to stay out late and have a good time—we'd earned it. So I left my jacket behind and went out with the guys to tear it up. The next morning I got up all hungover and was racing to get ready to catch the team bus. I was all packed and ready to go, and the last thing I had to do was put on my suit jacket. I put it on, and to my horror, the guys had cut off the sleeves. I was like, "Oh, shit!" Mike was very particular about us all looking good when we traveled, and I didn't know what I was going to do. So I ran down there, and when I got on the bus, the entire team started cheering and gave me a standing ovation, it was hilarious! Mike looked at me all serious and said, "You know the rules, you're not getting on this bus without a proper suit." I just looked at him, about ready to cry, and he started laughing hysterically. He said, "Mike, I'm so glad the guys have taken a liking to you, that's what being a team is all about. Go sit down, you look great!" It was pretty funny, I have to admit. Anyway, when I got back to Chicago, Steve Smith came up to me and gave me a $4,500 gift certificate to a really nice men's clothing store. He'd taken a collection, and the boys wanted me to look presentable, so they told me to go out and get a couple of new suits. I couldn't believe it—most Iron Rangers from northern Minnesota don't walk around in $2,000 suits—but I was more than happy to oblige. It was a really nice gesture, and it made me feel great, like I was finally a part of the team.

Brent Suter, Theo Fleurry, Al MacInnis, and Doug Wilson, I really respected those guys, as well, they were also really, really good captains. Brent was a real likeable guy who led by example. Theo and I played together in Calgary, and I think he was more comfortable wearing the A as opposed to the C, but a heck of a leader in his own right. I played with Al in St. Louis, sort of a soft-spoken guy whom I enjoyed playing with. He came to the rink every night ready to play. Dougie, meanwhile, he was a prankster and would always keep us laughing, that was how he got the team to gel together. If we had some tough losses, he would pick us up by getting us to smile and forget about whatever it was that was keeping us from winning. He kept us loose, that was his gift.

Sometimes your best leaders don't even wear letters. Mark Lamb was a guy like that whom I played with in Ottawa. I'm not even sure if he wore a letter or not, but it didn't matter because, as far as I was concerned, he was our team leader. He was a second-line checking guy, but he did it all. He blocked shots, he'd scrap, he'd sacrifice his body for the team—he was there for his teammates no matter what. He was there to win, period. Great guy.

Al Secord was the same way in Chicago; he was a great leader, too. Interesting story about Al.… Back when I was playing anyone could get sent to the minors. Everybody was fighting for a position each and every night, and it was tough. In my second year with Chicago alone, I got sent down on five different occasions. I will never forget one time I was standing out in front of the old Chicago Stadium with my bags packed, waiting for a cab to take me to the airport. I was pretty down, not knowing why I was being sent down and feeling pretty low. Al Secord, a great leader on that team, saw me out there and came out to talk to me. He put his arm around me, told me to work hard and that he was going to be pulling for me to get back up with the club. He told me that he appreciated me and what I did for the team, and that felt really good to hear that from a guy like him. Just then my taxi pulled up, and he said, "*Fuck* that, I'll drive you to the airport!" We visited along the way, and he really picked me up. It was a little thing that nobody knew about, but it meant the world to me. When I did get back up, you can rest assured that I had Al's back each and every night. He'd earned my respect, and I was going to be there for him no matter what. Little things like that, when guys go out of their way to help others in times of need, that goes a long way, in my eyes—both on and off the ice.

You know, all of these guys I mentioned here whom I was fortunate enough to play with over my career, they all led in different ways and all had their own styles. But there was one thing about each of them that rang true. None of them ever gave a shit about their individual stats. The team always came first. These guys were all character guys who were never afraid to go to battle, I just have so much respect for each and every one of them. It was truly an honor to have been able to play for them.

Lance Pitlick

While I never got to play with Scott Stevens, I tried to model my game after him. The way he could hit guys in open ice, he was the best. A true lead-by-example leader whom everybody respected. I was in awe of that guy. As for teammates, there were a few guys I really respected as captains. When I was in Ottawa, I was fortunate to have played alongside Daniel Alfredsson. He came in shortly after I got there, and you could just see the leadership qualities in him from the get-go. The way he prepares, the way he conducts himself professionally—he's the complete package. He's worn the C up there for a long, long time now, and I think that speaks volumes about the type of player he is. When I was in Florida, I played with Scott Mellanby, and he was very similar to Alfie in that he worked very hard and just brought his A game every single night.

At the end of my career, I played briefly in Colorado, and it was just an incredible experience to play alongside so many great leaders up there. Joe Sakic wore the C, but there were some other outstanding players on that team who could've worn it, as well—guys like Peter Forsberg, Rob Blake, Adam Foote, and Patrick Roy. Leadership starts in practice, and those guys were absolutely *the* hardest

Derek Plante on Why the Dallas Stars Won the Stanley Cup in 1999

We had a lot of selfless guys on that team. In fact, I think there were 10 players who had previously been captains on that team—either with Dallas or with other teams. As a result, they weren't afraid to stand up and say something if they felt strongly about it. It created a very open dialogue among us and that was very unique. To have that kind of leadership on your roster is just huge.

workers in practice. Without a doubt. Even if they were out partying the night before, they were first in line for every drill the next morning. That's just textbook leading by example, in my opinion. And I've never played against a goalie [Patrick Roy] who got so pissed off in practice when someone scored on him. Every shot was personal to him, it was unbelievable. That type of positive, competitive attitude, it's infectious to everyone else—and that's why that franchise was so dominant during that era. I was in awe of those guys, I really was. As a player, you had one choice, either push yourself to try to keep up with them or fall by the wayside and play somewhere else. It was an amazing culture they had created, and it started at the top with those veteran leaders. I just with I could have stuck around to play with them a whole lot longer than I did, because they made coming to work every day fun.

Larry Pleau

When I first got into the league with Montreal, my captain was Jean Beliveau. I was in awe of the guy, he was just larger than life to me. And he was a quiet guy who never had to say a word. His presence spoke volumes for him, I'd never seen anything like it. It was like royalty was entering the room whenever he walked in. No kidding. There was literally a silence that was automatically given to him out of a total respect that I have never seen before in professional sports because of who and what he was and how he handled himself. Everything that you could ever hope for in a captain, he gave you night-in and night-out, on and off the ice. He was the definition of the perfect captain, the ultimate professional. The only guy I could equate to Jean Beliveau today would be Steve Yzerman, but even Stevey Y was no Jean Beliveau, in my opinion. He was just that good.

Shjon Podein

While I greatly admired guys like Craig MacTavish, Chris Drury, and Peter Forsberg—who were all amazing leaders —the best captain I ever played for, without a doubt, was Joe Sakic. Joe hardly said a word, he just let his actions speak for him. Every day he led by example, on and off the ice, and as a family man. His preparation, his performance, his willingness to give everything he had on a nightly basis, his leadership—the guy was just a consummate professional. He made a huge impact on me; I was in awe of him. Not only was he an unbelievable hockey player, he was truly an incredible human being.

The one moment for me that completely sums up Joe Sakic came just moments after we had won the Stanley Cup in 2001. Our entire season had become about us getting the Cup for Ray Bourque, who'd come to Colorado after a lifetime in Boston on his final quest to win a championship. We all wanted to win it for him so badly. I will never forget the moment right after we won it, we were all celebrating and could hardly wait to see Ray hoist that big beautiful

Cup over his head. Joe, as our team captain, got to raise it first. That's one of the great traditions in the NHL, the guy who wears the C gets it first directly form Commissioner Bettman. Joe, being the selfless guy he is, took the Cup from the Commissioner but, instead of taking a second to raise it up and experience the thrill of having thousands of fans go crazy, handed it directly to Ray so he could have that feeling. It was epic. Epic. I don't think there was a dry eye in the house. No kidding. He took the focus and spotlight off of himself and put it on somebody else. Tell me that doesn't epitomize leadership to a tee? Joe Sakic: best captain ever.

Rob Ramage

When we won the Cup in '89 with Calgary, it was all about Lanny McDonald. I will never forget watching him raise the Cup. What a moment. He was the captain and was the old veteran we were all playing for that year. He was in and out of the lineup during the playoffs, and Crispy [Coach Terry Crisp] put him in for Game 6, where we clinched it, and sure enough he scored a big goal. It was unbelievable. So, when he hoisted the Cup, there were not a lot of dry eyes in the house. Everybody was pulling for him to finally get his moment with Stanley. Everybody. This was going to be his last season, and everybody was rooting for him. What a wonderful person, a true professional. He was so deserving. To see him out there smiling with that big old red beard, just classic.

Tom Reid

When I was playing with the North Stars, I really admired our captain, Teddy Harris. He wasn't the greatest hockey player in the world, but he was one of the most respected.

He'd come to Minnesota from Montreal, a hallowed franchise, and had already won a bunch of Stanley Cups. We were a young expansion team, and he stepped into the role of team leader beautifully. Teddy was one of those guys who truly led by example. If there was a problem out on the ice, he was the first guy there to defend you. He was a gentle, quiet guy, except when he got mad—then watch out. He was tough and he was fiercely loyal to his team- mates. He was never afraid to jump in and drop the gloves, and I would say he was probably one of the best fighters I ever saw. He was always ready to go, he loved it. Our first big rival was St. Louis, back in the late '60s and early '70s, and they were really physical. Teddy was always ready to go against their tough guy, Bobby Plager, and that gave us so much confidence out there. He would neutralize him and in turn give us momentum, it was amazing. In one critical playoff series that we wound up winning, afterward Bobby was quoted as saying, "Did you see how many times I hit Ted's fist with my face?!" Those two used to battle, they were warriors. Overall, though, Teddy was just a terrific captain. He was a great leader, very well liked in the locker room, and overall just a super guy.

Doug Risebrough

In Montreal we had some just outstanding captains over the years. When I first got there, we had Henri Richard, who was followed by Yvan Cournoyer and Serge Savard. Bob Gainey came next, and he was the guy I probably connect- ed to the most, he was a great captain. In that organization they tended to go with the more senior players to wear the C, which is always a good way to go. If you were asked to wear the C in that organization, it was a huge responsibil- ity. There were no nights off, and it meant that the media

Doug Risebrough skates in a game in November 1983 as captain of the Calgary Flames. Photo courtesy of Getty Images

was going to turn to you when things weren't going well. It was a tough job, and it required a special kind of player. Bob was just that type of player. He was driven, he was accountable, and he worked hard every day. He was also well respected in the locker room and could relate to the guys. That's important. Most of the good ones lead by example versus leading by conversation, and that was Bobby to a tee. He was very consistent, too, you could count on him to bring the same level of intensity night-in and night-out. The players admired him for all those reasons, and that was why he was such a good leader.

Gordie Roberts

I played with a few great captains over the years. For starters, I was very fortunate to have won a couple of Stanley Cups with Pittsburgh later in my career, and our captain there was one of the best of all-time, Mario Lemieux. He was the heart of that franchise, just an incredible leader. He had the unique ability to not only elevate his own game to another level but everybody else's, as well. I'll never forget our Stanley Cup run in '91 when his back was so bad that he had to have a trainer tie his skates. He played through pain all the time, and at an incredibly high level, too. The way he could overcome obstacles and find ways to persevere was just unbelievable. He had a calmness to him, too, in that even when things weren't going well, he wouldn't panic. When you have a dynamic leader like that who is just so passionate and so incredibly good at what he does, everybody automatically just follows along. Even beyond the ice, the way Mario handled the media pressure on a daily basis, he was just a true professional.

Another guy who was really good was Ray Bourque. He was a real character guy, very well respected. I played with Ray in Boston, and that guy was the epitome of consistency. He was a coach's dream. He came to the rink with a good attitude every single day. He worked hard, never complained, and led by example. He treated people with a great deal of respect, too, which was a quality I really admired about him. He set the bar so high, he really did. Now that I'm in coaching, and on the other side of the game, I appreciate what he was able to bring to the table on a nightly basis even more. He was just a tremendous all-around player and leader.

Rick Tocchet, meanwhile, was more of a fiery, vocal leader. He was never afraid to call guys out in the locker room between periods if he didn't feel like they were playing at the top of their game. He'd voice his opinion in front of everybody and hold you accountable, which was his leadership style.

Brian Rolston

I've played for some pretty amazing captains over my career, guys like Joe Sakic, Scott Stevens, and Scott Niedermayer. These were all guys who didn't say a whole lot in the dressing room but were all incredible leaders in their own way. Guys talking about getting fired up to play doesn't really do a whole lot for me. It's much more meaningful if they go out and make something happen out on the ice. I remember in the Stanley Cup Finals against Detroit, Scott Stevens had some just huge hits that absolutely swung the momentum toward our bench. There was no better open-ice hitter in my opinion than Scotty, he had that down to a science. As players, you feed off that energy and personal sacrifice. There was no question that he was the catalyst who propelled that team to the championship.

Nick Schultz

I've really enjoyed playing alongside Mikko Koivu here in Minnesota. He has so many great leadership qualities. He grew up as a coach's kid, and his brother has been a captain with Montreal for a number of years, so leadership obviously comes very naturally for him.

Brendan Shanahan

My first captain was Kirk Muller, and I had so much respect for him. He was an intense, selfless player who always put the team first. Always. He was very young at that point, too, still learning the ropes in the NHL. No matter what, though, it was always about the team and always about winning. I will never forget an incident involving Kurt back when I was a rookie with New Jersey. We were just entering the

Steve Smith on Doing the Right Thing

I remember talking to Lee Fogolin one time about when he gave up the C to Wayne [Gretzky] in the early '80s when we were with Edmonton. Gretz was young but clearly had emerged as Edmonton's team leader not only out on the ice, where he was shattering the league's scoring records, but also in the locker room. Lee recognized that and proudly handed it over to him. He knew that it was best for the team, so he did the right thing. It could have been an awkward scene, but Lee made it into a positive one. Lee stood for everything a consummate professional stood for, in my opinion.

second round of the playoffs, and I was up and down with the black aces at that point. [Teams have backup players in the postseason ready to play in case there is an injury to a starter and are commonly referred to as "black aces."] Most of these guys were either rookies who didn't play much or call-ups from the American League. All of their teammates were out playing golf, but they were all there, hoping for their shot. There were about 10 of us and maybe one or two of us would get the call, or maybe none of us—nobody knew. It was tough to be there because you wanted to be with the team, and instead you had to just practice and prepare yourself in case they needed you. We were on a difficult schedule, too, regarding practice times and extra skating, and we even had our own bus. It was frustrating and lonely, to be quite honest, and our enthusiasm was waning at that point. Anyway, I remember Kurt coming up to talk to us one day after practice. He said, "Guys, I just want you to know how much we all appreciate how hard you're all working and all the extra time you're putting in to help us stay focused and prepared. I know it must be tough not getting to play, but should we need one of you and you come in ready, it could be the difference between us winning and losing. So keep up the hard work, and most importantly, thank you." Here is our team captain, who is only like 22 years old at this point and must have what feels like the pressure of the world on his shoulders, coming over to acknowledge us lowly black aces. He probably had so many more important things on his mind at that moment, yet he wanted us to know that we had a very important role and that he valued us. It meant so much to us, it really did. We got so fired up after that, we were ready to go to battle for him. I will always remember that moment, it was an example of extraordinary leadership that I will never forget.

Neil Sheehy

When I played with Calgary, we had tri-captains—Doug Risebrough, Lanny McDonald, and Jim Peplinski—and each guy brought something different to the table. It was a great system, it really was. First was Riser, who was the ultimate warrior. He was older and very well respected. Every game he put on the armor to go to battle. Every game. I had so much respect for him as a player because he didn't have a big body, yet he played big. And he played that way every night, regardless of whom we were playing. Man, that guy was so tough. Just awesome. When you have a leader on your team who plays bigger than he is, it becomes contagious, you just want to emulate that.

I remember one time we were going through sort of a slump and we just weren't playing well at all. The coaches were staying positive, but nothing seemed to be working. Finally, between periods of a game we were losing, Doug came into the locker room and let us have it. He had some choice words for all of us about our attitudes and our work ethic, and then to really make his point he flipped the garbage cans, kicked the tape cart, and knocked over the drink table. It was quite the scene. As a young guy at the time I couldn't believe my eyes. It certainly got my attention, that was for sure. We responded, though, right away, by going out and playing well that next night and from there we turned it around. As a veteran who'd been through a lot of battles in Montreal, Doug had the credibility to do things like that— and it was extremely effective. I certainly tried to emulate my game after his style, I really looked up to Dougie.

Lanny was like the team dad, just a great guy. I will never forget my first call-up from the minors to play in the NHL, it was on Christmas Eve. They put me up in a hotel, and I was pretty nervous. Then I got a call from Lanny, this larger-than-life player who I'd seen on TV and read about, who invited me over to his house for dinner with his wife and four kids. What a classy gesture. And he did that for all the young guys, too, to welcome them and make them feel at home. I learned a lot about what it means to be a leader both on and off the ice from him. He was very involved in the community and overall was what you would call a true professional. On the ice, he was our go-to guy. Whenever we needed a big goal, we could always count on Lanny. Great player, but beyond that he was just a very special person who had some special attributes as a human being. He brought the team together and got us to gel in very unique ways.

Pepper, meanwhile, he was a little bit younger and he kept us loose. On the ice he worked hard and would stand up for his teammates. Off the ice he was just a tremendous person whom everybody really liked and respected. He had a great sense of humor and helped us gel in ways that seemed to complement what Doug and Lanny brought to the table.

Steve Smith

I was fortunate to have been able to play alongside Wayne Gretzky and Mark Messier in Edmonton, and in my opinion there's not too many leaders in the history of the game who were better than those two guys. What made them unique was the fact that not only were they great leaders, they were also top-end players. Your leaders aren't necessarily always going to be your best offensive players, but in that situation it was the case. Another great captain I played with was Dirk Graham in Chicago. He was a completely different player from Gretz and Mess. Dirk was more of a gritty guy who would do whatever it took to help his team win. His teammates really respected him. Opposing players hated to line up across from Dirk because he was painfully difficult to play against. He led by getting dirty and digging through the trenches. So two polar opposite approaches to leadership, yet both extremely effective.

Eric Staal

As a kid I looked up to Joe Sakic. What a humble, down-to-earth leader. I watched him lead Colorado to a couple Stanley Cups and then watched him wear the C for Team Canada when they won the gold medal. He was never a flashy player, just very modest and went about his business. Whenever there was a big game, though, he rose to the occasion and played his best hockey. He was seemingly always right there in the thick of things when it mattered most. That's what great leadership is. When the chips are down, he comes through and performs to the best of his abilities. I really admired that as a young player, and his style has certainly rubbed off on me, too.

As for who I look up to as a player today? Playing in

Carolina for my entire career I've been fortunate to have played under two great captains in Ron Francis and Rod Brind'Amour. Both had similar styles in that they were very hard workers on the ice and quiet leaders in the dressing room. They both had a really hard work ethic, too, especially in practice. I definitely tried to pattern my own style after that because I saw early on how much the guys respected that effort on a daily basis. I learned a lot about intensity from Rod. To watch him work so hard on every faceoff, that was amazing. He took such pride in that and was so good at it, one of the best. As a young player, you watch and you learn, so to see how both of those approached every game was really helpful in my development as a player.

Mark Stuart

I learned a lot while playing with Zdeno Chara in Boston. He wasn't the most talkative, rah-rah guy, but he led by example. He worked hard every day, took care of his body, and was just there for everybody. He was a pro. He knew the game, knew how to carry himself, made the right choices, and always represented the team the right way. Then, on top of all that, he'd stick up for every one of his teammates out on the ice. He was never afraid to get physical out there, and the guys really respected that. At 6'9", he was a pretty intimidating dude! What else can you say about the guy? He's a textbook professional. Great captains don't have to say much, they just have a presence about them that everybody is drawn to. He definitely had it.

Another great captain I really looked up to in Boston was Mark Recchi, who wore the A while I was there. He was a great veteran player, very well liked and respected in the locker room. I remember one time we were really struggling as a team and just couldn't seem to get out of it. So Mark invited everybody over to his house, wives and girlfriends, too. He hosted a team party, and it was awesome. He got us together, and we all had a good time, it was nice. Sure enough, we started winning games right after that. Whatever it was, it worked. It's important to do that, to step back and get out of the office every now and then. Mark knew that we needed to get out and have some fun, so he facilitated that for us. That's what great leaders do, they recognize problems and find solutions without anybody asking.

Gary Suter

Chris Chelios comes to mind first and foremost. He came to work each and every day, he was a grinder. We first met in college at Wisconsin and then played together in Chicago and also on a couple U.S. National teams. On the ice, he was sort of a junkyard dog, meaning he would do whatever it took to help the team win. Off the ice he was always making sure everyone did stuff together. That's huge, it really is. He was the guy who helped foster the team chemistry that every organization needs in order to be successful.

As a player, Chris played bigger than he actually was. Literally. I mean he was like 5'11" and maybe 185 pounds—he was not a very big guy. Well, I remember one time when we were playing together in Chicago. We were playing St. Louis, and they were all over us, so Chris took it upon himself to go out and fight Chris Pronger—who's like 6'6". He didn't win, but he sent a clear message to the rest of us that we needed to start playing a whole lot harder— which we did. That was his way of waking everybody up, I suppose. That was Chris, though. He was vocal and wore his heart on his sleeve, and guys respected that. He was a warrior on the ice and a great friend off the ice.

Bryan Trottier

I will never forget as a kid watching Jean Beliveau hoist the Stanley Cup over his head. He was Montreal's captain, the guy wearing the C, and that really stuck with me. I looked up to him, and from that moment on, I wanted to do the same. What a great leader. I wanted to be a guy who carried myself like Jean Beliveau. On the ice he was just a tremendous hockey player. Yet off the ice he was so quiet and so polite and had such integrity. He was just the complete package. Early on I loved watching guys like Jean, as well as a guy like Gordie Howe, who was not only such a talented hockey player, but also so tough. I was lucky. I played through several different eras of hockey—the '70s, '80s, and '90s—and holy cow there were some terrific captains during those years. I was fortunate to have played alongside Dennis Potvin in Long Island. Great guy. I played with Mario Lemieux in Pittsburgh. Just an unbelievable talent. He had such a presence. You learn bits and pieces along the way, and I certainly learned a great deal about hockey and about life from my teammates over the years.

Wes Walz

I played briefly with Steve Yzerman in Detroit, and that was a real thrill. What an amazing captain he was. I had been in the minors and joined the team for a few months for the stretch run. I think I learned more about leadership in those few months than at any other time in my career. I just sat back and watched how he handled himself, and I was in awe. I remember late in the season, with just a few weeks to go, I saw him working out on the bike in the training room. Stevey wasn't a man of many words, so figuring this might be my only shot to strike up a conversation with him, I jumped on an empty bike next to him. I asked him why he

The New York Islanders' Bryan Trottier faces off with Toronto Maple Leafs goalie Ken Wregget as the puck goes flying by during a January 1987 game.

was busting his ass so hard in practice every single day. I mean, he was on that thing between periods, before practice, after practice—it was crazy how hard he was pushing himself. We had already secured a high playoff seed, and I figured he would be taking it easy like so many of the other guys and conserve his energy.

He sort of smiled as he looked at me and then proceeded to tell me that he was preparing his body for the playoff grind that was about to ensue. He knew that he needed his conditioning level to be at its peak in order for him to be the most effective player he could be, so that was what he was doing. He knew that with all the travel coming up, along with the other duties that a captain has to deal with—like talking to the media—he wouldn't have a lot of time for that. So he was building his energy and endurance as much as he could to get ready. I was just blown away by that. Here I was, a 20-something-year-old kid trying to cut my teeth and find my way in the National Hockey League, and here is this superstar captain who has clearly earned a day or two off, working harder than anybody else on the team. I don't think I was ever more inspired by anything in my life.

From that day on, I vowed to try to push myself and be that hardest-working guy on whatever team I was on. Because that's how you earn respect in this game, through hard work and leading by example. Later, when I wore the C in Minnesota, I tried to work twice as hard as everybody else just like Stevey did. I wanted guys to see me pushing myself. I wanted them to see me put in the work and the hours after games and after practices—and then go out at the age of 34 and fly around on the ice like a 24-year-old. That was my goal. And those were the leadership qualities I learned from Steve Yzerman all those years prior.

Erik Westrum

I'd say the captain I probably looked up to the most throughout my career was Shane Doan. We played together briefly in Phoenix, and I thought he was a great leader. He was so good at making everybody feel like they were a part of the big picture. He had the unique ability to connect the fourth-line healthy scratch guy with the first-line All-Star centerman. He had a gift to be able to do that. I remember coming into training camp right out of college, and there were some big-name players there at the time, guys like Jeremy Roenick and Keith Tkachuk. I was pretty intimidated by those guys and never really interacted with them. Shane, meanwhile, came right over to say hello to me and then and introduced me to a bunch of other guys. He made me feel so important. He gave me confidence. It was awesome. Even out on the ice, he'd work with you and push you, always trying to make you better every day. He just embodies everything good about being a captain. He was the hardest-working guy on the team. He shows determination, he's ultra-competitive, and overall he's just a great guy. What more could you ask for in a guy who wears the C? You're not a hockey fan if you don't root for Shane Doan. I couldn't be happier to see that franchise finally turn the corner and get deep into the playoffs. Shane's been there through the lean years, and nobody deserves to hoist the Cup more than he does. He's the foundation and identity of that team, I really hope it eventually happens for him.

Tom Younghans

When I was playing with the North Stars, our captain was Paul Shmyr. He was by far the best captain I've ever run across throughout my entire career. He joined our team in 1979 after playing in Edmonton. But after the WHA folded, he came in, and they gave him the C right away. We had just gone through a merger with Cleveland, and there were a lot of new faces on the roster. We were a young team, and there was a lot of drama and jealously going on. And to make matters worse, there were probably three or four different cliques. None of them got along, either, it was bad. The guys genuinely didn't like each other, which pretty much killed the team chemistry. Players genuinely like each other on good teams. This was clearly not the case. What Paul did, though, was to break down those walls and get us to come together as a team. He got us communicating and he got us to relax and just have fun. It seemed like he cared about everybody else more than himself at times. He was just a great leader with a lot of charisma, and that was why we all followed. We got better and better as a team, and eventually everybody got along to the point where we liked each other. It was incredible. We needed somebody like Paul to bring us together and be our leader. I'd bet dollars to donuts that if he wasn't there, we would never have gone as far as we did. Guys would have had successful careers individually, but as a team...no way. Two years later, that team was playing in the Stanley Cup Finals.

Steve Yzerman

Bryan Trottier was a guy I really looked up to early on in my career. He was a quiet guy who just went out and played a no-nonsense style of hockey, which I really respected. He kind of did it all out there, too, whether it was scoring goals or being a team leader off the ice. Just a really good guy.

CHAPTER
3

SO HOW DO COACHES AND GMs *REALLY CHOOSE* THEIR CAPTAINS?

It's never an easy process to choose a new captain. Make the right choice, and you will be rewarded handsomely with a player who brings a clear identity to your franchise. Make the wrong choice, and you (the coach or general manager) could be out of a job in a hurry. Yes, it's that important to pick the right guy. Each team is different, though, and for a lot of teams it's about picking the right guy for the right time. Do you have a young team, a veteran team, a team with a lot of foreign players? All of those factors weigh in to the final decision. Ah, decisions, decisions...

Do you go with a grizzled veteran, a guy whose experience and presence speak volumes without saying a word? In today's game, that might be Niklas Lidstrom, Rick Nash, Chris Pronger, or Daniel Alfredsson. Maybe you want to go with a young guy, a future superstar in the making? Perhaps that's Sidney Crosby, Alexander Ovechkin, Jonathan Toews, Eric Stall, or Ryan Getzlaf. Or you could go with an emotional leader who doesn't say much but just delivers each and every night. In today's game that could be Shane Doan, Jarome Iginla, Brendan Morrow, Joe Thorton, Dustin Brown, or Ryan Callahan. The right captain

Nashville Coach Barry Trotz on Captains

To me, a captain is accountable; he speaks for the betterment of the group; he gets the coach's message into the locker room; and he has a caring attitude while getting and keeping everyone in line…. [He] embodies what the Nashville Predators are all about on and off the ice—hard work and professionalism.

Source: "A 'C' of Responsibility," by Shawn P. Roarke, Impact! January 2003

becomes your identity with the fans and in the media. Boston's toughness is epitomized in the 6'7" hulking frame of Zdeno Chara—who just so happened to lead his team to a Stanley Cup championship in 2011. Not a bad choice.

If you're with one of the Original Six franchises, steeped in history and tradition—Montreal, New York, Toronto, Chicago, Boston, Detroit—then you'd better trade for somebody good, because your fans aren't going to accept anything less than the best. That can be tough, too, because that means you've now got to take the C away from your current captain. Talk about a difficult conversation. Maybe you'll get lucky, though, and have that conversation with somebody like Trevor Linden, who was always all about the team. Trevor had been given the C by the Vancouver Canucks at just 21 years of age, then one of the youngest captains in league history, and most assumed he'd serve as the team's captains for 10 to 15 years, easy. Linden's world came crashing down in 1997 when the organization brought in none other than six-time Stanley Cup champion Mark Messier. Yes, the same Mark Messier who had captained the Rangers past Vancouver in the '94 Stanley Cup Finals just a few years before. How would "Captain Canuck" react? With class, of course. He welcomed Messier, and before anyone could say a thing, he gave him the C off his chest. He said it was out of respect and because it was just the right thing to do. That's why he remains the most popular captain in franchise history even to this day.

Maybe you already have your guy in place, but he's getting long in the tooth. Great organizations never seem to miss a beat with regard to succession plans. Look at how the Red Wings seamlessly passed the torch from Steve Yzerman to Niklas Lidstrom—talk about consistency. Or how about when Sidney Crosby took over for the great Mario Lemieux? Just incredible to see that small-market franchise, once on the verge of relocation not too long ago, back on top and winning Stanley Cups as in the days of old.

So that's the deal for *who* you choose, but then there's the whole dilemma of *how* you chose. Do you pick "your guy" or do you let the players vote? Interesting, very interesting…I also wanted to try to delve into the coach-captain dynamic, and shed some light into that unique relationship. You know, the bond between coach and captain oftentimes runs deep. Their relationship starts off as adversarial, but evolves over time into a working partnership—even a friendship. I came across a lot of inspirational stories in writing this book, and one that particularly stood out was the relationship between Canadiens defenseman Butch Bouchard and his coach, Toe Blake. Bouchard played for Montreal for 15 seasons, 1941 to 1956, and wore the C for eight of them. Late in his career he suffered a severe knee injury that slowed him down considerably.

By 1956 Butch could barely stand on the knee and couldn't suit up for the latter half of the season. As luck would have it, in his final game ever that season, the Canadiens beat Detroit 3–1 to capture the Stanley Cup. Coach Blake, out of respect and admiration, had Bouchard suit up for the game. He sat on the bench until the very end of the game, when Blake sent out his old warrior for the final minute to enjoy what would ultimately be his last shift. Blake wanted to say thanks for his service and let him proudly conclude his illustrious career on a high note. As the buzzer sounded, the elated Bouchard led his teammates over to congratulate their net minder, Jacques Plante. With the fans going wild, NHL president Clarence Campbell called for the team captain to come out to center ice to accept the Stanley Cup, which Butch gladly did.

Neat stuff, which hopefully sheds a little light onto what goes on behind the scenes in this most interesting of associations...

Scotty Bowman

I wore an A for a time as an amateur player but never wore the C. Anytime you are singled out as a team leader, it's a prestigious honor. As I got into coaching and management, I quickly learned the importance of finding the right guy for the job. It's often a tough decision, too, because you really want to get the *right* guy for the job. And getting the two alternates is equally important. As for selecting the guys to wear letters, I always let the coaching staff weigh in on the decision. I never let the players vote, however, that was just something I didn't believe in. There were a lot of qualities I looked for when choosing the right captain. Good captains have to have a lot of patience. They have to be able to make decisions based on what's best for the team, not necessarily what's best for themselves. And they have to be good leaders who will work hard every day in practice. That's so important, to have someone who is going to lead by their example. Beyond that, I always looked for someone I could have a good relationship with. Your captain is your go-between with the players, and you have to have an open line of communication with that person in order to be an effective coach. I was very fortunate that I have had some outstanding captains to work with over the years: Steve Yzerman in Detroit, Mario Lemieux in Pittsburgh, and Serge Savard in Montreal, just to name a few. Highly respected captains like that don't come around very often, that's for sure. Putting the C on natural leaders like that is what sets average teams apart from the great ones.

Bobby Clarke

We as the coaching staff made the decision—it was never left up to the players. It's generally a pretty easy decision. The coach knows who the leader is on the team. There's a lot of leaders on the team, though, so it's about choosing the leader with the right personality for the job. Your captain can't be too quiet and reserved, he's got to be able to shake things up from time to time. He can be soft-spoken and more of a lead-by-example kind of a guy, but behind the scenes in the locker room, he's got to be able to get after guys if need be. The good ones have to be able to speak up and ultimately be responsible for their teammates.

Bill Clement

When I was playing in Calgary at the tail end of my career, I had a pretty tough experience regarding this. As a team, we went ahead and voted on who we thought should be the team captain. Jim Peplinski, one of my good friends on the team, kind of went around afterward and asked a bunch of the guys whom they had voted for. Pep then told me that without a doubt I'd won the majority of the votes. It was extremely flattering to know that I had the respect of enough of my teammates to be named as the team leader. I'd worn the C in Washington earlier in my career and was ready for the challenge. Shortly thereafter, once the votes had been tallied, it was announced that the captain had been chosen by the organization…and it wasn't me. It turned out that our coach, Al MacNeil, didn't care too much for me. At all. We had battled each other for a while regarding ice time and a host of other issues, and this was his final way of telling me how he felt about me, I suppose. I had no respect for the guy, plain and simple, and in the end it cost me the C. I certainly understood why management wouldn't want a guy who hated his coach as their captain. As it turned out, our GM, Cliff Fletcher, let me go following the season. He was going younger and knew that I wasn't going to be a part of the team's long-term plans, so it was easy for me to take a philosophical approach about it. It was easier for me to accept his rationale versus Al's, but nevertheless, it was a tough situation all the way around.

Curt Giles

I coach high school hockey in Minnesota nowadays, and choosing our captain is very important for us. What we do is ask a lot of questions and interview a lot of people. The biggest thing, I think, is asking our graduating seniors who are leaving the program about who they think would make a good captain. We have a lot of respect for those guys and value their opinions and input regarding which kids are the best leaders coming up. You get a different view-point from those guys once they are gone and no longer have to play politics. Beyond that, we look for kids who lead by example, who are respected by their teammates, and who obviously work well with others. You've got to put the C on the right kid, it really matters.

Phil Housley

For all the years I wore a letter in the NHL, it was always the coaching staff that chose the guys, never the players.

Some teams do it that way, though, but it can be risky. Now that I am in coaching myself, I can see why. The coaching staff needs to pick their guy to be captain. There are jobs on the line, and they want to make sure that they have the proper guys in place. They need to be sure that they guy they pick can be an effective communicator back and forth between management and the players. It's not a popularity contest, it's about finding the right guy to not only lead the team but also deal with the media and that whole side of the game, as well.

I'm a high school coach in Minnesota now, and it's always an important decision to me who wears the C for our teams. It's not always about picking the best player, either. First and foremost, I look for character. That's the most important thing for me. You want guys who are going to best represent not only the team but the entire community, both on and off the ice. Your best captain might be a role player who's a really hard worker and who's looked up to by his teammates. He needs to be someone they respect and someone they will listen to. He needs to be someone who is going to make smart decisions off the ice and not care about peer pressure. He needs to be a really hard worker in practice. Is the role going to be a burden on him and

Dean Blais, Former Head Coach of Columbus Blue Jackets, on Captains

It all starts with your captains, who are your leaders. You can't make leaders, you either have them or you don't. All it takes are a couple of bad apples to ruin the whole barrel. Sometimes as a coach, you know that you have a championship-caliber team, but without that chemistry and winning attitude, you won't win. You need your leaders to keep everybody in line.

prevent him from being the type of player he hopes to be? You have to ask yourself that question, too, because you obviously want someone who wants the job. Your leader sort of sets the tone and leads by his example, so it's an important aspect of your team chemistry.

Don Jackson

As a coach today, I can tell you that I learned about leadership as a member of the Edmonton Oilers. In my opinion, it's so important to have your natural leaders as the captains of your team, not necessarily your top players. There is a big difference. Great players don't always make great leaders. In Edmonton we had both, and that was a big reason why I think we were so successful. Great leaders get everybody involved. Even though I was a role player, the "20th man" on the roster, as I used to consider myself, the leaders on the team made me feel very, very important. I really appreciated that, and as a result, I wanted to work hard for them.

Barry Melrose

I have a unique perspective on captains. As a player, I wore it in junior and then later wore the A for the Cincinnati Stingers in the WHA. Later, as a coach, I quickly learned just how important they are. Captains were very, very important to me when I coached. I firmly believe that you're not going to win anything as a team without a great captain. To be chosen is both an honor and a sign of respect. It means you're a leader. The teams that I coached, I always picked the captain. I'm always surprised when I hear about a situation where the players picked their captain. In my opinion, it's way too important of a decision to let the

Bruins Coach Robbie Ftorek on Why He Chose Joe Thornton to Wear the C

There are a lot of guys who are qualified to do that job on this team. It was something I had to think about quite a bit and do a lot of the pros and cons. When it came down to it, we felt this was the way we wanted to go for the right reasons. There's a whole cast of characters in the dressing room, there's no question about that. Joey is able to flow with all of them, and it's an important key. He can have an ear to the guy who's not playing, he can have an ear to the guy who's fighting, he can have an ear to the guy who's struggling as a goal-scorer or to the defenseman who just got toasted.

Source: "A 'C' of Responsibility," by Shawn P. Roarke, Impact! January 2003

players vote. Friends vote for friends, and then it becomes a popularity contest. Not good. Your captain isn't your most liked guy on the team, he's your most respected guy on the team. I think it's very important that, when the captain gets up and speaks, he doesn't care if the guys like him or not. Good captains get up and say what they believe in and what they believe is best for the team. Again, it's much more important that the captain is respected than liked.

When I was coaching, the guy I picked to be captain was an extension of myself. I felt that the captain had to believe in the same things I believed in as the coach. He was the guy I depended on to say the right thing at the right time. He was a guy I expected to make the right decisions outside the rink. If the guys were out late screwing around for a road trip, I'd expect him to grab them and remind them that curfew was in 15 minutes. He had to make tough decisions, many of which are very unpopular, and then stand by them. Most importantly, though, he was the guy I depended on to be my voice in the dressing room. That's *very* important to a coach. If he didn't agree with everything I said, I told him that we could talk about it together in private, to discuss it. But it was *very* important that we *never* disagree with each other in front of the players. We were a unified front, no matter what.

When I took over as the head coach in L.A. in '93, Wayne Gretzky was already wearing the C. He injured his back in training camp that season, though, and we didn't know when he was coming back. So I named Luc Robitaille as my captain, and it turned out to be one of the smartest moves I ever made because he really thrived under the C. It made him a better player. In fact, he set a record that year for goals by a left winger with 63. He just became a different guy with that C on and really emerged as a team leader. It was an amazing transformation. Wayne wound up coming back midway through the year, and of course, I gave him the C back. Luc was cool with that, too, which was very classy on his part. Wayne was one of the greatest captains in NHL history, so out of respect I did what I felt was right. I was worried it would upset the team chemistry, but it didn't

Craig Dahl, Former St. Cloud State Head Coach, on Dealing with His Captains

Communication is really important, so I meet with my captains once a week to touch base with them and get feedback about different things. That gives the players a voice, a say in what is going on, and then they feel like they are more able to lead the others.

at all. In fact, Wayne came back refreshed and invigorated and wound up leading us all the way to the Stanley Cup Finals that year. We wound up losing to Montreal, but it was an amazing run we put together down the stretch.

What can you say about Wayne Gretzky? He played so hard every single night and just made everybody around him better. He played on the road, he played at home, he scored points at will on anybody and everybody—they call him "the Great One" for a reason. He loved to practice, he loved to be with the guys, he was great with the media, and he just loved to play hockey. As a captain, he commanded respect. I mean, when the best player on the planet with a handful of Stanley Cup rings stands up in the dressing room, people listen. The guy was just unbelievable. It was a real privilege to be his coach.

Lou Nanne

When I was the GM, I would talk it over with my coach, and we would make the selection together. You can't just pick the best player, nor can you just pick the most popular player. As for who we chose, we wanted someone who we felt had the respect of his teammates. We wanted somebody who was committed to winning. We wanted someone who could be a liaison between management and the players and would help us facilitate a proper working relationship together. We wanted someone who we knew was going to work extremely hard every time he was out on the ice, in practices and in games, to lead by example. There were a lot of different criteria that we wanted, so it was no easy task. You had better do your homework on that guy, though, before you put the C on his jersey, because the microscope will be on him at all times. You need the right guy for that role, it's extremely important.

Nowadays you see coaches rotating the C and rewarding different players and whatnot—I never cared for that approach. I think you need to do your homework and then go with one guy. He's your leader, period. The reality is the guys in the locker room know who the captain is whether he's got a C on his jersey or not. Your veteran players, the guys who lead by example, they are the ones who are the most respected players on the team. When things go wrong and the shit hits the fan, those are the guys they all turn to.

Michael Peca

I'm the coach and general manager of a junior team nowadays, on top of also coaching my son's peewee team. Choosing captains is really important, even at these levels. For me, character is everything. I've never felt that the best player on the team should be the captain. Rather, I think the captain should be the best leader on the team. You have to find the *right* guy for the job. You need a guy who has the ability to say, "Jump on my back," or, "Follow me." Finding the guy with the right personality and character is tough, but oh so important. They're hard almost to describe, those intangible qualities, you just know them when you see them. Leadership is key. The guy I've already picked out to be the captain on next year's team is being recruited to play hockey at West Point Military Academy. He embodies leadership, and I know he's going to be a great captain for us. So it really matters whom you pick. That guy sets the tone and leads by example at every practice and in every game. He's *your* guy. You can see teams over history who've made a poor selection as captain, and it really has a negative effect on the hockey club.

Larry Pleau

When choosing, it should be the general manager and coach who decide, *not* the players. The C is not a popularity contest, it's serious business. You can get input from the players, but at the end of the day, it has to come from management. You need to be comfortable with *your* guy. He's your liaison between our office and the locker room, so you have to be able to trust him. That's key. We need him to be able to convey our message in there, otherwise we're going nowhere in a hurry. Once you get that guy, then you pick your assistants—collectively that becomes your "leadership group." Every team has them, and they're critical to the success of your team.

There are *so* many important characteristics that go into finding a good captain, but it all depends on your team that season. It all depends. It might not be your best player or even your best leader, and it can't be a fourth-line player who gets eight minutes a night, either. You really have to ask these tough questions and weigh all your options. Maybe you look over your roster and say to heck with it, and you just go out and trade for the guy you want or sign him as a free agent. That's a possibility, too. You can never limit your options. You might ask a guy to be your captain, and that guy might turn you down because he feels like the "real" captain, the leader the players look up to and respect, is already in the locker room. That happens, too. He doesn't want to step on anyone's toes and cause drama, so he'll just respectfully decline. I've seen that, too. You just never know with this stuff.

You have to really dissect what your structure's like. Do you have a young team? Or is it a veteran team? What do you need from your captain? Do you need a guy who can pass the message along to players from management the right way? Do you want somebody who's just gonna be a rah-rah guy? Do you want a hardass who's gonna get after guys and hold them accountable in the locker room? Do you need a guy who's going to work his ass off in practice every day and lead by example? Do you want a young guy who you can groom into the role? And, if so, do you have the veterans on the roster to help teach him how to become a leader? If not, it won't work. Do you want an older guy who can show the kids how to be a professional when it comes to preparation and training in the weight room? Maybe you want a tough guy? Or a really intense guy? Do you want a guy who's really polished with the media? Or do you want a guy who can do all of these things? Good luck finding that guy!

I've had some good ones over the years. In St. Louis we had Al MacInnis and Chris Pronger, who did a great job for us. And then in Hartford I had Davey Keon, who was a great captain in his own right. Look, if you have a natural leader like Al MacInnis on your roster, consider yourself extremely lucky. Guys like that don't come around very often. What that does is free you up to make some other decisions, like who's going to wear the As. Maybe you can do a good cop/bad cop. Or give an A to an up-and-comer or to a veteran who's going to be your rah-rah guy in the locker room. Either way, when you have a great captain in place, it really gives you a lot of flexibility from a coaching standpoint.

As the coach or general manager, these are the questions you need to ask before the start of every season. Yes, it's *that* important. Trust me. There's a *lot* of discussion and thought process that goes into this. Timing is everything with this stuff, but you can't screw it up or it will come back to bight you. If you don't get the right guy who can get you to

Don Brose, Former Mankato State University Head Coach, on Communication

I tried to get my captains involved as much as possible. I always tried to make sure that the captains were elected on a leadership basis and not on a popularity basis. I also explained to the captains that I was going to be very hard on them and that they would have to be on a different wavelength because they would be the go-betweens for the players and coaches.

the next level, it could set the entire organization back for years. I've spent many a night asking myself and my staff these questions, analyzing the data over and over, and the older and smart I get—it still never gets any easier.

Mike Ramsey

Having been on the coaching side now and being a part of the selection process for who wears the C has given me a different perspective about it. As an assistant coach with the Minnesota Wild, we selected a captain on a monthly basis. Because we were an expansion team, Jacques [Lemaire] thought this would be a good way to get more guys into roles of leadership, as opposed to just naming one guy. When you had one guy, like most teams do, you live and die with that guy. That doesn't always work out, so we wanted to try something different. We would use it as a motivational tool, to reward guys and honor them for playing well. Every month or two, we'd all sit down and hash it out, and it wasn't something that we took lightly, either. It was usually a four-hour meeting, followed by a dinner conversation, concluded over breakfast. We'd finally all agree on whom we wanted to pick as a coaching staff, and then Jacques would change his mind, so we would have to start all over again. It was fascinating to see how it would change guys and boost their confidence out on the ice. Just to see their eyes light up when they saw the C on their jersey for the first time, that was special. Some guys would get real emotional about it. I will never forget when we put it on Wes Walz. He hit the ice and was so fired up that he sprinted a victory lap. The guys went nuts, so it became an instant tradition. From that moment on, whenever a new captain was announced, he would take a lap around the rink while his teammates cheered him on. It was a lot of fun. I think the biggest thing for me is that your captain doesn't necessarily have to be the best player on the team. Your best player might be your top scorer, but that doesn't mean he's your best leader, so it's important to make that distinction. Players lead in different ways, and as a coaching staff, it's up to you to find the guys who best represent what you are trying to accomplish as a team. We really mixed it up. Heck, one time we gave it to Matt Johnson [an enforcer], and that was an extremely popular pick among

Phoenix Coach Dave Tippett on His Team's Longtime Captain, Shane Doan

Shane is one of those guys that leads by example. He's one of the hardest-working players you're going to find in practice. He goes into every game with preparation, and detail into every game is at the forefront of what you want any captain to be. You take the hockey side of it as well as who he is as a person and how he lives his life. He's just a stand-up guy. Every teammate will tell you is a wonderful person.

Source: "Coyotes, Kings feed off captains' emotional investment," by Kevin Allen, USA Today, May 12, 2012

the players. He was such a well-liked guy and would do anything for his teammates, so in that instance it went over extremely well. Other guys, like Brad Bombardir and Brian Rolston, wore it for longer stretches. There was no rhyme or reason to it, we would just use it as a reward, or to mix things up. We wanted to develop team leaders, and this was a great way for us to do it. The press always wants to talk to the captain when things aren't going well, so this was an opportunity for them to deal with those types of things, as well. For a month or two, that guy was the team's figure-head or spokesman, which some guys enjoyed being and others didn't. The bottom line with it for us was that it was going to be used as something positive and rewarding that would ultimately bring the guys together in a productive way.

Glen Sonmor

Believe me, as the head coach, finding the right captain is very important—it sets the tone right out of the gates. So you have to get the right guy in there who's going to help execute your game plan. I was one of those coaches who used to let the players vote on whom they thought the captain should be, but then I'd count the votes! I wanted to make sure I had *my* guy in there. I always felt that if you had a real strong personality on your team and he was obviously the leader in the locker room, then you needed to do whatever you had to do to get the C on that guy's jersey. I'd lean on the older guys to find out who that guy was. It wasn't a popularity contest, though. You weren't looking for the most liked guy, you were looking for the most respected guy. Big difference. You wanted someone the other guys would follow. The key, though, was to make sure that guy was a hard worker in practice and that he would set a good example. If you pick a guy that didn't do those things, it will all blow up in your face.

It's important because he is your go-between, your liaison between the organization and the locker room. If there was a problem within the rank and file, maybe a little squabbling going on, I needed to know about it. So I needed to be able to trust that guy, and vice versa, so that he'd be able to talk to me openly and candidly about it. Hell, a really good captain might even tell you, the head coach, when you were getting out of line and screwing up. I appreciated that, too, I really did, because sometimes during that long grind of a season you can lose your way. The coach and the team captain have to have a strong, positive relationship. He's the guy you wind up sitting next to on buses and planes and at breakfast quite a bit, so he might as well be somebody you like—at least that's how I saw it.

I had some great captains when I was coaching the North Stars. Paul Shmyr wore it when I first got there in the late '70s, and he led us all the way to the Stanley Cup Finals in '81—where we ultimately lost to the Islanders. Oh boy, that one still stings. Paul was the social chairman of the group, always making sure to get everybody together for dinner and drinks on the road, stuff like that. To pay for the party fund, he even set up a mock tribunal system for the players whenever they would do something wrong. He was the judge, and the players would all serve as the jury. Paul would present the case, and then everybody would vote, thumbs-up or thumbs-down. If a guy took a bad penalty or didn't work hard in practice or whatever, they'd throw him on trial! If he lost, and believe me, they *all lost*, he had to pay a fine—which then went into the beer fund. I even got put on trial once when I sent the team bus to the wrong

Mike O'Connell, Boston Bruins GM

It's quite an accomplishment to become captain. No other sport really recognizes a captain like hockey.

Source: "A 'C' of Responsibility," by Shawn P. Roarke, Impact! January 2003

arena in Vancouver. I pleaded my case and tried to blame it on the bus driver, but they made me pay up anyway!

It was a neat tradition, and the guys loved it. Fun, silly stuff like that builds team chemistry, it's really important. And it forced the guys to be accountable, too, which is extremely important. As the coach, you don't want to waste your time dealing with the petty stuff like that, so if you have a captain who deals with those things, it's a big help. Paul was just a natural leader and was really a great help to our coaching staff. He unfortunately signed with Hartford as a free agent that next year, so I gave it to Tim Young. Great kid, but he had a bunch of injuries that year, so I wound up giving the C to Craig Hartsburg. Craig was a great fit and wore the C for us for the next six seasons. He was an outstanding captain. He was a really hard worker, and the guys trusted him. Once you get a guy like that whom you like, you leave him alone and let him do his thing. Don't fix it if it ain't broke!

CHAPTER
4

WHAT'S THE DEAL WITH PLAYERS-ONLY MEETINGS?

Ever wonder what's going on behind those closed door players-only meetings? Some work and some don't, that much I can tell you. We read about them in the newspaper usually following a big loss, or sometimes after a long losing streak. We hear about them because the players will maybe mention them as a turning point, a hallmark, a catalyst they look back upon that somehow swung the momentum for the team and got them back on track. If done effectively, they can be just the wake-up call a team needs to find their mojo and get the wheels back on the bus. One thing I found, though, is that players-only meetings are like Vegas, baby. What's said in the locker room, *stays* in the locker room!

Keith Ballard

They can be very effective if done properly. You can't have them too often or they lose their effectiveness. One of the trends I think we are seeing more of today is teams going with a leadership group, as opposed to just one captain who runs the whole show. In Vancouver, where I play, we have five captains—four As and one guy who wears the C. They don't always come from losing streaks or from not playing well, either. We're a veteran team, and I think those leaders really have a lot of control over how the team plays.

213

We don't control the Xs and Os, per se, but we make sure everyone is prepared and that everyone's focus is where it needs to be. We've had several this season [2011–2012], and they've been very positive for us. It lets us as players voice our opinions as well as dictate our expectations to one another. I think good coaches encourage them, really, because they allow the players to air their dirty laundry and figure out their own issues among themselves without the coaches having to get involved.

Bill Clement

I've seen plenty of players-only meetings over the years. They work, but only if there's an agenda. More than anything, when the players get together to hash things out, it creates a forum of open and honest communication that otherwise doesn't exist. It's a chance for players to vent, but with the insulation and protection of all of their other teammates sitting around them. They can say things in a safe environment, without worrying about retribution or punishment from the coaches or management. That's what they do, they create a forum or dialogue, that ultimately lets guys clear the air. Players learn not only a lot about their teammates in these types of meetings, but also themselves. Their ultimate goal and purpose is to help the group rededicate itself to the common goal, which is usually winning the Stanley Cup. The challenge afterward is for the team captain to be able to convey the information back to management in a safe, productive, and meaningful way. He has to be careful not to throw anybody under the bus and say something that was deemed as confidential or off the record. It can be tough.

Phil Housley

I've sat through many of these over the years. One of the more memorable closed-door meetings I was a part of came early in my career with Buffalo. Gilbert Perreault was the team captain, and we were struggling, so he got us all together to hash things out. He didn't yell and scream at anybody or throw anyone under the bus, but rather he started a dialogue for us to talk through some things. He didn't care about the past, he wanted to know what we were all going to do from that moment on moving forward. He cared about the team and wanted us to come together so we could get out of the funk we were in. So we went around the room and talked it out, focusing on the positive things that each person brought to the team. You know, as a player you don't know just how important you actually are to a team until your peers tell you. We all left refreshed and energized, and it gave us a real lift out on the ice. We got back on track shortly thereafter and turned things around. I will never forget that, it was awesome.

Dave Langevin

I'll never forget a team meeting we had that Clark Gillies called right before winning our first Stanley Cup in '80. The playoffs were just about to start, and we were going to be playing Boston, which had a really tough team in those days. We had lost to the Rangers in the playoffs the year before, and the media had been spouting off about how we were soft, that we lacked toughness, and that if opposing teams came after us, we'd crumble. Well, none of us wanted that reputation, so we just started talking about how we were going to get rid of it. We knew that we were going to have to take their tough guys head on. Just then, Clarkie stood up and said, "All right, boys, I'm gonna take care of [Terry] O'Reilly!" Then Garry Howatt stood up and said, "Then I got Stan Jonathan!" [Bob] Nystrom then stood up and said, "I got John Wensink!" The rest of us were so pumped up at that point that we all stood up and basically said, "We've got everybody else!" That was a defining moment *right there*. That was when we became a team. In my eyes, that was it. We all decided that nobody was going to push us around anymore. That was us drawing a line in the sand. That was our moment right there where we said this is what it's going to take to become champions. I bet Clarkie fought O'Reilly five times that series, and he pummeled him. He even beat Al Secord, too, who was no slouch. Talk about leading by example. We just fed off of that energy and rode that momentum past the Bruins and right on to winning what would be our first of four straight Cups.

Barry Melrose

Sure, everybody calls players-only meetings. When the team is struggling, you get your captain to call one and you let them air it all out. Nine times out of 10 they don't help, but as long as the players *think* that they've accomplished something…that's all that matters.

Mark Parrish

I tried to read guys and see where they were. Sometimes I would call a players-only meeting and other times I would do one-on-one's with guys, it really depended on the individual situation. Maybe it was just taking a guy to lunch or out for a beer to cheer him up. As captain, you have to be a good listener and just be there for guys—sometimes it's as easy as that. Other times, you need to kick the coaches out of the locker room and get loud. Sometimes you need to do whatever it takes to get the guys to speak their minds. Sometimes the captain will have to break some sticks and toss some water bottles to get the guys' attention. The captain may call a guy out in front of the entire team and take him to task. That's his role, to hold guys accountable. Maybe your team is in a slump or there is some big off-ice distraction going on. Whatever the case may be, this is an effective way to let the guys clear the air and voice their opinions. The bottom line is that sometimes players need to hear criticism or critical feedback from the other players, as opposed to the coaches. It just takes one player who gets in the coach's doghouse, who is sulking, to disrupt your team's entire chemistry. Believe me, misery loves company, and it can become contagious. So a good captain will recognize this and try to put an end to it before it snowballs into a bad situation for the entire team. It can be difficult to do that stuff, but it's necessary sometimes. That's what true leadership is, the ability to do that kind of stuff without even thinking twice about it. You know it's not going to be easy, you know you're going to feel bad about it later, and you know you're going to piss some guys off—but you under-stand that it's for the good of the team, so you just do it. If I ever say something to a younger player and realize later that I was maybe a bit harsh on him, then I will for sure take him aside after the fact to apologize and explain my reasoning for whatever I said. Sometimes being the captain can be lonely, but that just comes with the job, I suppose.

Lance Pitlick

Every now and then, maybe in the midst of a bad slump, we would have one. The captain would find a dive bar where we could use the back room, and we would all go in and have it out. We'd order beers and try to solve the world's problems. Looking back, nothing ever got solved in those things. It was just the act of getting together, outside of the locker room, and hanging out with each other.

Sometimes the coaches will facilitate them, too. I remember playing in Hershey years ago, and we were in this terrible slump. Our coach, Mike Eaves, was at his wits' end. He bagged us ["bag-skates" are intense practices with no pucks], he brought in a sports psychologist, he gave us time off, he did everything he could think of to turn it around. Nothing worked. Finally, he called us into the locker room after practice one day, and when we got in there, he had three giant coolers of beer sitting on the floor. He said, "Boys, I don't know what else to do. So we're gonna sit here and empty these coolers until we figure it out!" We sat around, let our hair down, laughed, and sure enough, we won the next night!

Mike Ramsey

What happens in the room, what's said in the room…stays in the room. Enough said.

Joe Sakic

Fortunately, we had a lot of success in Colorado, so I never had to call one very often. As captain, you would do it a couple times a year, though, to get everybody on the same page and let them speak their minds. You'd do it usually when you were in a slide, and if done properly they were very effective. It was a great way to clear the air and let guys talk about whatever it was that was bothering them, either on the ice or off the ice. It was best to just talk about it and nip it in the bud before it grew into something bigger and potentially more of a distraction.

Colorado Avalanche center Joe Sakic gets past Chicago Blackhawks defenseman Gary Suter as he heads for the goal during a game in April 1997.

Nick Schultz

We had one back in '07 that I will never forget. We'd lost like nine in a row on the road, so we all got together and closed the doors behind us. Guys really opened up and let it all out. It was tough, but some things had to get aired, and they did. It worked, too, because we turned things around and went on to win like 10 in a row on the road after that all the way to winning the division title. So they can be effective if done properly, no question. It was just the wake-up call we all needed.

Brendan Shanahan

The players-only meetings were very meaningful because it was just the guys. It was behind the scenes, never for show or headlines, and that was important. Calling one at the right time could be huge for the team, depending on whether or not the air needed to be cleared. If done properly and in the right context, these types of gatherings can really be effective.

Scott Stevens

I'd call them every now and then, sure, especially right after a big game when guys were still hot—typically after a loss, when guys needed to blow off some steam and clear the air. They could be quite effective if done properly. The key, though, was to make sure what was said in the room stayed in the room. If that trust was ever broken, then all bets were off.

Wes Walz

I didn't call too many players-only meetings. Those were reserved for when things were *really* going bad. I chose instead to have it out between periods, right then and there when things weren't going well. I'd tell the coaches and trainers and equipment guys to just get out of the locker room, and then we'd have it out as a team. I would never throw a guy under the bus and embarrass him in front of the team, but there were times as the team leader when you had to get vocal and hold guys accountable. If you felt like guys weren't giving enough effort, then it was up to you to get them to give a little bit more. A lot of guys think that they're giving enough, but in reality they really don't realize that they're not playing with their hearts. I didn't do this very often, though. I was a firm believer in picking your spots with stuff like this. Every now and then, when it really mattered, that's when private gatherings like this could really be effective. Knowing when to say the right thing at the right time is crucial for any leader, and that all comes with experience. When I wore the C, I was a veteran player and felt confident in doing those things.

CHAPTER
5

WHAT LIFE LESSONS DO YOU THINK YOU LEARNED FROM WEARING A LETTER THAT YOU'VE NOW BEEN ABLE TO APPLY TO BUSINESS?

In the final chapter, I wanted the players to reflect and ponder just what it meant for them to be named as a captain. Then I wanted them to think about all the life lessons they had learned during their journey, to consider how those lessons applied to success in business life after hockey, and to share these lessons with others who want to learn about leadership and become captains in their own world. The answers here were deep and profound, some really eye-opening things came to the fore-front. The big takeaway for me was that there simply is no one right way, there's lots of different ways to find success. The key, though, is finding *your* way. Good luck!

Adrian Aucoin

For me it was all about the power of the team. When I was playing in New York, I had a bunch of neighborhood friends who worked on Wall Street. I remember one time them all telling me that, if I ever needed a job after I was done playing, it would be no problem for me. I asked them why they thought that, figuring it was just because I was a professional athlete or celebrity, but they said it was because I was a part of a team. The fact that I was the assistant captain at the time really stood out with them. And they knew that hockey players, as opposed to other professional athletes, were especially unselfish with regard to sacrificing their personal stats for the betterment of the team. They knew that our mentality was all about the team, and about how we all wanted to make everybody better—so that the entire team could get better and ultimately win championships. That was the reward at the end of the day. They then explained to me why so many big companies were desperate for that type of leadership. Sometimes in the business world a lot of the big companies forget that. They forget that you have to make the company stronger, because that's how everybody gets rewarded. I found that just fascinating.

David Backes

I've learned a lot about how to manage people, and to get the most out of them. I think that starts with being positive, too, and to not be that guy who is constantly harping on guys all the time. Negativity is no good for the locker room, so I never wanted to be that guy. For me, I care so much about every one of my teammates—that just comes out, I guess, with the way I lead. When you have those contentious moments out there, when you have to get in someone's face or give them the business because you feel that they

Larry Pleau on Mark Messier Leading the New York Rangers to Their First Stanley Cup in 54 Years in 1994

Who can forget Mark Messier, the captain, practically carrying that team on his back during the playoffs that year? He had guaranteed the win against New Jersey in Game 6 of the conference finals and then backed it up with a hat trick. We then won it the following game on Stephane Matteau's double-overtime game-winner, which was just an amazing moment and one I will never forget. Then, in the Finals, to be up three games to one on Vancouver only to watch them force a Game 7—which we won dramatically at home in the Garden. It was amazing, it really was.

need to produce more or give more effort—that's taken as constructive criticism for the good of the team and not just a personal slam. It's business. Being the captain means making tough, unpopular decisions, a lot. And that's no fun. But you have to do it, that's your job. So if you can do it positively and with respect, then it's a lot easier to have those conversations. Guys will respect you if you lead by example and actually walk the walk, not just talk the talk.

Keith Ballard

To be looked upon as a leader is a big responsibility. Whether it's the leader of a team, a business, a family, or any organization or group, it's an honor and a privilege to be the leader. You have to have certain attributes. You have to be willing to do the right thing every day. It requires self-discipline and the ability to make unpopular decisions that you feel are best for the group. You have to have the kind of charisma and character that inspires others to the point that they become motivated to do things that they wouldn't normally do. Great leaders have those attributes.

Brian Bellows

Real leaders have the ability to make the people around them better. Whether it's complimenting them or helping them or showing them how to do it, they find ways to bring everybody up to their level. Sometimes, if you sacrifice a bit of yourself to help the people around you, it makes all of you better. The whole product becomes better. In return, you gain insight and actually make yourself better. You can't be selfish in a team sport like hockey, it just doesn't work. I coach youth hockey today, and I've found that's a tough concept to get across to 13- and 14-year-olds. They either get it or they don't.

Rob Blake

For me, it was about being able to relate to everybody on the team, which included all sorts of different people. As the captain, you have to be able to talk to your top scorer, the goaltender, the rookie who just got called up from the minors, the Russian guy who can't speak English. You have to be able to relate to them and you have to somehow make them all feel like they are a valuable part of the team. From there, you have to get them all driving toward the same common goal. Nobody said it was easy, and I suppose that's why only one guy on the team gets to wear the C.

Ray Bourque

For me, it's all about your attitude and how you approach your job on a daily basis. It's applying everything that you learn along the way toward becoming a better person. It's a combination of work ethic, passion, preparation, leadership—it's all of those things together that make you successful in whatever you do in life.

Rod Brind'Amour

It's about choices, consistently making the right choices. As the captain, you learn pretty quickly that there is a microscope on you and that people are watching your every move. So you have to do the right things. That's the life lesson for me, doing the right thing and making the right choices. Sometimes that can be tough, and certainly unpopular with people, but as a leader that's what you have to do. You have to be able to look yourself in the mirror every night and ask yourself if you made the right choices that day. Did you work as hard as you could? Did you give it your best? Did you try to improve? Did you make a difference? I think if you can do those things consistently, then you'll find success in whatever you do.

Neal Broten

The big thing for me is just treating people with respect. It's the old golden rule, treat people how you want to be treated. Nobody likes to be talked down to, no matter what they do in life. So I just tried to treat people right, and in so doing, hopefully they felt compelled to treat me the same.

Andrew Brunette

The big thing for me was to just be myself. That's how you earn respect, by being yourself. You can't pretend to be somebody else as a leader, you have to figure out your own style. It might take time and effort, but eventually you will find it—and when you do…you'll have success in whatever you do in life.

Bill Butters

Consistency. It's a long season when you play hockey. You're going to win some and you're going to lose some, but it's really about your long-term approach. You're going to have ups and downs along the way, and it's ultimately about what you learn from those ups and downs more than anything else. If something doesn't go your way, learn from it and then move on. We all have success as well as setbacks in life on a daily basis. If you stay consistent in your approach, though, whether it's your faith, your marriage, your business, or whatever it is—and you know that there are going to be good days as well as bad days—things will eventually work out. You can't let the good days take you too high and you can't let the bad days take you too low. You have to be consistent and you have to stay grounded. Good leaders, the guys who are respected by their teammates or their coworkers, are consistent with what they say and what they do.

Ryan Carter

For me, it's about not what you say, but how and when you say it. It's doing and saying the right things at the right times in order to help your team in any way you can. It's about conducting yourself as a professional at all times. Quite honestly, had I not ever been a captain, I probably wouldn't have thought about those things before. But luckily, since I was early on in my career, it really helped me to become more of a leader now that I am in the NHL.

Zdeno Chara

Whether you are a professional athlete, an entertainer, a businessman, a musician, or whatever, the most important thing, in my eyes, is to do your best every day. You have to show up every day and do whatever it takes to be the best. We can never become complacent and think we know it all, because we can always get better through hard work and preparation. Always. As leaders, we are here to serve others, that's what being a good human being is all about—regardless of whether that's in sports or business.

Kelly Chase

For me, it's confidence. That's the life lesson for me. If you have confidence, you can accomplish anything in life. You can't worry or give a shit about what other people say about you. You know, I played with a chip on my shoulder. I was never drafted, and I just had to fight for everything I got in this game. Players used to razz me about not getting very much ice time, about being a goon, you name it—I've heard it. So I took all of that negative energy and channeled it into motivating myself to get better. I came from nothing and really carved out a long playing career that I am very proud of. Even today I am very fortunate to still be in the game as a radio analyst, and I also own several businesses. I'm very proud of what I've accomplished because I had to do it the hard way. I mean, I started out with absolutely zero. My dad died when I was young, and I moved away to be on my own shortly thereafter. So I've just always had this chip on my shoulder. When people say bad things about me or try to knock me down, that only makes me stronger. The stronger I get, the more confident I get, and the more confident I get...the better off I am. I think I'm a better leader now than I've ever been because I made a lot of mistakes along the way. But I've learned from them and grown from them, and I know that my best years are still ahead of me.

Tom Chorske

I've always relished the opportunity of competition and tried to meet it head on. So showing up every day and putting in the effort, that's the big thing for me. And it's not just showing up, it's showing up with a good attitude. Perseverance is key, too. You take your licks, you pick yourself back up, and you try again. That's hockey and that's life.

Bill Clement

The big takeaway for me is that being a leader requires making tough choices and having difficult conversations. It's tough to be a great leader. If you are a true leader, then

Johnny Bucyk on Leading Boston to Its First Cup in 30 Years

Winning the first Stanley Cup had to be the biggest thrill. Although I was wearing an A, I was still the captain because we had three assistants that year and I was the No. 1. I don't know what the difference was except I had an A instead of a C, but I was presented the Stanley Cup on behalf of the team in Boston. In those days, the captain took the Cup and skated around the rink, and I got the opportunity to do that, right in my home rink. It was a thrill I'll never forget. It was a big honor. In those days, you couldn't take the Cup home with you, but just to have a picture of me with the Stanley Cup was outstanding.

Source: http://www.hhof.com/htmlSpotlight

sometimes you have to stand up and say things that are not only difficult today but will possibly alienate you from part of or most of the group. If the message that you are delivering comes from the right place, and it's supported by the right values and principles, however, then that loneliness and alienation will pass. *And* you can look in the mirror afterward and say, "I did what had to be done and said what had to be said, all for the betterment of the organization." Leaders are confident in their convictions and know that standing up for what they truly believe in is way more important than winning a popularity contest. That's true leadership, in my eyes. Look, it's tough to find great leaders. Really good, strong, respected leaders are extremely difficult to find. Many, many times the guy wearing the C on a lot of teams is simply the best player. And, in my opinion, there is very little correlation between the best player, skill-wise, and his ability to lead others. Putting up numbers isn't leadership. As an analyst, I see far too much of this in the game today. The bottom line is that it's hard to find quality leadership, on the ice as well as in corporate America. The best teams find them, though, and put them in positions to succeed, and that's what separates them from the rest of the pack.

Ben Clymer

For me, it's just about treating people right and having a good work ethic. Good captains embody those qualities and exemplify them tenfold compared to the average person walking the street, and probably threefold compared to the average NHL player. It's in their nature. You know, we all grow up getting to play this amazing game because our parents are willing to make sacrifices for us along the way. They get up early to drive us to practice, they stand out in the cold to watch us, and they work hard to pay for all the equipment and ice time. I think that selfless attitude gets engrained in us, like it's a part of the culture of the sport. It certainly did for me, anyway. So that's it, if you work hard and treat people right, I think you're going to have success in whatever you do in life.

Matt Cullen

It all sort of boils down to this: you have to walk the walk. Leadership by example is just that—you have to get in there and do it. Anybody can talk the talk, but real leaders roll up their sleeves and get dirty. There's nothing worse than sitting in a locker room listening to some guy talk about accountability when he shows up late and leaves early. Leaders earn respect through sacrifice, through prepara- tion, through making the right choices, through outworking everybody else, and by being a good person whom people can trust and believe in.

Natalie Darwitz

Communication is the big thing for me. It's crucial for suc- cess in whatever you do. I'm not the most rah-rah, give- a-big-motivational-speech type of person. I'm more of a lead-by-example type. So, for me, the biggest challenge was always the communication piece. How do I communi- cate to my teammates effectively in order to effectively lead the team? That was the question I was constantly trying to answer as a player, and am stilly trying to answer today as a coach. Everybody is different in the way you get something out of them. So it was figuring out how to get to Player A, who relates to something completely differ- ent than Player B. You can get to Player A with a kick in the pants, whereas getting to Player B might involve a pat on the back and some encouraging words. One you can yell at to get through to, whereas the other you have to be calm and supportive. Both are good players and both are motivated to do well, but it comes down to effective communication to be able to get through to them in order for them to succeed. Because, as a coach, you know that it's critical that everyone is involved and motivated, otherwise the team won't do very well.

Jim Dowd

For me, it was just all about the team. I learned that as a kid, growing up one of seven kids in New Jersey. My parents couldn't come to all my games, obviously, but afterward they would always ask me the same questions: "How did the team do, did you win?" "Were you prepared?" And most importantly, "Did you have fun?" They never asked me how many goals or assists I had, they didn't care about that stuff. They wanted to know how the team did. That's always stuck with me, even today as I coach kids. It's not about the individual stuff, it's all about the team. And the team isn't just necessarily your teammates, either, it's everybody in the organization. I used to come to the rink and make sure to say hi to the Zamboni driver, the janitor, the bus driver, the trainers—everybody. I wanted those guys to know that they were all a part of the team. Some guys are above that but not me, that's who I am.

Mike Eruzione

Respect. I've always been taught to respect people and to respect myself. As a captain, or leader, you want people to respect you for who you are and what you stand for. To get that respect, though, you have to earn it by being a good person. You have to make the right choices, you have to work hard, and you have to lead by example. And most importantly, if you want other people's respect, you have to show them respect first. I'm not a real deep person, I just understand that I'm kind of a kid who grew up with a lot of old-fashioned values. Respect is at the core of those values for me, it's how I live my life. Show people respect and you'll have success in whatever you do, it's as easy as that, in my eyes.

Tom Gilbert

Being competitive is the big takeaway for me. If you're willing to work your butt off and fight for what you want, you're going to find success in whatever you do in life. You have to look at it like it's a battle every single day. That has to be your mentality if you really want to get ahead, I think. You can't be complacent and just expect good things to happen to you. Being a professional athlete, I'm naturally extremely competitive and I hate to lose, so hopefully that translates into success for me once I enter the real world after I'm done playing hockey. If not, I'm in big trouble!

Curt Giles

You have to stand for something. Sometimes it takes a lot of guts to put yourself out there and stand up for what you believe in, but people respect you even more when you do, in my opinion. As a leader, you're going to be called upon to make some tough decisions. That's just a part of the deal. Being the leader isn't a popularity contest, you've got to put yourself out there. Some people will agree with you and some won't. That's life. Great leaders make tough choices and then stand by them. If you take that mentality into the business world, you're going to find success there, too.

Clark Gillies

Self-discipline. When I retired from hockey, I retired from hockey. I didn't want to get into coaching or management and bounce my family around any more than I had to, so I went into business. I had plenty of offers to come back as a coach, but I was ready to just become a fan. I chose to get into the world of corporate finance with Smith Barney, and it was a pretty big learning curve. I didn't know a whole lot about it when I got into it, so I had to work twice as hard as everybody else. I was in the office every morning at 7:00 and didn't leave until 7:00 at night. And all I did all day long was cold-call people I didn't know. It was awful, and I struggled. It would have been very easy for me to call people in the tri-state area of New York, New Jersey, and Connecticut, and say, "Hi, this is former Islander Clark Gillies, and I'd love to earn your business." I would've probably had a ton of new business had I chosen to do that, but I didn't want to take that route. I knew that I needed to thicken my skin by getting some rejection. I needed to pay my dues so that I would truly learn the business, without taking any shortcuts. So I chose to call people in Ohio, California, Washington, Texas, and Florida. Most of the people had no idea who the hell I was, and that was just fine by me. For six months I pounded the pavement and learned how to deal with a whole bunch of rejection. It was like my rookie hazing all over again, just brutal. I learned so much during that time, though, and was so glad that I chose to take that route. I've been doing it for nearly 25 years now, so it's been going great. Discipline. That was what it was all about. It's a choice. The same discipline that I learned and employed on the ice, I used in growing my new business. Success doesn't come easy, that's for sure. Along the way you're going to have a lot of disappointments, but eventually, if you stick with it and remain disciplined, things will eventually work out for you.

Bill Guerin

The nugget of wisdom for me was just the power of leading by example. I remember one time when I was the captain of the Islanders, we were playing New Jersey and it was a pretty tough game. There had been a couple fights and things weren't going our way. We were trying to create an identity for ourselves at the time, and I felt like I needed to step it up. As the guy wearing the C, I just felt like I needed to be a part of that. Most older captains don't have to do that stuff at that stage of the game, but to me I guess that's what leading by example is all about. So I jumped over the boards and dropped the gloves, too. I couldn't sit back and watch everybody else make sacrifices without making some of my own. I wanted the young guys to know that I was all-in, and hopefully that would rub off on them. The bottom line is that, as the leader, you simply have to do things that you don't like to do sometimes.

The captain isn't just another player. He's the one who's looked upon each and every night to not only set the tone for the rest of the team but also to do the right things on and off the ice. He's the guy who has to make tough decisions in the locker room. He's the guy everybody looks to when things are at their worst, too. He's the guy who's responsible for digging the team out of the hole, because that's just a part of the job. He's the face of the franchise. So, for me, that was the big takeaway, knowing that others are depending on you and are expecting you to lead them.

Bobby Clarke Gave Up the C to Become a Player/Assistant Coach

In 1979 Philadelphia Flyers winger Bobby Clarke was named as a player/assistant coach. In order to do so, however, he had to relinquish his captaincy due to NHL rules. As a result, Mel Bridgman was given the C. That season the Flyers went on a 35-game winning streak, the longest in NHL history. The team ultimately made it to the Stanley Cup Finals before losing to the New York Islanders four games to two. During the playoffs, Clarke went on a tear, scoring an incredible eight power play goals. When asked about the move, Clarke was blunt. "It was horrible," he said. "I didn't want to do it, I wanted to remain captain. Pat Quinn was the coach, and he asked me if I would do it. I said no because I didn't think it could work, and it didn't. It was a disaster. But, at that particular time, Pat thought it was the right thing for the team. So I tried it. I couldn't wait to be done with that and just go back to being captain."

They're counting on you to deliver, to step up, no matter what. Knowing that people are looking to you for leadership and to set an example is very humbling. It's an awesome responsibility.

Ben Hankinson

Attitude is the big takeaway for me. It's contagious...either way. If you have a good, positive attitude, that rubs off on everybody else. And if you have a bad attitude, it brings everybody down. I learned that from my mom, about the importance of always being positive. I always tried to use my sense of humor to make guys laugh and keep them loose, so for me that was a big part of having a good attitude. Beyond that, it was all about putting the team first. If you do what's best for the team, or your company, then you're going to have success. It's that easy. If you focus on yourself and your individual accomplishments and accolades, you might have short-term success—but not long-term. Talent only gets you so far in sports and in business. It comes down to other factors, like working hard and being a team player. It comes down to making sacrifices, like blocking shots or playing whatever role is asked of you. Hey, I didn't want to be a fighter, but I was willing to do it in order to help out my team. I wasn't very good at it, either, but my teammates appreciated me stepping up and doing it. That meant a lot to me. So I think the people who are willing to make those sacrifices and work hard and do whatever they can to support their organizations, those are the ones who will have success over the long haul. Teams that are full of selfless guys like that win more often than not.

Casey Hankinson

Accountability was the big takeaway for me. We all make mistakes, guaranteed. Owning those mistakes, acknowledging them, and then moving on, that's what it's all about. People respect you when you just own it and don't make excuses. Say you're sorry, take your medicine, and then work hard to make sure it doesn't happen again. That's it. People don't want to deal with BSers on the ice any more than they want to deal with them in the business world. If you screw up, admit it and go on. Don't dwell on it and don't blame others. It's as simple as that.

Derian Hatcher

Leadership to me is a lot about how you hold yourself. That says a lot about you, believe it or not. Little stuff like that matters to me. I always tell my kids that when they talk to people to make sure they don't droop their shoulders, that they look the person in the eye, and that they give them a firm hand shake. People will follow you if they trust you, and that starts with how you hold yourself, in my opinion.

Kevin Hatcher

There certainly are life lessons from being captain that you can relate to business. I'm a multiple business owner in the Detroit area, and when it comes to achieving success, I relate everything back to sports. I relate everything to having a team philosophy, which means you have to have great leadership at the top. All the best organizations do, whether that's in sports or in the corporate world. If you surround yourself with good people, from top to bottom, you're going to have success in what you do in life.

Brett Hedican

I learned that you're not going to have your A game every night. So you need to find a way to get the job done with your B game. Hockey teaches you that you're only as good as today, not yesterday. Hockey keeps you humble that way. Over a grueling 82-game regular season schedule, plus the playoffs, you're not going to have your legs every night. You're going to have injuries and setbacks along the way, but you just have to stay the course. Nobody is outstanding every night, but true professionals do the little things in order to maximize the number of nights that they are outstanding. Anyone can have a great night, but to do it over and over again, consistently…that's what it's all about.

For me, that's following a standard of excellence to which I try to hold myself every day. That's what good leadership is all about, holding yourself accountable. Your teammates will either conform to that attitude and philosophy and jump on board or else stand out like a sore thumb. Great leadership is contagious. That's how it was the year we won the Stanley Cup in Carolina, we had so many outstanding leaders all pulling in the same direction that, if you didn't conform, you were pretty much ostracized. In Carolina we worked. Hard. That was a prerequisite. You couldn't just punch in and punch out. You had to come in before practice and stay late after practice. That was the expectation for every man on the roster, regardless of his role. If you weren't up for that, then that wasn't the team for you. That was our culture, and we all believed in it. Once everyone believes in it and buys in, that's when amazing things can happen.

I'll never forget one day midway through that Stanley Cup season, we had what I would call a "perfect practice." No kidding, it was flawless. I'd never seen anything like it, everybody was just working and clicking. It was amazing. After practice our coach, Peter LaViolette, came into the locker room and said, "There's no question, if you continue to play like that, I guarantee you we are going to win the Stanley Cup." He was right.

Darby Hendrickson

You're going to have adversity in life, but it's how you choose to respond that really counts. To continually improve and get better in whatever you are doing requires making the right choices, consistently. It requires a level of toughness, of resiliency, of discipline, that quite honestly most people don't even realize they have. The bottom line is that there are going to be ups and downs along the way, but it's all about how you respond to that adversity that matters.

Phil Housley

The big takeaway for me is to never be satisfied. You've always got to prove yourself each and every year, no matter what. If you go in with that attitude and you're well prepared, then you're never caught off guard. I've always felt like you're only as good as your last game, and even as good as your last season. There are no guarantees in hockey or in life. You have to earn it through hard work and dedication, each and every season. In fact, I always came into training camp every year with the same attitude, like I was trying to earn a spot on the roster. It didn't matter that I'd been a team captain. That was *last* season. Things change, and I always wanted to be prepared, I was never satisfied. I just never took anything for granted in this business, never. That attitude helped, I think, and was a big reason why I was able to play 20-plus seasons in the NHL.

Brett Hull

For me, it was about realizing the importance of everybody's role on the team. You have to respect each individual and his contribution to the team, regardless of what it is. You can't win with just your top six forwards and two defensemen, there's a lot more to it. You need those guys who kill penalties, who block shots, who change the momentum of a game by getting into a fight, who do all the little things that quite frankly many of the top guys don't or won't do.

There are so many aspects to the game that make you a winning team, and it took me a long time to figure that out. So I learned that in order to be successful as an organization, you have to embrace your role players—because you're not going to win a championship without them.

Chris Kunitz

To me it's about paying attention to the details and doing the little things. It's blocking a shot or finishing on your forecheck or going to the net or not being out of position defensively. Little things become big things if they aren't done properly, so it's important to always focus on being able to execute the details.

Tom Kurvers

The game of hockey is basically a shit storm on ice, and it's the captain who's got to be able to deal with all the problems and drama both on and off the ice and then make sure his team reacts to all of it the right way.

Jamie Langenbrunner

I think the big thing for me is being able to deal with so many different personalities. Communication is huge. When you're the captain, it's your job to be the team spokesperson sometimes, and you need to be able to speak on everybody's behalf. You need to make sure that you say the right things and that you do the right things so that the team stays together. Sometimes you have to get on somebody for some reason, and other times you have to bring something to somebody's attention—which can create an uncomfortable situation. That's just a part of the job, though, and you have to do it. How you say stuff, though, that's the key. You have to be able to do it in a positive and constructive way that is encouraging—otherwise it can be tough. That's what being a good leader is all about, having those types of conversations with the understanding that it's not personal. Everybody else can shy away from that stuff and just worry about your own business, but not if you're the captain. That's your job. Hopefully, you say the right stuff, and the situation resolves itself, otherwise it can be difficult. So being a good communicator is probably the biggest thing for me.

Dave Langevin

Never give up. You're going to encounter adversity along the way, but if it's important enough to you, then you have to find a way to do it. Life is like a puck thrown in the corner. Two guys are going for the same goal, yet only one is going to get it. One's going to work harder to get the puck, and the other one isn't. It's as simple as that. I coach kids today, and that's what I always tell them. You're the only one who says when it's over. Period. Nobody else. Growing up, I had aspirations of going to college and then playing in the NHL. A lot of kids laughed at me. I just told myself, I don't care what people think. I'm going to do whatever it takes to fulfill my dream and go where I want to go. Those doubters and naysayers motivated me, they pushed me to work even harder. When I finally accomplished my goal, it was just that much sweeter.

Igor Larionov

Responsibility. When you are in charge of leading a team, whatever the size, details matter. Everything comes back to

Montreal Canadiens Hall of Famer Yvan Cournoyer on What It Meant to Wear the C

I was named captain of the team by the players. Everybody voted. It was a tremendous honor to be captain of the Montreal Canadiens after the Rocket [Richard], Jean [Beliveau], and Henri [Richard]. That was quite something to be named, and it gave me great confidence to be captain of the team.... As captain of the team, I played harder than I ever had played in my life. I enjoyed representing the team. We were a very close team. There was no French or English. When we lost, we lost together, when we won, we won together.... I think a captain then was more like an assistant to the coach. I was the mediator between the coach and the players. Today, if there's a problem, the players say, "Talk to my agent."

Source: http://www.hhof.com/htmlSpotlight

you, win or lose, and it's your responsibility to make sure your teammates are prepared and ready to play. When you are the leader, everybody looks up to you, and you can't let them down. That means making the right choices and doing the right things, all the time, on or off the ice.

Reed Larson

The big life lesson for me was something I got from my parents as a kid, and that's just to be a good person. Do things the right way, don't cheat or take shortcuts, or cut people down to get what you want. To me, your reputation is priceless. People do things for money or for fame or whatever, but to truly be successful in life you have to have integrity and do things the right way. I don't care if that's in hockey or in business, those values and principles ring true for whatever you do in life.

Troy Loney

It's just leading by example, plain and simple. I know that's cliché, but that's it. If your team is working hard, then as the leader you've got to be working harder than your team. That's just how it goes. That applies to hockey and it applies to business. It's no secret. If you have high expectations for your teammates, then you better be out there leading the way. You can't expect them to put everything on the line unless you do the same. In hockey, if you're not speaking the truth and you're being a phony—saying one thing and doing another—it becomes real obvious, real fast. Players don't respect guys who are all talk but can't back it up. It's no different in business, either. You can't be saying one thing and doing another, you'll never get ahead and you'll certainly never gain anybody's respect.

John MacLean

Hard work. Really, what else is there?

Todd Marchant

Sacrifice is the big thing for me, I think. Being a captain is a big responsibility, and a lot of people don't realize that. You have to separate yourself and your personal goals from the good of the team. That can be tough. You have to be willing to sacrifice your personal stats and recognition in order to help the team win. There are captains and assistant captains I know of who have had trouble with that. Sometimes they get so worried about the team not playing well that they forget about their own game and about what they need to be doing on a nightly basis in order to be successful. So the good all-around captains are the guys who can not only do both but do both well. Being a good leader and being a good player at the same time, that can be tough, but the best captains find ways to get the job done. Not only do they play good hockey, they also get their teammates to elevate their games—which is huge. Even if they have a bad game, they have to come in the next day and pick everybody up. Sick, tired, injured—it doesn't matter. They need to get everybody up and ready to go. It's a delicate balance. But the captains who are willing to make those personal sacrifices for the greater good of the team are the ones who are most respected—and usually most successful. I've tried to apply that same logic to my everyday life, as well.

Paul Martin

To be able to work with all sorts of different people and get along with them on a daily basis, that's the big takeaway for me. In an NHL locker room, you have strong personalities from various people who come from all over the world, many of whom speak different languages. So, as a leader, you have to be able to not only get along with everyone, you have to be able to effectively communicate with them in order to find success for the team as a whole. That might mean making a lot of sacrifices along the way, but in the end, if you are able to bring everybody together, then the whole team will win—both on and off the ice.

Basil McRae

I think it's never taking anything for granted. For me, every day I got up and put two feet on the floor and then headed to the rink. Every day was a challenge for me. I felt like I had to prove myself every single time I stepped onto the ice. Heck, I played five years in the minors, so every day I played in the NHL was a bonus for me. You just never know what tomorrow holds. In hockey you could get injured, you could get sent back down to the minors, you could get benched—you just never knew. So I tried to play every game like it might be my last. I love that song "Live Like You're Dying" because you never know what tomorrow may bring you.

Marty McSorley

I learned a lot about leadership from my coach in Edmonton, Glen Sather. Glen showed me that in order to be successful you have to surround yourself with great people, and then you have to trust them to do their job. He didn't micromanage people, he let them do what they were paid to do. He let our leaders lead and he stayed out of the way. He'd give them responsibilities and then he would step back and trust them. Sometimes those people would fail. But if he believed in them, he would stick with them, and eventually it would all work out. So for me it's about getting the right people on your team and then trusting them to do their jobs.

Barry Melrose

Leadership is working harder than everybody else and then doing the right thing when no one's watching. I tell my kids all the time that it's easy to be a follower, but the world is always looking for leaders. People respect leaders. Captains are leaders. Be a leader.

Joe Micheletti

Hard work. More than anything, that's what it's all about...
hard work. Nothing comes easy in life, you have to work
for it in order to create your own luck. My mom and dad
were both extremely hard workers, and I was the fifth of
nine kids, so hard work was nothing new to me growing
up. Whether it was helping Mom with the dishes or laundry
or helping Dad outside, we were always working on something from as early as I can remember. I certainly never got
spoiled as a kid, that's for sure! Work ethic was an expectation in our household up on the Iron Range in northern
Minnesota. Everybody worked hard.

Mike Modano

Communication was the big thing for me. When you are
the captain, it forces you to learn how to communicate
with people—all sorts of people with all sorts of personalities. I think that I learned to be a pretty good listener along
the way, too, which helped me to better understand what
people's strengths and weaknesses were. I learned that
everybody had his own way of motivating people and that
it was up to me to be able to be an effective communicator
so that I could figure those ways out. I needed to know what
made each individual tick. I needed to know what they
needed to hear and what they needed to see. Sometimes
that meant not saying a word, just observing. The better I
was at all of that, the better off the team was going to be.
So it was important.

Kyle Okposo

The biggest thing for me when I became captain was the
fact that you can't change who you are. Whether it's getting

promoted in business or getting a letter in hockey, being a leader shouldn't change you. Whoever promoted you obviously sees your qualities, so you have to stay true to yourself. It's easy to get caught up in it and think that you need to become someone else, maybe someone who held that role before you. But that doesn't work, people see right through that. You have to be yourself, always.

Joel Otto

Great leaders have the ability to bring teams together. They can unite them and get them to rally around a common goal. Great leaders are rare, that's what makes them so unique.

J.P. Parise

Responsibility was the big thing for me. I learned to really think things over before making instant decisions. When you're captain, it's a different mind-set. When you are just a player, everything is about you. But then when you wear the C, everything becomes about the team. You realized that there were other people that were going to be affected by your actions, and that's a very powerful thing, no kidding. So it really forced me to become more responsible and to think through things before I just did them. Yes, very often I would have to stop and count to 10 before just reacting. It made me a better person, and that thought process carried over into my life after hockey, as well. Now, whenever I make a decision, I stop and ask myself how that decision is going to affect the others who are involved in it. I'm not perfect at it, by any means, but I have gotten a lot better at it over time.

Zach Parise

I think it's leading by example, for me. I feel like I am more of a lead-by-example type of captain, not so much of a vocal guy. It's easy to be a captain when the team is winning and everyone is having a great time. It's tough to be captain when you're losing or in a slump, because the media and the fans and even the players look to you for answers. So it's up to you to get things turned around and in the right direction. For me, that wasn't so much about calling a players-only meeting or yelling or screaming, or any of that kind of stuff. For me it was about working hard, doing the little things, and staying positive. I know that, if I do those types of things, eventually we will get it figured out and get back in the right direction. When you wear the C, everybody looks to you for guidance and leadership; how you choose to respond makes a big difference. There's probably no one right way, but for me, it's to work hard and lead by example.

Mark Parrish

Attitude is everything. One of the hardest things to be able to do during the course of a season is to stay positive. It's a long season and things are going to happen—you're going to get bumps and bruises, you're going to get hot and cold, you're not going to agree with the coach all the time—but through all of that, you have to stay positive. That's your job as captain, and that can be tough. When it comes right down to it, the only two things you can control are your attitude and your work ethic. That's it. There are so may things that are out of your control in this game, so many—injuries, a coach who doesn't believe in you, politics, trades, you name it. You may have a bad stretch or even a bad season or seasons. But if you can stay positive and work hard, no matter what, you're going to eventually find success and be rewarded. Again, it may take time, but the opportunities are there for the guys who work hard and are positive. It's the old cliché, the harder you work the luckier you get. It's totally true, you see it over and over again. The teams who work the hardest and stay the most positive through thick and thin, they are the ones who tend to get the bounces in their favor more often than not.

Michael Peca

Accountability. Being responsible for your own actions is what it's all about, whether you're on the ice or in the business world. True leaders don't need others to hold them accountable, they just do the right things and make the right choices. At the end of the day, you want to be somebody people look at and say, "You know what? I want to be like *that* guy." And not for what he has or what he's done, but for the type of person he is and how he lives his life with integrity.

Mike Peluso

The big takeaway for me was something I got from Steve Smith while we were on our Stanley Cup run in Chicago together. We eventually lost to Pittsburgh in the Finals, but along the way we went through a lot of ups and downs. I will never forget Steve telling us all in the locker room one day, "Guys, remember...no highs and no lows." I think we won like 11 in a row to get there, and some of the younger guys were getting cocky and confident. Steve saw that and really reinforced to us that we're going to have good days and bad days, but the most important thing was the ultimate prize—the Cup. Steve had already won a bunch of championships in Edmonton and knew that there were going to be peaks and valleys. Boy, was he right. "Settle it down, boys, let's channel it," or, "Tomorrow will be a better day." I can still hear his voice all these years later, reminding us of all the momentum shifts that take place in each and every game we played. Unfortunately, we never won the Cup that year, but that life lesson really stuck with me. Even today, with all the little victories and setbacks we have in our everyday lives, you have to keep an even keel. I'm not afraid to admit that I've had my share of struggles away from hockey in my own personal life, with depression and whatnot—from all the head injuries over the years—and I keep having to remind myself of Steve's words. It's certainly helped me along the way.

Lance Pitlick

What I try to instill in my own kids and in the kids I coach is something I learned from Herb Brooks many years ago: "Plan your work and work your plan." The bottom line is that, in order to be successful in anything you do, you have to have a goal and then you have to work hard in order to achieve it. Effort is everything. There are three principle characteristics that I want people to say about our team every time they see us practice or play: 1) we work our butts off, 2) we play as a team and move the puck, and 3) we take short shifts. You work as hard as you can for a minute or two and then get off so that the next guy can do the same. For me as the coach, I try to create an environment in which everybody feels like he is a part of the team. I try to delegate responsibility. And lastly, I try to get people to overachieve. I want them to try to do things that they otherwise thought was impossible. That's it.

Shjon Podein

Great leaders are great listeners. I realized early on in my career that it was much better to listen than to speak. We had leaders on our team for a reason, but it took me a while to figure that out. Eventually, when I just sat back and listened to the veteran guys who had been through the wars and had had success, that's when things started to make sense for me. They knew what it took to get to the next level, and they'd been through many failures and success, both on and off the ice. So, once I shut up and let them get through to me, it was really liberating. It allowed me to make better choices, which resulted in fewer mistakes, and as a result I really grew as both a player and a person.

The guy who taught me most about this was Ray Bourque. Ray is one of the classiest people I have ever met. I remember in '01 playing together in Colorado, he had just come over from Boston, and we all wanted to win the Stanley Cup so badly for him. Well, en route to winning it that year, I will never forget an incident during one of our big playoff series. We were down three games to two, I can't recall who we were playing, and everybody was pretty uptight. Right before Game 6, Ray came in and gathered all the veterans on the team together. He didn't yell or call anybody out or criticize anyone, he just asked questions and listened. He valued their input and expertise and he acknowledged it. We all wanted to get to that next step, but none of us were really sure how to do so until Ray came in and brought us all together. The way he took in all of that information and processed it and then gave everyone constructive advice—it was amazing. It got us all focused on the same goal, it gave us a purpose. He then asked us, as leaders, to pass that information on to our linemates. He was asking us to be accountable, and we all bought in right then and there. The fact that he was willing to listen to a fourth-line ham-and-egger like me, it made me want to work even harder for him. It was an extremely powerful moment for me and one I will never forget.

Mike Polich

I was never a real rah-rah type of a leader, but rather more of a lead-by-example kind of guy. I just worked hard and tried to get everybody to follow along. Hard work and preparation were the big takeaways for me. What you put into it is what you're going to get out of it. My old coach at the University of Minnesota, Herb Brooks, used to always say, "Competition without preparation is suicide." That was it for me, I never forgot that. Our practices were brutal, he worked us so hard because he wanted us to be over-prepared. He never allowed us to become complacent, either. Ever. He never let us get too high or too low. If we were winning, he'd work us even harder. We prepared hard every week for each opponent and never took them for granted. He always told us that we weren't good enough to win on talent alone, becoming the best required training and preparation. No shortcuts, just hard work.

I remember one time we had just won a big series over our biggest rival, Wisconsin. I had a pretty good series and scored some big goals for us, which felt pretty good. We were back on the ice Monday morning for practice skating laps. I was sore and was trying to ease back into the swing of things. Just then Herbie skates over to me and says, "Michael, heck of a series this weekend. Great job. Listen, we've got another big series coming up this week, and it looks to me like you're taking the day off. Your teammates are looking to you and watching you as the captain to see what you're doing and how you're preparing. So let's pick

The Mark Messier Leadership Award

One of the fiercest competitors to ever play the game, "Mess" was the quintessential leader—a captain among captains. His extraordinary leadership was honored in 2007 when the NHL created the Mark Messier Leadership Award, which recognizes a player who exemplifies superior leadership qualities, both on and off the ice.

Leadership [for me] probably started when I was a stick-boy for my father when he coached senior teams. I watched how he interacted with players. He had a very good knowledge of hockey and all of its elements. And [the leadership also came with] playing with great players and watching what they did. Then there's Glen Sather [Edmonton's president, general manager, and coach during the dynasty years] and Ted Green [an assistant coach with the Oilers during that same era]—I learned a tremendous amount from them. They were guys I really respected. The odyssey that [Sather] shared with all of us was something I learned a lot about. John Muckler [another coach in Edmonton] was an unbelievable technician. You learn from all the people you come in contact with and, of course, through winning, you gain experience and, unfortunately, through losing you gain experience, as well. You start putting all these things together as your career evolves, and pretty soon you figure out what works and what doesn't, and that's what experience does. Pretty soon, you realize that relationships are important and learn to cultivate those and extract the best you can out of everybody, and I think that is what leadership is.

Source: http://www.hhof.com/htmlSpotlight

it up. Show these young guys what it means to be a leader."
Wow. That was Herbie, no days off. You won a big series...
big deal. What are we going to do next week? He demanded our best and he expected our best. That's why the guy
won three national championships in seven years. He was
a perfectionist and demanded excellence. That attitude and
mentality was pounded into us on a daily basis, and I guess
it's always stuck with me. I've been selling real estate for
30-plus years now, and those life lessons are as true today
as they were back then. Hard work and preparation, there's
just no substitute.

Tom Reid

For me, it was learning how to deal with people and how
to deal with solving problems. After all, there's three sides
to every story...my side, your side, and the truth. And that's
always going to be the case, it's never going to change.
So, as a leader, you have to be able to work with people
to solve problems and find resolutions to conflicts. As the
captain, that can be tough because you have to be able to
represent the players as well as the coaching staff—you're
the go-between. I always found that, if you can diffuse
situations as quickly as possible, it was usually the best way
to go. If you have a little problem within an organization,
get to the bottom of it fast, otherwise it will fester and grow
into a big problem. Once that happens, you have a cancer
on your hands that can take down your entire team. At that
point, people start getting traded, cut, and fired, which is
no good for any organization.

Doug Risebrough

It was the compassionate side for me. I was more of a
hard-driven player, and I had to learn to become more

compassionate toward others. I had to become more understanding of the fact that not everybody was like me. If you want to reach people, you have to be a good listener and be more understanding of them. It took me a while to figure that out, but once I did, I became a much more effective leader. Captaincy is all about encouragement, in my eyes. Great captains have the ability to encourage everyone around them in positive yet tough ways. They find ways to get guys involved and build their confidence as opposed to breaking it down. They give their teammates a chance to succeed on their own strengths, which is really a unique attribute. It's easy to be a great leader when you are surrounded by great players, but what separates the good captains from the average ones is their ability to lead teams full of mediocre players. To be able to get the most out of guys who aren't feeling as good about their game or who are in a slump, those are the guys you need to be able to reach out to and connect with. And to do so, in my opinion, requires a level of compassion that is unique to certain leaders.

Gordie Roberts

I think it comes down to consistency. Barring any major injuries, the guys who are able to stick around for a lot of years have a certain mental consistency about them. The players who are able to stay in the league for a really long time, they do the right things day-in and day-out. They work on the fundamentals, eat right, sleep right, take care of their bodies, and do all the little things that are necessary to stay healthy on and off the ice. Those are the guys who got the most out of themselves and, as a result, were productive well into their thirties and even forties. What it all boils down to is that they know how to be a pro. I know a lot of guys who had a ton of talent but only played for five or seven years. The difference between those guys and the guys who played for 10, 15, or even 20 years is that level of consistency.

Brian Rolston

Leadership is a daily process. You have to make the right choices every day. If you apply yourself to the best of your ability, work hard, and treat people right, you'll find success in whatever you do in life. That's what being a professional is all about.

Joe Sakic

Being a good leader to me was just about doing things the right way. That's it. If you are genuine and respectful and responsible, and you work hard, then good things are probably going to follow. That's it.

Nick Schultz

I think it's accountability. Whenever things aren't going well, people look to the leaders for answers and guidance. They want someone to stand up and take responsibility. That's what the captain has to do, he has to be that guy. That's always stuck with me. Whether it's playing hockey, raising kids, running a business, or whatever, people respect leaders who don't make excuses and are accountable.

Brendan Shanahan

I think it's the ability to read people and to be able to encourage or motivate them the best way possible for the good of the team. Great captains, guys like Mark Messier, Steve Yzerman, and Kirk Muller—they just have this incredible ability to recognize specific people on the team who needed either a nudge or a hug. Either way, something good was going to happen after that conversation—you just knew it.

Neil Sheehy

For me, it's knowing that you're being counted on by your teammates and then coming through for them. It's humbling to be considered a leader on a team of your peers. When they put that letter on your sweater, you realize that you're a part of something bigger than yourself. It makes you realize that you're always being looked to and counted upon to help the team win. It's a lot of pressure and a lot of responsibility, yet it's extremely gratifying and rewarding, as well. Today, that attitude resonates with me in how I treat my clients. I just always want to be there for them and work hard to represent them the best way I know possible. I look at them as my teammates, and just like when I was playing, I still want to do whatever I can to help us win.

Bobby Smith

I think it's a combination of being realistic and optimistic. In hockey, after a team wins five in a row, a good captain or coach or leader will always keep things in perspective. When asked about it by the media, he'll say, "Yeah...but so-and-so and so-and-so are really having a hard time, and we gotta get these guys going," or, "Yeah...but this can't continue as long as player A, B, or C are struggling as much as they are," or, "Yeah... but we've got a conflict in the dressing room." They never give the impression that things are going great, they always leave some room for improvement or for skepticism. They don't want the guys getting cocky, they want to be realistic and keep them on an even keel. And it goes the other way, too, with regard to being optimistic. Maybe the team lost five in a row, and now he has to face the press. "Yeah...but the problem we had a week ago we've solved and we're feeling good about ourselves," or, "Yeah...but so-and-so is playing better and we're not gonna panic, we're just going to play our game." Stuff like that. And it's the same thing in business, as far as I'm concerned. You have to be realistic when you're having success, to keep yourself humble, and you have to be optimistic when things are going poorly, so you can stay the course and eventually work your way out of that slump. Good captains, good coaches, as well as good business leaders—they find ways to say just the right things at just the right times.

Steve Smith

Whether you wear the C on your jersey or not, it's all about being a good teammate. Sure, you have to work hard and all of that, but beyond that it all comes down to being a re-spected team player. The team aspect of this game is clearly second to none, and it's certainly the same in business. It requires a team, complete with a solid supporting cast, to achieve success in anything you do in life.

Eric Staal

For me, it's just staying the course. There's going to be ups and downs along the way in hockey and in life. No team wins 'em all. There are times when things are going great and everything's the way you want it to be, and other times when it's not. So it's about keeping those same intangibles in place—like work ethic, your drive, and your will to try to get better each and every day. That, in my mind, is the biggest thing you learn as not only a hockey player but as a parent, husband, or businessperson. It's easy to do well when things are going good. Your true character comes out when things are going bad, and that's when you have to stick to your principles.

Mark Stuart

I think the big thing for me is communication. As a captain, you have to call guys out every now and then and hold them accountable for things. It's not fun, but it's your job. I've found that there's a time and a place for everything, and if you find that right time to talk to people, you'll probably have more success when it's all said and done. You have to pick your spots. I like talking to guys one on one, versus in a group setting. You never want to embarrass anyone or anything like that. So much in hockey goes unsaid, and a good captain will be able to break down that communication barrier and open a dialogue. And you have to be positive, too, and make sure to find good things that the person is doing. People need to be patted on the back a lot more than they need to be yelled at. You have to reward guys for their hard work and for being accountable, that's important. Good captains are good at doing these things. They support their teammates no matter what but are able to show some tough love along the way, too. If you're a respected leader, then the player you are talking to is going to listen and try to make improvements in his game. If not, then you are going to have problems and are probably not going to be wearing a letter for very long.

Gary Suter

For me, it was about learning to deal with the highs and the lows. Whether it's in hockey or in life, you're going to have successes and you're going to have failures. It's how you deal with them, however, that matters. You can't get too high and you can't get too low, you have to stay steady and keep plowing forward. That's it.

Darryl Sydor

To me, it can all be summed up with one word: *professional*. To be a professional means you have respect for the game and respect for your teammates. It means you understand your role, too, because everybody has a job to do on the team. If everybody on the team worried about doing his job to the best of his ability, and they all held themselves accountable to that, then there's no stopping that team.

Bryan Trottier

I think the bottom line with great leaders is that they are able to make everybody feel important. There's a quiet respect that evolves when that happens from captain to player and from player to captain. Everybody feels appreciated. Everybody feels a sense of responsibility through a role that they have. Everybody feels a sense of accountability through that role as well, to play hard and to be a good teammate. When that type of leadership is embraced, that's when teams really thrive. Being a leader means being a lot of things. It means being confident. It means being able to make tough decisions. It means carrying yourself in a certain manner, with dignity and respect. It's all of those things. It's also about being humble. Great captains don't walk around the dressing room saying, "Look at me, I'm the captain!" For great leaders, it's all about the team. So I tried to learn from each and every experience I had, whether it was on or off the ice. That's what life's all about. Watching and learning in order to get better, whether it's in hockey or running a business or raising kids. You make mistakes, you own up to them, you learn from them, and you move on. That's it.

Wes Walz

For me, it's just how you handle yourself. When you're a leader, everyone looks to you. So your demeanor on and off the ice really matters. Guys are looking to you to see if you get frazzled under pressure. Since I retired from playing, I've been an assistant coach in the NHL and also gotten into doing TV analysis. Every time I address the team to teach them something or to go over something, I think about my demeanor. Every time I go on the air to break down a play or to talk about something important, I think about my demeanor. So it's become engrained in me, I suppose, to think before I act and to realize that people are watching you even when you don't think they are watching you. You have to handle yourself the right way, and at all times, that's the bottom line.

Erik Westrum

Wearing the C means you're a leader, and that gives you confidence. When you believe in yourself and in what you're doing, nothing can stop you. It also breeds success in the people around you because they're going to buy into whatever it is you're trying to get them to do. Great leaders inspire others on their team, whether that's in hockey or in business, it's the same principle.

Steve Yzerman

Determination. It takes a lot of determination to reach your goals, whether they are in hockey or in life. To become a champion in hockey, you have to pay a price. The Stanley Cup playoffs, in general, are really a test of your will. They are a test of your ability to stay strong and deal with adversity. If you can do those things and persevere, then you will be successful. It won't guarantee you a championship, but it will guarantee you an opportunity.

Detroit Red Wings beloved longtime captain Steve Yzerman, shown during a game in Detroit in April 2004.